ACCESSING YOUR MULTIDIMENSIONAL SELF
A KEY TO COSMIC HISTORY

by Stephanie South
(Based on GM108X transmission from Votan to Red Queen)
"We are but the secretaries, the authors are in Eternity"

Yellow Galactic Seed Year

Accessing Your Multidimensional Self: A Key to Cosmic History
Copyright © Galactic Research Institute

 Yellow Galactic Seed Year (2014)

All rights reserved by the Galactic Masters.

ISBN 978-0-9767759-5-9
www.lawoftime.org

Original Graphics by Valum Votan (José Argüelles), Kin 11 and Red Queen (Stephanie South), Kin 185
Computer enhancement by Kelly Harding Kin 240 and Jacob Wyatt Kin 201
Book Design and Layout by Kelly Harding Kin 240. Cover Design by Jacob Wyatt Kin 201
Copy Edit by Forrest O Farrell Kin 140, Jacob Wyatt Kin 201, and Seamus Hiestand Kin 218

Prayer of the Seven Galactic Directions

From the East, House of Light,
May wisdom dawn in us so we may see all things in clarity!

From the North House of Night,
May wisdom ripen in us so we may know all from within!

From the West, House of Transformation,
May wisdom be transformed into right action so we may do what must be done!

From the South, House of the Eternal Sun, may right action reap the harvest
so we may enjoy the fruits of planetary being!

From Above, House of Heaven where star people and ancestors gather,
May their blessings come to us now!

From Below, House of Earth,
May the heartbeat of her crystal core bless us with harmonies to end all war!

From the Center, Galactic Source, which is everywhere at once,
May everything be known as the light of mutual love!

Ah yum Hunab Ku evam maya eh ma ho!
Ah yum Hunab Ku evam maya eh ma ho!
Ah yum Hunab Ku evam maya eh ma ho!

In Dedication to Valum Votan

ACCESSING YOUR MULTIDIMENSIONAL SELF
A KEY TO COSMIC HISTORY

CONTENTS

Foreword: Interplanetary History – The Context ... 7

Introduction: The Skeleton Key ... 15

Introduction Part 2: Numerical Proofs of Prophecy ... 23

PART I: ENTERING THE COSMIC MYSTERY PLAY
Chapter 1: From Vela Pulsar to Cosmic History ... 27
Chapter 2: Becoming A Cosmic Thinker ... 33
Chapter 3: Activating the New Frequency: 13:20 ... 43

PART II: ENTERING THE UNIFIED MIND OF THE EARTH: NOOSPHERE
Chapter 4: Defining the Mind of Gaia – Noosphere ... 53
Chapter 5: Empowering Telepathy ... 65
Chapter 6: Balancing UR: Universal Recollection ... 75

PART III: RETHINKING THE UNIVERSE THROUGH COSMIC SCIENCE
Chapter 7: Attuning to the Sun, Solar System and 7 Rays ... 87
Chapter 8: Integrating the Plasma Universe and 7 Psychic Centers ... 95
Chapter 9: Realizing the 13 Dimensions ... 109

PART IV: APPLYING THE SYNCHRONIC CODES
Chapter 10: Enchanting the Numbers ... 121
Chapter 11: Liberating the Planet Holon ... 135
Chapter 12: Universalizing the Planetary Grid ... 147

Chapter 13: Synchrogalactic Yoga ... 157

Appendix: Foundations of the Synchronic Order ... 195

Foreword: Interplanetary History – The Context

To understand the vast scope of this book, we must first understand the purpose and context of the *Cosmic History Chronicles*, which is based on the *Galactic Mayan Mind Transmission*, known as GM108X.

The mission of the Galactic Maya has its origin in the stars. The different star systems comprise one intergalactic federation. This mission began a long time ago (by Earth standards) and is anchored in the Pleiades with various jumping off points, including Arcturus, Antares and Sirius. The Pleiades is also known as the "shining anchor" as our solar system rotates around Alcyone (the Great Central Sun), the main star of the Pleiades, in a 26,000-year cycle.

The mission is multidimensional, though with special focus on the Velatropa sector. This is the region of our galaxy defined by the pulsar Vela, located in the Orion arm of what we call the Milky Way galaxy—more specifically, Velatropa 24: the intergalactic code name for our Sun, Kinich Ahau.

Our solar system is at the center of a 6,000-light year diameter area defined by the pulsar Vela (V), a remnant of a supernova oscillating at an incredible rate of speed. A pulsar is an advanced, evolved late state of what was once a supernova. Keep in mind that Vela is only a small (but potent) "microbe" in the galaxy.

This mission has as its object the surveillance of the planetary system of Velatropa 24, with special focus on the five inner planets: Mercury, Venus, Earth, Mars and Maldek (now the Asteroid Belt). *The Arcturus Probe* describes how this area of Velatropa 24, including Earth (Velatropa 24.3), became the free will quarantine zone. This is also the area of an unfolding program known in scriptures as "the fall" or "original sin."

It was known by other beings in different parts of the galactic system, that within the free will quarantine zone there would be a process of learning that would focalize the karmic debris of many world systems into one structure that would inevitably come to a point when the process could go no further without disturbing the entire Kinich Ahau system.

Once the problem was quarantined to the Velatropa sector, the "guardian angels" could keep their eyes on it, and as it got closer to the appointed hour, they would increase surveillance. Why is this necessary?

In the process of the evolution of this star system, planet Earth (V.24.3) became separated from the natural timing frequency that the rest of life in the universe is functioning on. The reason for what is referred to as the Mayan civilization and the Mayan system of astronomy and mathematical calendrics was to help re-set Earth onto the right course of *time*. Mayan mathematics are the jewel of this galactic knowledge system brought to our planet.

The Sirian High Command first began to assist this course of events by understanding the battle playing out in the collective human mind. A remedy known as Dreamspell was sent from Sirius through the Arcturian force field to help humans bridge dimensions and realign with their multidimensional destiny. The Dreamspell codes that were transmitted to José Argüelles/Valum Votan actually describe the harmonic registration of movements toward stabilizing the system of Kinich Ahau (Sun or V.24).

The harmonic registrations of the planetary orbits in relation to each other create, over time, synchronization cycles called "Dreamspells"—the specific Dreamspell code for this time is referred to as *Timeship Earth*. The Timeship Earth Dreamspell codes are mathematical codes for re-instrumenting the human species according to a galactic/harmonic timing frequency.

These codes were stepped down into the practical format of the 13 Moon/28-day calendar (synchronometer) and are based on the cycles of Sirius. This is all part of the Galactic Mayan mission. The Galactic Maya are planetary navigators and mappers of the larger psychic field of Earth, the solar system, and the galaxy beyond. They are a telepathic culture. This means that their perceptions, modes of knowing and communication come from a high degree of telepathic attunement with the cosmos.

The galactic "Mayan" calendar is not what it appears. The purpose of this (13 Moon/28-day) calendar is ultimately to ensure that Earth is synchronized with the new galactic beam. As synchronic engineers, the Galactic Maya first deposited these codes in the form of what we call Mayan civilization and then—as a new, planetary dispensation came the *Dreamspell* codes. After the Dreamspell was brought forth, many more fourth/fifth-dimensional gifts followed that defined a terrestrial path back to the stars, known as the synchronic order.

On one level, the goal of these tools is to keep the planet from self-destructing and on another level, it is to stabilize the consciousness of the planet into a cosmic resonance with the local galaxy so that this has an effect on the Sun. As the Sun goes through its internal convulsions, a stabilization of the solar frequency is created which shifts the consciousness on this particular planet. This is a unique situation in the final stages of the experiment within the Velatropa sector, with the V.24 star (our Sun) and V.24.3 (planet Earth) as the central points of focus. Pacal Votan is chief among the engineering team of this experiment.

PACAL VOTAN: CHIEF ENGINEER

Pacal Votan is a superconscious synthesizer whose purpose is to, through his higher-dimensional consciousness probes, define the parameters of this particular experiment, spanning from 104,000 years ago to the present. This may seem like a vast amount of time for one being to be responsible for, but this is only a small slice of time in the higher galactic cosmic timing cycles.

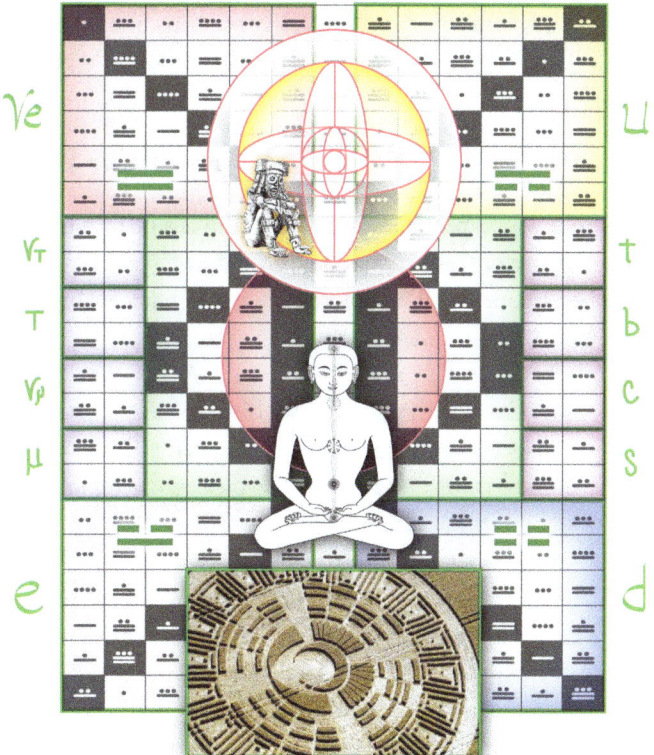

The star Sirius is the focal point of this system and, along with other centers such as Tau Ceti and the AA Midway station, it is involved in the long distance transmission of the planetary and solar engineering experiment. This is actually occurring in another part of the galaxy in tandem with a Type 4 cosmic civilization and a network of galaxies in this sector of the universe.

Type 4 cosmic civilizations have completely transcended the use of material instrumentation and operate with a supergalactic consciousness and an absolute understanding of universal design principles of the cosmos. Through this knowledge they can *radiogenetically* transmit those principles to Type 3 cosmic civilizations.

Type 3 cosmic civilizations are the most advanced stages of the material plane and are operating with telepathic means but are also grounded in the physical plane and are able to transmit the telepathic surveillance vehicles that we call UFOs.

Pacal Votan is from a Type 3 "Mayan" civilization, which is scattered in different colonies throughout this and other galaxies. Type 3 cosmic civilizations are direct receivers of the transmissions from the Type 4 cosmic civilization that is conducting the experiment. Pacal Votan's incarnation came after much surveillance in order to stabilize a cultural node in what we call the Chiapas area of southern Yucatan, Mexico.

In that process of cultural stabilization he created the foundations of the galactic research base. In these different bases, information was taken from the resonant readings of the planetary field and transmitted to the higher telepathic mind of himself and several other agents working closely with him. At his *disincarnation* he left instructions, including oral and telepathic to his spiritual successor, and as "deposits" into the noosphere, as well as in a prophetic lineage transmission: GM108X.

Telektonon Prophecy

The Telektonon prophecy of Pacal Votan is a distant transmission of the guardian spirits of the Earth. The purpose of this prophecy is ultimately to ensure that the Velatropa system becomes stabilized at a higher frequency. The key to this is the relationship of V.24.3 with the other planets in the solar system in relation to the Sun.

The orbits of the planets within our solar system maintain different frequencies of different stages and levels of consciousness. However, it is the V.24 star (the Sun) that is actually undergoing a massive inner transformation in the process of stellar evolution. The Sun's process is directly related to the stabilization of human consciousness.

According to the Telektonon Prophecy, the experimental zone of Velatropa is also known as the realm of the lost worlds, which is the repository of karmic errors. This karmic stream traces back to Maldek, the fifth orbit of out solar system which was shattered by the perturbations from the massive sixth planet Jupiter. This in turn destroyed the electromagnetic flux tube circuit that aligns the orbital harmonics of the planets with the Sun (Kinich Ahau).

As the locus of the primal shattering, the orbit of Maldek sustains the vibration of the lost chord and the cosmic haunting of a paradise lost. From Maldek the error was transferred to Mars whose civilization was incinerated, wiping out Mars' flux tube system. Then the karmic residue was transferred to Earth (V.24.3). Since the Earth functions as a whole system, stress on one component of the system actually stresses the whole order

We have incarnated in order to correct these karmic errors and to create a new collective reality. Every karmic stream that we correct helps to reconnect the memory circuits of the lost worlds in the human mind. This is a key theme of the *Cosmic History Chronicles*.

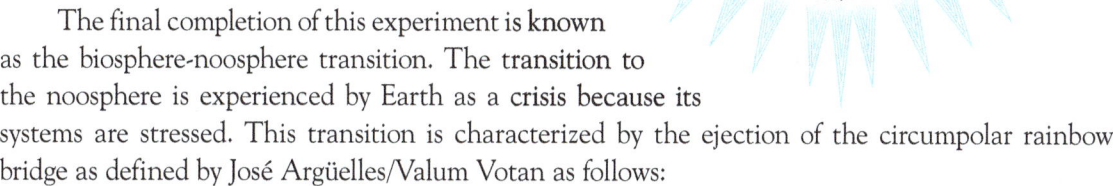

The final completion of this experiment is known as the biosphere-noosphere transition. The transition to the noosphere is experienced by Earth as a crisis because its systems are stressed. This transition is characterized by the ejection of the circumpolar rainbow bridge as defined by José Argüelles/Valum Votan as follows:

The Rainbow Bridge is a galactic engineering project in tune with the stellar evolution of our local star, the Sun. It is a cosmic event. The point of it is to establish a telepathic matrix, bonding a critical mass of humans with the planet's etheric, electromagnetic and biopsychic fields. Through such a matrix, at the target date point, the collective telepathic mind is intended to engage the auroral flows from both of the Earth's magnetic poles and entrain them into joining each other permanently, creating a circumpolar rainbow bridge around the Earth.

GALACTIC BEAMS AND THE AA MIDWAY STATION

Hunab Ku, the center of the galaxy, is like a powerful radio station that sends out beams, each with a different program. Scientists call these beams density waves because they tend to be of low frequency, like gravity. These beams affect galactic evolution as they are encoded with cosmic memory plates or holograms of the memory field of an entire epoch of evolution.

At the center of the Hunab Ku is the galactic time atom or *sole atom*. What we think of as black holes are actually the entrance and exit points of this galactic time atom (which has no sides or dimensions). From the intersections of the galactic time atom emanate different streams of transmissions.

Accessing Your Multidimensional Self: A Key to Cosmic History

The AA Midway Station is located interdimensionally above the planetary midpoint between Jupiter and Maldek (Asteroid Belt). Also known as "the Mother Ship", "AA" refers to the two star systems—Antares and Arcturus—that monitor interplanetary affairs in the Velatropa 24 solar system. After the collapse of the experiment on Mars, a joint partnership was formed between the advanced intelligences of Arcturus and Antares to monitor events on the Velatropa 24 solar system and particularly on events that would be occurring on Velatropa 24.3 (Earth).

Through the surveillance (or remote viewing) conducted by the AA Midway Station, virtually everything that occurs on this planet is known and observed. The AA Midway Station is an aspect of the larger operation known as the Galactic Federation. The Galactic Federation uses the AA Midway Station as its principle surveillance unit for the Veletropa 24 star system and its environment.

Everything that occurs at the AA Midway Station is reported to and accessed

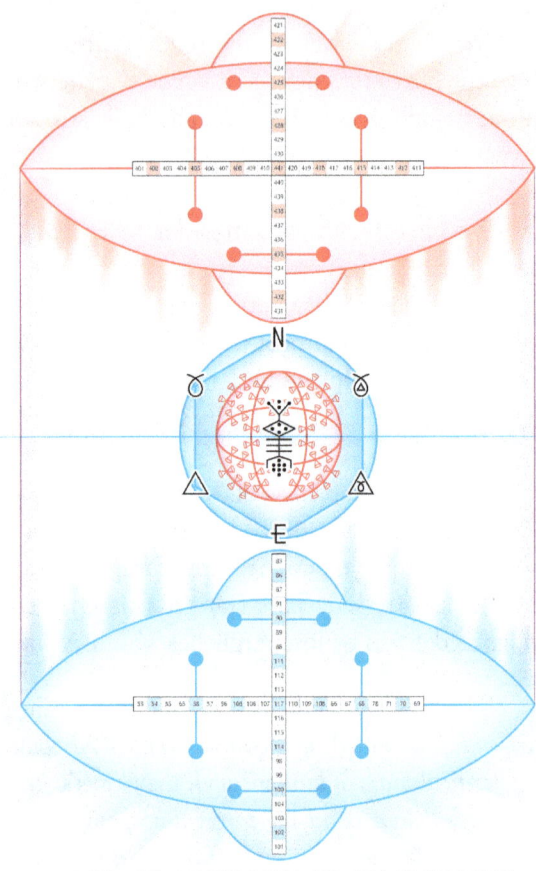

AA Midway in Red & Blue Time Phases Simultaneously
[Alpha-Alpha Dominant Red, Beta-Beta Dominant Blue]

ALL INFORMATION GATHERED IS ORGANIZED MINIMALLY AS PLANETARY MENTAL AGGREGATES – MAXIMALLY AS GALACTIC MENTAL AGGREGATES

by the Galactic Federation. This data is, in turn, correlated with the records kept in the seventh-dimensional akashic library archives or what we might call the Master Record. The next hierarchical level of command then assesses that information and may or may not give further commands or instructions to the AA Midway Station.

The Galactic Maya are synchronic engineers that help guide events on planets and star systems to ensure that they are in synch with the program of the galactic beams. There are many types of beams for the many phases of the evolutionary development of consciousness. The most recent beam of 5,125 years (13 Baktuns) exactly matched the human historic cycle that completed on December 21, 2012. José Argüelles/Valum Votan discovered that the beam consists of thirteen large frequency cycles, which the Maya call *baktuns*. Each frequency cycle or baktun is like a radio channel with its own unique quality. Each of these cycles is affected by and builds upon the previous cycle. The affect of this particular beam was to accelerate human activity, increasing material technology until the third dimension was thoroughly exhausted with more information and population than it can process.

When this beam reached its exponential point it began to phase into a process of Galactic Synchronization, preparing Earth for its next stage of evolution. This is the meaning of July 26, 2013, Yellow Galactic Seed, the point at which the Earth opened to receive a new galactic beam of higher consciousness and knowledge, triggering the collective return journey to our multidimensional origin.

VELA SYSTEM DEFINED (HIERARCHY OF LEVELS OF GALACTIC INTELLIGENCE)

V.24.333	Internal system of the human (chakras)
V.24.33	The human
V.24.3	Planet Earth (subsystem of the star)
V.24	The star (Sun)
V	Vela (sector of the galaxy where the star V. 24 is located)
V.0	Vela Pulsar (located in the Orion Arm of the Milky Way galaxy (G))
V.00	Hunab Ku, the center of the Milky Way Galaxy (G)
G	Galaxy is a function of Universe (U)
U	Universe is a function of Cosmos (C)

The Galaxy is a function of Universe; and Universe is a function of Cosmos. Cosmos represents all the different dimensions that the Universe contains. V.24.3 and V.24.33 are the summation and culmination of this process. The human body (V.24.33) is the microcosm of the Galaxy, Universe and Cosmos which is realized through its 7 chakra generators (V.24.333).

Vela is a function of G, the local galaxy. G is a function of GN (galactic neighborhood), which is a function of the total whole system universe. In turn, the universe is a function of the seven universes—the septenary universe. Was everything created simultaneously, since it all exists simultaneously?

INTRODUCTION: THE SKELETON KEY

The evolutionary vehicle of life on Earth is shifting. The foundational structure of human knowledge is changing. Everything must be radically re-envisioned.

Accessing Your Multidimensional Self: A Key to Cosmic History opens us into the realm of a new galactic knowledge base as woven through the seven volumes of the *Cosmic History Chronicles*. The key premise of Cosmic History is that there is a divine plan of exquisite order and intelligence that endows all creation with a rhythm, a pattern and a form that, however diverse, is a single unifying whole.

Planet Earth is the focus of the resolution of the "War of the Heavens." The War of the Heavens refers to the galactic patterns of karmic influence that scatter and settle residually in the orbital harmonics of different star systems. This war traces to the destroyed planet Maldek (now the Asteroid Belt). The memory of the dissolution of Maldek contains the knowledge of the origins within this star system of the process of Cosmic History unfolding in the involution of spirit into matter. On Earth, this "war" translates into the drama of the struggle of spiritual forces within the materialistic cauldron of artificial time.

The purpose of Cosmic History is to imprint new galactic frequencies into the noosphere (planetary mind) that arouse a positive image or order of reality. This order of reality is galactic in nature. All genuine renewal and reformation of knowledge comes from a living revelation.

The root of Cosmic History is based on a *between the worlds transmission* known as GM108X: Galactic Mayan Mind Transmission. Cosmic History articulates not the past world but the coming world. The origin of this transmission lies far outside the Earth and predates the present historical cycle by hundreds of thousands of years. It is the information stream that contains the knowledge pertaining to the science that defines how we arrived to this particular star system. This knowledge is not only being transmitted to our world but to other worlds simultaneously.

This transmission is part of a prophecy or terma (hidden treasure) and is the final stage in the prophecy cycle of Nah Chan, Palenque. There are two parts of this terma: The terma of the tomb of Pacal Votan and the terma of the tomb of the Red Queen. In 1993, José Argüelles realized that the entire tomb of Pacal Votan was actually a prophecy in the form of a terma, a hidden "text" or treasure. This prophecy reveals that the spiritual history of the planet is a single integrated circuit that can be accessed through the *synchronic order*. The 13 Moon, 28-day calendar (synchronometer) defines the synchronic order as a universal fourth-dimensional matrix that unifies all other systems.

Accessing Your Multidimensional Self: A Key to Cosmic History

This transmission is also part of a galactic lineage. The living transmission of GM108X establishes the Galactic Mayan spiritual lineage on Velatropa 24.3 (Earth). This is the first time that the Galactic Mayan Mind transmission had been accessible on this planet. The Galactic Mayan lineage represented at Palenque was re-established through Valum Votan (José Argüelles) and Red Queen (Stephanie South). By passing the transmission, the lineage is established and returns to the matrilineal—which is a key purpose of Cosmic History.

First Cosmic History Transmission

The first Cosmic History transmission began on March 12, 2002 (Kin 173) with a blast of interplanetary recollection regarding Maldek, the destroyed planet. In a vision, Valum Votan witnessed a series of interdimensional scenes followed by the vision of a master time molecule at the center of the Earth. He understood this time molecule as the synthesizing structure that holds the information templates of Cosmic History. These templates were deposited into the master time molecule within the crystal core of the Earth as a time release program by Pacal Votan at the beginning of the 13-Baktun cycle of history.

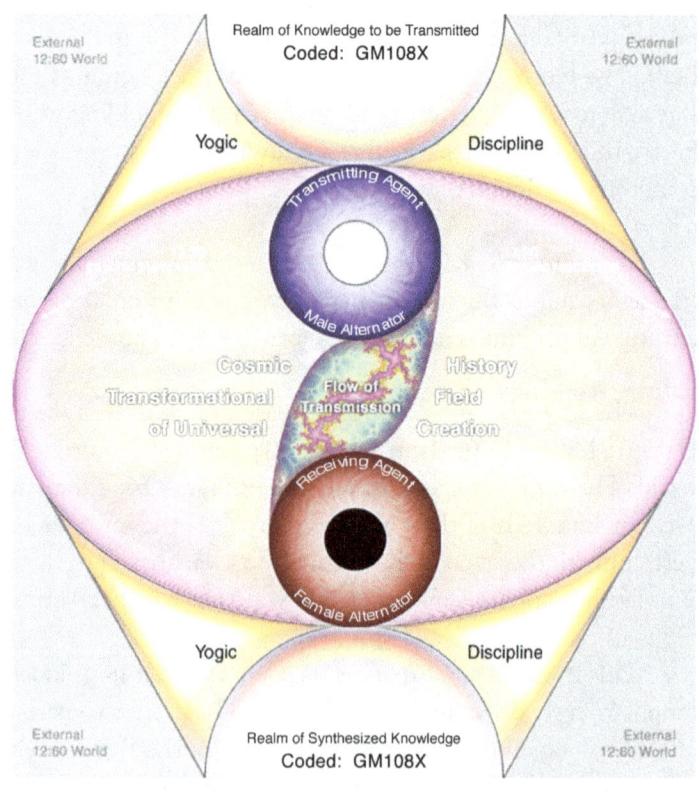

To release the information stored within the Master Time Molecule, Valum Votan and Red Queen established a daily discipline consisting of yoga, pranayams, mudras and daily transmission. Continuity was supremely important so that all points could be tapped and released. The purpose of this transmission was to establish the GM108X lineage in order to engender a new consciousness and knowledge base on planet Earth.

Nine days before the first Cosmic History transmission, Valum Votan was honored in a ceremony at Teotihuacán, Mexico on March 3, 2002, Kin 164, Yellow Galactic Seed. (Kin 164 also codes Galactic Synchronization, July 26, 2013, the commencement of a new galactic beam and cycle).

On this day, atop the Pyramid of the Sun (the place where he had his initial vision 49 years earlier), Valum Votan was honored by nine Indigenous elders as the "Closer of the Cycle", the one to bring forth the new knowledge to humanity. Teotihuacán is known as "Place where the Gods Touch the Earth" or "Place Where Men Become Conscious of Their Godly Powers."

Cosmic History is a point of origin in time rather than space. The initial vision was followed by 260 days of consecutive transmission. This set the foundation of the knowledge. By any standards, this succession of tutorials on multiple themes was a stupendous effort requiring maximum focus and concentration. The *Cosmic History Chronicles* are like one sentence with seven words, and each of those seven words is a number that unfolds into different subtopics and synchronic themes. By absorbing the resonant force of these teachings the mind is reformulated at a higher frequency, opening us to the seventh day of creation.

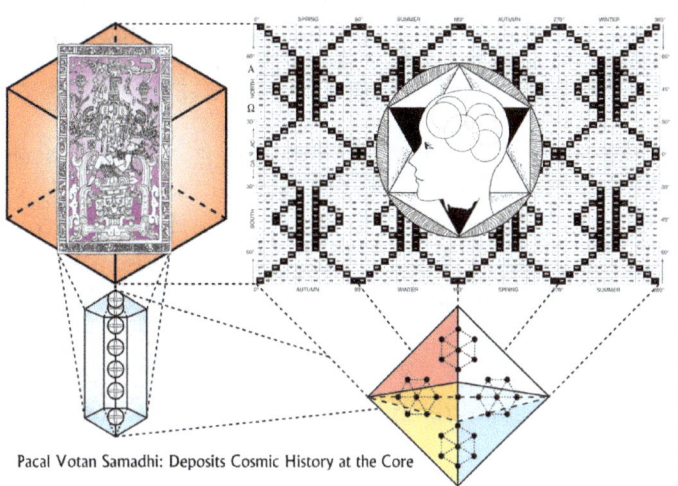

Pacal Votan Samadhi: Deposits Cosmic History at the Core

The pure mindstream of the GM108X samadhi, as transmitted from Votan to the Red Queen, is a "between the worlds" transmission, and contains the essence of the Cosmic History teachings. The GM108X transmission beam is directed through the North and South poles and is stored at the Earth's core within an octahedron magnet that holds the poles in place. Around the core, there is a resonating tympanum that is perceived as an "inner Earth." From this core, specific information resonates out and is received according to the present stage of evolution. This information includes different modalities of thought, culture, life, spiritual truth and ways of being that radiate from the core of the Earth to the psi bank; they then filter down into the surface life of Earth as inspirational thoughtforms.

Tomb of Pacal Votan

The unique tomb of Pacal Votan, comparable only to the tomb in the Great Pyramid of Giza, was discovered June 15, 1952, Kin 218: White Planetary Mirror. The discovery was initiated in 1949 in the temple atop the Pyramid of Inscriptions, when archaeologist Alberto Ruz cleared a large pile of rubble and noticed a tile tube sticking up from the ground. This tube, it was discovered, ran all the way from the tomb at the bottom of the Temple of the Inscriptions, up the side of the stairs, all the way to the floor of the temple on top. This tube, which Ruz called a "psychoduct", came to be known as TELEKTONON, or Earth Spirit Speaking Tube.

In the chamber where the tomb is found are sculpted representations of the Nine Lords of Time and Destiny. Beneath the intricately sculpted sarcophagus lid was found a jade mask, which represents one who has acquired a "true face," that is to say, knowledge, wisdom and enlightenment.

When the tomb of Pacal Votan was opened in 1952 a mind stream flowed out and some of the particles landed into the mind of fourteen-year-old "José Argüelles" when he was atop the Pyramid of the Sun in Teotihuacán one year later where he received his first vision of what he would later understand as GM108X.

The Telektonon Prophecy of Pacal Votan began to reveal itself to José Argüelles on Kin 144 (26 July 1993). This began the first year of the Seven Years of Prophecy: 1993-2000. The Telektonon Prophecy states: "Telektonon is no word at all, but number multiplying itself from within God's unending meditation that we choose to call creation."

Five days after this initial contact, José received a telepathic transmission that revealed him as "galactic messenger 108X." He first became aware of the "108X strand" in 1981 when he was writing *The Art Planet Chronicles—The Making of the Fifth Ring*, a novel set in the future from the perspective of the star system Arcturus. He understood the essence of this strand as a consciously focused beam of information that had been (and was being) transmitted from different planets and star systems, referred to as GM108X.

This was a direct mind transmission, making him an emanation of Pacal Votan's mind stream. An emanation is not dependent on sequence of rebirth (reincarnation), but rather is an essence passed through telepathic transmission of information based on a system of coded knowledge. The purpose of this transmission is to stabilize human consciousness at a higher frequency, opening the mind to other dimensions of existence. This stream of knowledge is set apart from historical streams while simultaneously encompassing them all.

Tomb of Red Queen

Forty-two years after the discovery of the tomb of Pacal Votan, another tomb was discovered in Palenque on June 1, 1994, Kin 194: White Crystal Wizard. The new tomb was discovered in Temple XIII, adjacent to the west side of the nine-storied Temple of the Inscriptions where lay the sarcophagus and crypt of the Great Pacal. It was hailed as the most sensational discovery since the discovery of Pacal's tomb. This tomb was identified as the "Tomb of the Red Queen" due to the red-colored sarcophagus lid painted both on the inside and outside. When the lid was lifted, red cinnabar powder flew everywhere, revealing the skeletal remains of a female along with sumptuous amounts of jade, pearl and other semiprecious stones and shells.

It was immediately assumed that the person in the tomb was a member of noble lineage and that the body belonged to a ruler of high hierarchy. It was natural to think this since the sarcophagus was similar in so many respects to that of the sarcophagus of Pacal Votan. But unlike the tomb of Pacal—which is laden with hieroglyphic inscriptions—neither the temple, the crypt nor the sarcophagus of the Red Queen bear a single inscription. Not a single glyphic clue was left as to her identity, much less of the date of her interment, which confounded all experts. Only a piece of ceramic pottery outside of the crypt was found to have a date, AD 697.

THE TWO TOMBS: KEY TO COSMIC HISTORY

To understand the *Cosmic History Chronicles*, it is important to understand its origins through the human originators and archetypal exemplars, Valum Votan and Red Queen. Archetypes are primordial form patterns, cosmic structures. What is being exemplified by the twin archetypes is a principle of *Galactic Mayan mind transmission* based on the discovery of the two tombs.

Just as the placement of the Red Queen's tomb in Temple XIII (being adjacent to that of the tomb of Pacal) is so obviously deliberate, so the lack of any hieroglyphic clues or dating also seems to have been intentional. However, the virtually identical sarcophaguses were outfitted with twin masks, which represent signs of wisdom.

The male tomb is inscribed and is therefore historical; the female tomb is uninscribed and is therefore post-historical, beyond the cycle, waiting to be inscribed. Hence, Votan the transmitter, the inscribed one; and Red Queen, the receiver, the uninscribed one. Red is the color of initiation and the "Queen" represents the feminine matrix that generates or gives birth and from which the new being flowers.

The tomb is the ark of interdimensional passage between the world systems. Its prophecy is a message of the passage from one time and its world system to another time and its world system. For each time as held by the belief in it creates a world system. The mystery of the tomb symbolizes a vessel passing between the world systems and its mystery is a tribute to the harmony of the divine order of the time.

Cosmic History Rooted in the Synchronic Order

Cosmic History is rooted in the synchronic order, a systematic set of codes discovered by Valum Votan that reveals the larger evolutionary patterning. The first stage of the Cosmic History was received by his human anchor, José Argüelles, beginning in 1983 with the writing of *Earth Ascending: An Illustrated Treatise on the Law Governing Whole Systems*.

After Earth Ascending, the foundational stage of Cosmic History was then continued with Votan's subsequent work, *The Mayan Factor: Path Beyond Technology*. These vast and revolutionary works form the base program of Cosmic History and were soon followed by the discovery of the Law of Time (1989) and the synchronic order (See also *Time, Synchronicity and Calendar Change* by Stephanie South).

All of this knowledge and information, as one unified program, was synchronically timed as a coded prophecy. The Law of Time and synchronic order are part of an advanced time science left on Earth by the Galactic Maya. Proof of the existence of the Law of Time and the prophecy of Pacal Votan lies in the prophetic numbers that weave together a tapestry, revealing a vast order of synchronicity far beyond any one person's ability to create.

Underlying the synchronic order is the same radial matrix that is present in the structure of the noosphere (Earth's thinking layer, see chapter 4) and the psi bank regulator (mechanism of the noosphere that registers fourth-dimensional time, see chapter 5). This means that the whole of Cosmic History is embedded in the noosphere. While one can talk about it, the synchronic order must be practiced and exemplified to be understood.

Terma/Terton

This Cosmic HIistory transmission is born through the alchemical marriage of male and female that brings to birth a higher knowledge. When Cosmic History "sounded", Votan and Red Queen became spontaneously immersed in a type of invisible force field that began to unlock telepathic memories and perceptions. This knowledge is based on terma, or hidden treasure and in this case it is known as the *Terma of the Red Queen.*

In the Tibetan tradition, terma comes from Padmasambhava, who is the terton (or transmitter). But it is his (female) counterpart Yeshe Tsogyal who hid the terma. So where did the terma come from? We cannot say that Padmasambhava was the greatest terton without acknowledging that it was Yeshe Tsogyal who hid the terma. Terton comes from the Tibetan tradition, but to understand Cosmic History we have to understand this phenomenon in a universal way. Valum Votan is a terton, or hidden treasure finder. The terma of the Red Queen came about when one cycle was closing and another was opening. The cycle cannot close without having a regeneration—in this case a regeneration of the human knowledge base.

In this regard the roles of terma and terton are that of text concealers and text finders or treasure concealers and treasure finders. It is said that the concealer of the terma knows who the finder will be. There are various kinds of terma—some terma is hidden in the ground, some is symbolic, some is pure mind terma, which is triggered by something that was hidden being revealed—like the Tomb of the Red Queen.

GM108X

The GM108X mind transmission, the prophecy of Pacal Votan and the science of the Law of Time are inseparable. The Cosmic History transmission takes account of all facets of life and consciousness and is the introduction to a new order of knowledge on this planet. The key point to understand is that this fundamental shift and reformulation of human knowledge is actually something that can be transmitted from one human being to another. Therefore, it can become part of the acquired human knowledge base. Cosmic History is revealed knowledge that, through study and contemplation, becomes acquired knowledge.

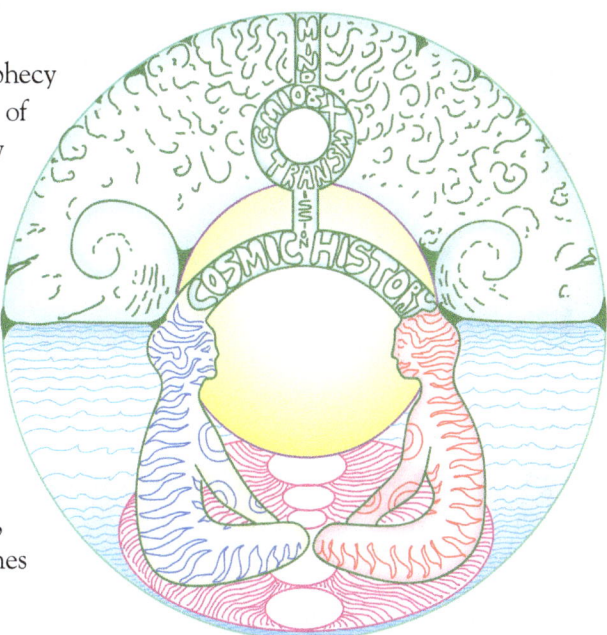

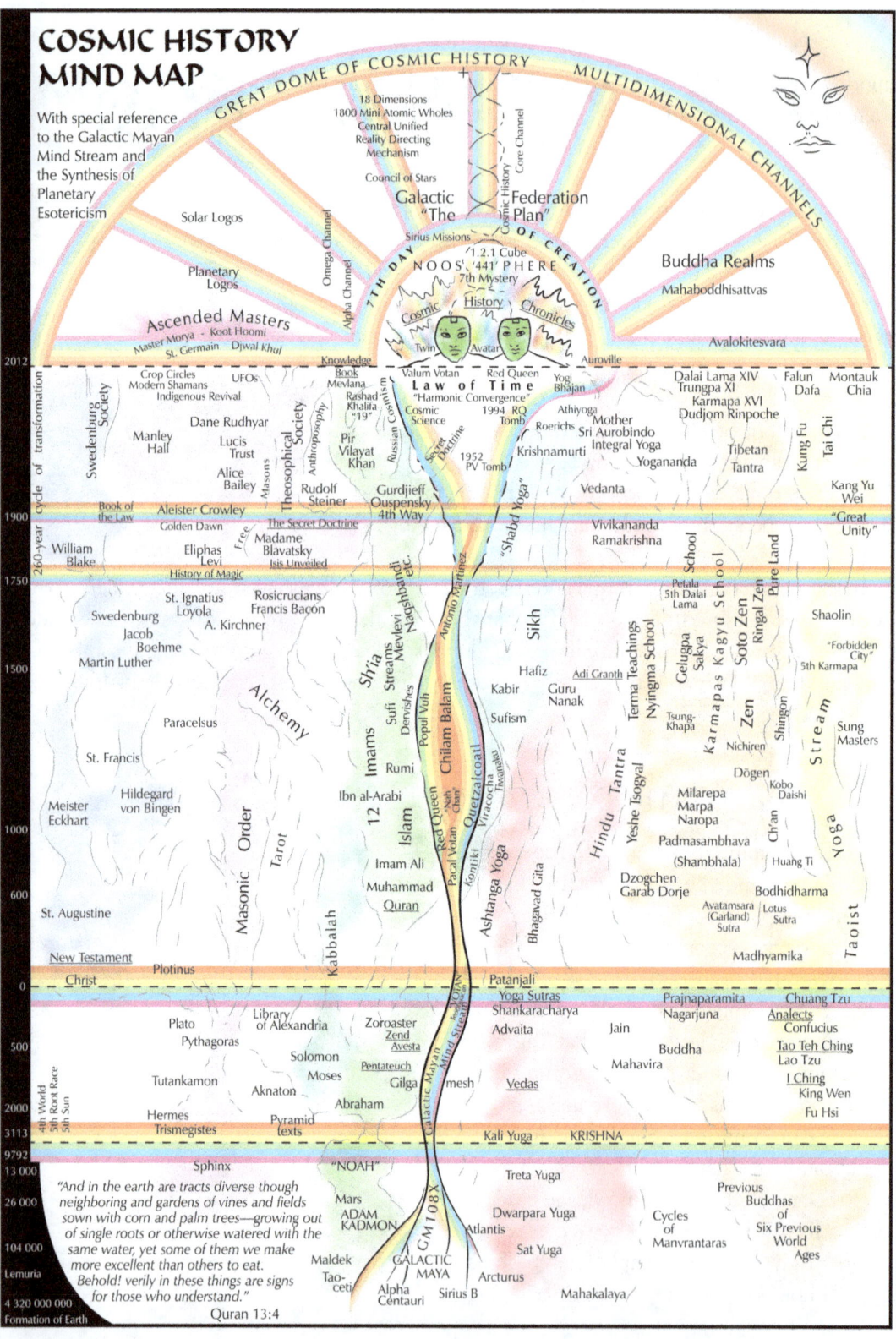

Introduction Part 2: Numerical Proofs of Prophecy

As a new program of galactic knowledge for the terrestrial sphere Cosmic History unifies all true traditions through the fourth-dimensional lens of the Galactic Mayan mind lineage. Cosmic History is based on numerical formulas occasioned by specific cycles of time. The Thirteen Moon Calendar is based on José Argüelles' scientific discovery of the **12:60** and **13:20** timing frequencies.

These timing frequencies are prophetically confirmed by the number of years between the date of the dedication of the tomb of Pacal Votan, AD 692, and the time of its opening, AD 1952 = **1260** years. There are **1320** years from the tomb dedication in AD 692 to the closing of the Thirteen Baktuns, AD 2012.

The **12:60** refers to the unconsciously accepted order of time that is artificial in nature, and **13:20** is the natural timing frequency.

The proof of the synchronic order is in the numbers. For example, note that José Argüelles/Valum Votan passed away precisely **1,328** years after Pacal Votan! And his entire life message was to spread the message of the 13 Moon/28-day calendar as a means to "change times."

Let's look at some of these prophetic correlations between Pacal Votan and Valum Votan. More of these synchronicities can be found in *Time, Synchronicity and Calendar Change: The Visionary Life and Work of José Argüelles*.

Pacal Votan, 603 – 683

Valum Votan, 1939 – 2011. Born on Kin **11** as an identical twin.

The affirmation for Kin **11**, Blue Spectral Monkey, ends with "I am guided by my own power doubled".

His date of birth was also his mother's 30th birthday and parents' **11th** wedding anniversary. Also he was born in the sign of Aquarius, the **11th** sign of the zodiac. Numerically, the Blue Spectral Monkey is written **11.11**. He passed away on Kin 89, the **11th** number in the Fibonacci sequence.

The great Pacal was **11**th in the lineage of the kings of Palenque, also known as Nah Chan, "House of Serpent." Pacal ruled for **52** years. **52** is also a fractal of **5200**. There are five **5200** periods in a 26,000 year cycle.

52 is the number of weeks in a year (364 days + 1), and is also the fractal of the approximate **52**-year cycle of the rotation of Sirius B around Sirius A. The Thirteen Moon calendar also runs in perfect 52-year cycles.

Born 1939: 19 + 39 = **58**. Kin **58** was the disincarnation day of Pacal Votan and the 2012 Day Out of Time (25 July).

There were **58** years between the time of José's first vision at Teotihuacán in 1953 and his passing in 2011. The Day out of Time 2012 landed on Kin 58 and was long count date Kin 11.

(Kin **58** was also the day that the present day "Red Queen" as Stephanie South first entered the tomb of Pacal Votan on June 15, 2000, the 48th anniversary of the discovery of the tomb of Pacal Votan).

In vigesimal mathematics (the mathematics of the Maya) 2.0.12 translates to **812**. **812** reversed is **218**. Kin **218** is the kin number of the discovery of the tomb of Pacal Votan (June 15, 1952). Valum Votan passed away in the Overtone Moon Year, Kin 109. 109 x 2 = **218**.

5 + **8** = **13**. "José Argüelles" has **13** letters. **13** Moon calendar. Temple **13** (of Red Queen).

He passed away in 2011 while living his Kin **31** year (**31** backwards is **13**). 20 + 11 = **31**.

3113 BC is the beginning of the historical cycle that concludes in 2012 (see *The Mayan Factor*). The cube of 11 is **1331**.

There are **60** years from 1952 – 2012. Kin **60**, Yellow Galactic Sun, is the birth sign of Pacal Votan. His tomb was discovered 1260 years after its dedication. 1260 is featured prominently in the Book of Revelation, and also the Book of Daniel, and is equivalent to 42 30-day months or 3 1/2 years.

The 11th chapter of the Book of Revelation talks about the two prophets exiled for 1260 days (1260 = false Babylonian timing cycle).

12 + 60 = **72** (age of Valum Votan when he passed).

From the time of the dedication of Pacal Votan's tomb to 2012 is **1320** years (13 + 20 = 33 = 11 + 22).

1320 rearranged is **2013**, the year of Galactic Synchronization and entry into the new galactic beam.

PART I

ENTERING THE COSMIC MYSTERY PLAY

CHAPTER 1

FROM VELA PULSAR TO COSMIC HISTORY

Cosmic History is a descent into interplanetary memory and knowledge which has its cosmic origin in the Vela pulsar. Our solar system is at the center of a 6,000-light year diameter defined by the pulsar Vela, a remnant of a supernova oscillating at an incredible rate of speed. A pulsar is an advanced, evolved late state of what was once a supernova. This Vela pulsar is what pulsed the information of the larger Cosmic History frame of reference, reaching all the way back to the point of the interval of lost time in eternity.

The Vela pulsar codes contain psychomythic clues and keys to unlocking the causes of the destruction of previous worlds in our solar system. The descent of Cosmic History includes the keys to previous programs that self-destructed (namely Maldek, now the Asteroid Belt) and reformulates these programs, opening a parallel universe or alternate reality option. This new knowledge is formulated in such a way that the events of the previous world systems are reconfigured in the presentation of the knowledge of Cosmic History.

How can we understand our interplanetary history and therefore understand Cosmic History? First we must consider: What is our place in the cosmos? In what direction should we orient our mind? Where have we come from and where are we going? These are the questions that Cosmic History explores.

All of reality is a language of signs and symbols. Everything that appears is a passing ephemeral manifestation, and yet, it represents some specific construct or value of another dimension. In other words, everything we see in the phenomenal realm has a hidden or "occult" meaning.

Cosmic History is based on the Law of Time. This Law defines an order of reality known as the *synchronic order*. All that exists constitutes the synchronic order. The synchronic order is a telepathic number science; it is the science of the future, which we will discuss in further chapters. To know or perceive the synchronic order requires a degree of self-reflective consciousness. Since the universal order of time is so vast, its' essence alone is all we can perceive or know.

A symbol is a sign that opens up, or makes transparent, insights and truths that were previously hidden. The Law of Time makes conscious what was previously unconscious through the symbols and codes of the synchronic order. This revelation also relates to the system of correspondence: everything we see corresponds to something we don't see. Everything on the earthly plane has its correspondence on the heavenly plane: as above so below. The purpose of the synchronic order, as a symbolic system, is to learn how to read a lower reality through the lens of a higher reality. In other words, the whole of reality is actually based on symbolic constructs projected from another dimension.

> *"Because it (reality) cannot be conceived of by the intellect and is free from all conceptual limitations from the very beginning, therefore it is called by the name mahamudra or the great symbol."* —Padmasambhava.

All of reality is an aspect of this great symbol, which is the mahamudra path. All of nature is a code. We are a code. Our human body is a code, a symbol. Time is a code. All of our experiences are coded. In the Sufi tradition everything is a sign—*dhikr*—pointing to the remembrance of God. Everything is a system of divinely orchestrated correspondences. What we see in phenomenal reality is not randomly arranged, but is the response to an underlying system that is precisely ordered, structured and meaningful.

The symbols contained in the synchronic order serve as signposts along the path, lifting us, rung by rung, from the conditioned grid of karmic reality, up the ladder to ever higher states of harmony. The symbols contained in the synchronic order are memory-generating patterns whose codes are defined by simple number relations. We currently live in a society that does not give credence to transcendent values, and therefore does not recognize the higher value of symbolic systems. Symbolic systems are a function of consciousness; they are a non-conceptual language of the transcendent reality.

Because our planet is a symbolic construct, it can be understood as a *timeship*, or a fourth-dimensional vehicle coded with all the laws of cosmic time. As this vehicle moves in time, it releases different levels of information according to a universal set of time-release programs. Cosmic History is part of this time-release program with its root in the synchronic order.

New Galactic Knowledge Base

The seven volumes of the *Cosmic History Chronicles* are derived from a memory stream that not only traces back hundreds of thousands of years, but also extends into other galaxies. However this is a new program of galactic knowledge to this terrestrial sphere that unifies all true traditions through the fourth-dimensional lens of the Galactic Mayan mind lineage.

Cosmic refers to *prajna*, wisdom or the absolute. History is *upaya*, skillful means or place of application—the relative. Cosmos is order and harmony, and harmony is universal. Cosmic order cannot be separated from our own process of perception. The absolute level of Cosmic History is a state of total harmony where every level of every part in all dimensions arrives at a perfect mathematically equal zero-point.

Cosmos is the absolute and history is the relative. Therefore, everything relative has a history. Everything historical is relative yet occurs within a vast complex of structure called the cosmos. The totality of the two creates a redefinition of reality; a reformulation of the human mind where everything is returned to wholeness and to an understanding that there is a GOD principle coordinating everything! (GOD = Galactic Ordering Dynamic, the Divine Master Matrix Source of ALL).

Knowledge Stored in Pyramids

Cosmic History and its prophecy is locked into the stones of Palenque—the focalization point of the GM108X Galactic Mayan Mind transmission on Earth. The root inspiration of Cosmic History comes from the tomb of Pacal Votan in Palenque.

Palenque/Nah Chan is the House of the Serpent or the House of Revelation and Regeneration. Revelation refers to the tombs and the regeneration refers to the living emanations of the tombs. The knowledge contained within Cosmic History helps to return the serpent to the stone or return the revelation—regeneration to the stone, so that the stone becomes awakened matter. Awakened matter becomes the living flesh of the previously unconscious planetary human. When the living planetary human becomes identified with awakened matter then it becomes possible for the perfection of the human soul to occur.

Sarcophagus lid of the tomb of Pacal Votan

As the body of Pacal Votan was laid in the tomb, a jade sphere was placed in his left hand and a jade cube in his right hand. The sphere is the absolute of the Absolute. The cube is the Absolute of the relative. All knowledge of Cosmic History is contained in and derived from these two structures: the cube and the sphere.

Our Place in the Cosmos

Cosmic History is a complete cosmology that focuses on the nature of the universe and recognizes multiple dimensions. From the point of view of modern science, cosmology is a branch of astronomy that deals with the original nature and structure of the natural world. Unlike modern science, the cosmology of Cosmic History is GOD-centered.

From the point of view of Cosmic History, cosmology is the understanding of the process of GOD's self-disclosure, understood as the unfolding of the universe. In other words the universe is the process by which GOD discloses Itself to Itself. The true cosmic scientist knows that only through submission to a higher power is the universe revealed; the universe is the unfolding of the thought and mind of GOD.

The cosmology of Cosmic History is understood through whole system design principles. These design principles are evolved through mathematical structures, platonic solids and the synchronic order. Cosmic History is ultimately a mind transmission stemming from the core matrix of Galactic Intelligence and rooted in the veneration of the whole Earth as a whole system. In this way the human is also viewed as a microcosm—a reflection of the macrocosm/universe or cosmos itself.

How can we understand ourselves as a microcosm? What is our place in the cosmos? How do we study Cosmic History as a cosmology?

First we should remember that in whatever we say or do, we are actually describing ourselves and how our mind works, or how we perceive things. If we want to have true self-understanding it has to have a context. Therefore it is important that we first understand ourselves in the context of the whole cosmos (rather than merely in the context of our home planet).

We can start by feeling the interconnectedness of ourselves with the Earth. We are interwoven into the Earth, and the Earth is interwoven into the solar system and the solar system is interwoven into the galaxy. If we really want to know who and what we are we have to first know what the galaxy is. What is this universe? Where did it come from? What is the purpose of life? Exploring these questions is a main purpose of Cosmic History.

Chapter 1 • From Vela Pulsar to Cosmic History

It is important to understand that we are not the first form of creation, and that this is not the only time of creation. Creation has existed through many times and gone through many different phases. So in order to know about ourselves we need to know where we came from, where we have been and what we have evolved from. Only then can we further understand what we are evolving into. These reflections lead us into wholeness—a complete perception of ourselves. In order to attain a holistic perception of the nature of the universe, including our context and place in the cosmos, a cosmology is necessary.

Cosmology is an important part of the objectification of the psyche. This means that our perception of the cosmos is also a description of the structure of our own psyche and mind. If we want to know our own mind, then we must know the nature of the cosmos; if we want to know the nature of the cosmos, then we must know the nature of our own mind. By hearing other descriptions of experience we can more clearly understand our own experience. Ask yourself, "How do I experience the cosmos?" "What is the cosmos according to the construct of my mind?" Consider the words of Padmasambhava: "All things, all phenomenal existence, everything within Samsara and Nirvana are merely appearances which are perceived by the individual's single nature of the mind."

The fact is that *we* are the universe and the galaxies that constitute the universe are no different than the cells in our bodies. Our perceptions are constantly fluctuating though there is ultimately only one mind. We always need to be thinking about what we are doing and why we are doing it. It is helpful to keep these three basic tenets in mind as we begin to absorb this new knowledge base:

1. Love, love above all.
2. You only advance according to your own effort.
3. In order to evolve, you must learn something new.

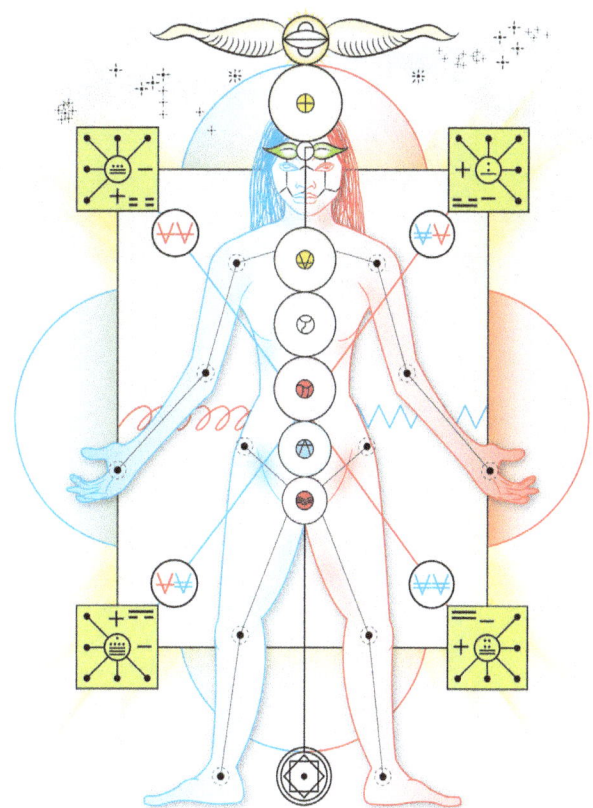

CHAPTER 2

BECOMING A COSMIC THINKER

Whatever appearances arise, all of them are just manifesting, like the images in a mirror that simply occur. Discriminate to see if your own mind is like this or not. —Karma Lingpa, Dzogchen

There is but One Mind that directs all evolutionary processes. Our mind is part of the Universal Mind. Each mind is connected with every other mind; and each mind, wherever it is located is connected with the whole world and cosmos. The cosmos is the sphere of consciousness. The Earth's biosphere is a microcosm of the cosmos, and we humans are a microcosm of the Earth's biosphere. We are each a magnetic field vibrating around our own nucleus and we want to learn how to vibrate with the cosmos.

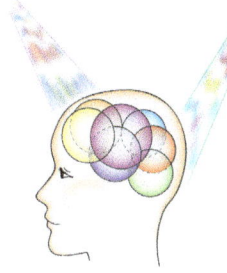

Every day we move through a particular time-space continuum where new situations, information and experiences arise, each one loaded with a variety of impressions. The quality of impressions that we register is in accord with our present level of consciousness. We are always seeking to integrate our experiences when new information is presented to us. How do we make sense of these impressions? Where do they come from? How do we determine if they are coming from our own, or from another's thoughts? How do we perceive reality correctly??

All beings see according to their own perceptions based on previous conditionings until conscious effort is made to break through these conditionings. Most people operate habitually and unconsciously according to programs inherited from family and are influenced by friends, media, environment, education and geographical location. Who we think we are is actually a set of programs running in a predictable order according to different cues and stimuli that create particular responses. These patterns play out in self-reinforcing feedback loops. Many people believe that these pre-recorded feedback loops are who they are and what reality is.

Up to this point in time, we have only been operating with a small portion of our brain capacity. We are so preoccupied by the external world that we let outside circumstances decide for us what 'reality' is so we do not have to think. We let the government do it. We let the Internet do it. We let institutions do it. We let the machine do it. How do we break out of this loop?

The first step is to recognize that the external world is only a particular hologram of reality. It is a collective dream. To break out of this collective dream and penetrate the deeper levels of reality, we must train ourselves to perceive differently. To change our perceptions of reality, we must first learn to think differently. This process requires an intentional exercise of will.

THOUGHTS ARE ELECTRIC

What is thinking? What are thoughts? What does it mean when someone says they are thinking?

What most people label "thinking" is recalling or replaying memories of the past, planning what they will do in the future, calculating and problem-solving (which also most often has to do with money, scheduling, and timing/planning). According to Cosmic Science (a branch of Cosmic History), a thought is more than an invisible set of words, but rather an *electronic line of force*. Electronic lines of force represent different levels of consciousness.

Cosmic History recognizes that the cosmos is filled with mind but that an unconscious artificial matrix has been superimposed over the human mind. So we are therefore in a process of deprogramming and unwinding the conditionings of our mind back to the Cosmic Source. In this process it is important to understand how the mind works.

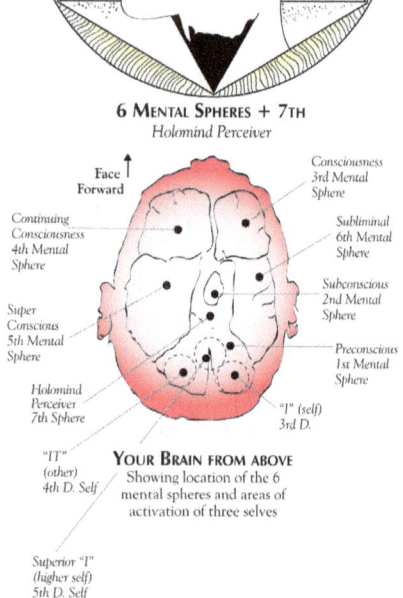

While modern science divides the dormant area of the brain into ten parts, kundalini yoga divides it into six parts. Cosmic Science also divides it into six parts: *six mental spheres*, plus a secret or invisible seventh, known as the holomind perceiver. The other six mental spheres include: preconscious, sub- or unconscious, conscious, continuing conscious, superconscious, and subliminal conscious.

These spheres are located in the brain, each serving a different function in the thinking layers of the cosmos. The brain is the computer or hardware and the mind serves as the grounding rod of the different levels of mind. Depending on the level of thinking we tune into, we ask different questions and get different answers.

At the center of each of these mental spheres are *alphas* (electronic fluids) that give rise to thinking. In other words, what we call "thought" is actually an electronic process that corresponds with interlocking information bits known as analphic engravings in a series. The act of thinking then is actually putting two or more pieces of information together through the correct or incorrect manipulation of a series of analphic engravings. These analphs are projected and registered in a conscious area of the mind, based on knowledge previously acquired. If there is no previously acquired knowledge, then we will try to establish correct thinking according to past analphic engravings. This means that new impressions are generally ignored in favor of what is already known.

Mental Spheres

The six (+1) mental spheres exist independent and apart from the brain and body and describe the processes and functions of the mind's various layers. By consciously activating and recognizing the different mental spheres, we activate dormant parts of our brain.

If the mind is left unexamined, emotions can be stirred up at unexpected moments by sequences of analphs. For this reason, we have to be continuously watchful of our mind as we enter the domain of Cosmic History. The only way that new impressions can be absorbed is if the thinking process is suspended so that fresh or unconditioned engravings can penetrate the mind. For this reason, Cosmic History operates within the fundamental base of Galactic Dzogchen, the integration of the highest mind teachings and meditation techniques with the construct of consciousness presented through Cosmic Science.

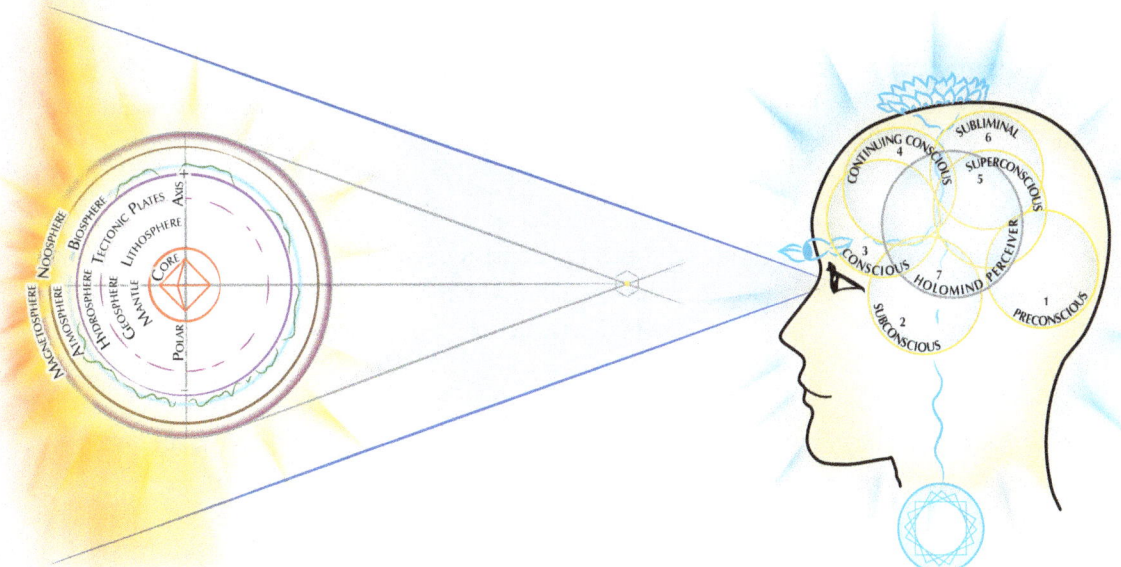

Study of the six (+1) mental spheres allows us new ways of perceiving and linking our daily experiences with the larger unfolding of the cosmic plan. Natural mind is the ordinary state of mind when it is totally relaxed and not thinking about anything. Galactic Dzogchen is the natural practice for directly experiencing your own mind—and of knowing the nature of universal mind.

Through conscious activation of the mental spheres, we can expand our mind and consciousness so that bit by bit, our vibration begins to change. This is a result of adopting new mental habits. Habits are accrued by a particular belief system. A belief system is an ingrained, habitual pattern of behavior and thought. What we repeat on a daily basis to create a semblance of continuity of life constitutes a belief system. The prevailing belief system on our planet today is the 'time is money' 9-5 work week. This belief system is held in place by the Gregorian calendar and mechanical clock and revolves around furthering material affluence of the dominant social order.

Knowledge is also a function of belief systems. For example, the belief system underlying Cosmic History is based on a unitive model—a belief in the supreme unity of all that is. It is also based on the belief that everything that grows is meant to transcend itself.

> **Engraving New Patterns**
>
> To overcome conditioned belief systems we must engrave new habits and patterns within our subconscious mind. Working with the mental spheres is a good way to identify where each of our thoughts is coming from. Conditioned thoughtforms are established as an infinite variety of sequences of analphs, electrical charges in the brain. These analphs carry stores of information commonly referred to as memories, forms of identity, or other sensations that arouse various patterns of conditioned behavior.

Holonomic Law

The whole is in the part, the part is in the hole. The law of holonomics establishes the unitary nature of All-That-Is, and thus works in tandem with the Law of Time. Everything in cosmos demonstrates order with a self-repeating, self-replicating holonomic consistency.

The two fundamental laws of holonomics as discovered by José Argüelles/Valum Votan are: 1) The law of whole systems which governs the uniform consistency of the appearance of all phenomena (including the imaginal realm); and 2) the Law of Time which keeps all phenomena unified by being synchronized in time. Everything is holonomic in structure, even thought. In reality, everything is cosmic!

Cosmic order is the very nature and structure of our inner and outer being. The mind takes the force of nature and projects it as thought. At this time, people are living largely in the unconscious sphere of mind.

Many who live in the realm of rote unconscious became "frozen" at some point in their life. At that point, they shut off the fresh incoming impulses as something occurred to make them distrust their own originality in favor of others' opinions. Once this habit is impressed and accepted by the conscious mind then the capacity for original thought diminishes. Our original creative spark is replaced in favor of attempting to please others and valuing opinions from the external world above our own inner voice. When this occurs we veer further and further from our connection with Source. Most people, to some degree or another, are living at this level of consciousness.

Cosmic consciousness is based on being present in every moment and no longer falling back into states of fear or conceptual errors. The Law of Time says that to reach cosmic consciousness one must break the spell of lower time and dissolve fear-conditioned factors that keep us locked into the unconscious. Most people are sleepwalking.

ACTIVATING DORMANT BRAIN POWERS

We are seeking to integrate fragmented circuits, activate dormant (or frozen) parts of the brain and restore creative imagination. This will allow us to express ourselves in authentic ways and thus unleash our galactic genius on behalf of furthering planetary consciousness. Discipline is essential to change. New patterns repeated on a daily basis over time erase negative or unproductive thought matrixes. Discipline helps engrave a new program until that program becomes second nature to our overall mindset.

The conditioned mind takes many experiences and filters them, sending many seemingly unnecessary thoughts to the subconscious. The unconscious is a vast store of unutilized or rejected thoughts and sense impressions. Though much may be useless, some may be valuable. This is where we develop our power of discrimination. The purpose of establishing the new galactic operating system is to establish a higher behavioral norm. This process stirs up our unconscious programming. With persistence, you will finally reach the point where the new operating system is so strong that you can immediately recognize unconscious programming.

We can begin now to explore how our brain works and how our mind evolves a personality from the workings of the brain. Are we using our minds effectively? How do we activate the dormant parts of our brain? Why do we behave the way they do? What are the steps of further integrating our human psyche, individually and collectively, into the natural cosmic order of planetary consciousness?

If everything we think and do is only coming from one tenth of our brain, this means nine tenths of our brain is pure untapped potential. Some yogis say that the silent parts of our brain have prana, but not consciousness. Why are different parts of the brain inactive? Because there is no energy circulating within them. What is energy? Energy is the factor of interaction of one element or component with another element or component. Everything both seen and unseen is comprised of energy.

Accessing Your Multidimensional Self: A Key to Cosmic History

According to Cosmic Science, energy is any phenomenon of nature that has a dynamic to it causing its fluctuation to appear, grow, or remain static. Energy is a momentum or force field created from the integration of electricity and magnetism. The main formulation of the Law of Time is T(E) = Art or energy factored by time = art. This means that all configurations of energy in the universe are intrinsically aesthetic.

To activate our dormant mind powers we must first lift our awareness and become cosmic thinkers. To become cosmic thinkers we must cultivate clear mind and then begin to occupy our minds with thoughts such as the purpose of creation, the reason this planet exists, the reason we are on this planet, the reason for all created forms and their destinies and the hidden forces and designs which underlie the world of manifestation.

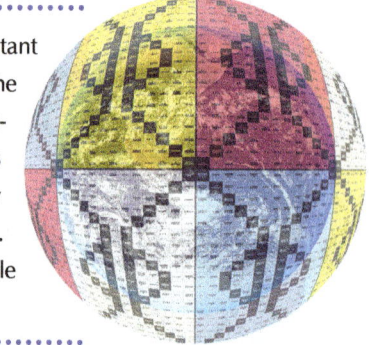

13:20 frequency remains constant throughout all phases of the evolutionarily spectrum of consciousness. 13:20 functions as law of time T(E) = Art (Energy Factored by Time equals Art). The Law of Time is perceivable as the synchronic order.

As Swami Vivekananda says: "Human nature likes to run through the ruts that are already there, because it is easy." By settling for the easy path, we continue to recirculate unconscious analphs or thoughforms. The Law of Time says that this is largely due to operating on a fictional third-dimensional timing frequency. Conditioned thoughtforms are firmly etched sequences of a variety of analphs, electrical charges in the brain that carry stores of information commonly referred to as memories, forms of identity, or other sensations that arouse various patterns of conditioned behavior.

To become a cosmic thinker requires turning the mind away from social or national identification and petty personal affairs to concentrate on larger planetary issues. Cosmic or multidimensional thinkers are interested in what is beyond the reach of the five senses and in the questioning of all human possibilities. This way of thinking is summed up by Arthur Rimbaud:

"I wish to discover all secrets, the mysteries of religion, nature, death and birth, the future and the past, the formation of the universe, non-existence. I am a teacher in creating the extraordinary. Listen!

This is the type of mind we wish to cultivate if we want to awaken the unexplored areas of the mind. Cosmic History demonstrates a whole systems integration of the new cosmic planetary psychology. In this model, a human will identify her/himself in relation to the natural cycles of (the) universal frequency, and in relation to the moon, the seasons, the movement of planets and in relation to the plant, animal and mineral kingdoms.

First Mental Sphere Preconscious (Paranormal Sphere)

This sphere contains karmic patterns, past life dormant analphs, racial archetypal memory and all other primal instinctual programs and autonomic functions. This mental sphere serves as the resonance chamber of the physical body where paranormal faculties are developed and stored. This sphere is the producer of all parapsychological phenomenon and paranormal faculties. It is the place of all untapped psychic energy. Corresponds with radial plasma Dali and Hyperplasma Alpha-Alpha: Profound Samadhi.

Second Mental Sphere: Sub or Unconscious

The Unconscious is the mental sphere that contains conditioned and acquired thought reflexes. This is the repository of rejected conscious stimuli, and of the automatic derived complexes perceived as reality. The unconscious also contains material that may have once been conscious but is now repressed.

Third Mental Sphere: Waking Conscious

This mental sphere contains fleeting and moment-to-moment awareness and is responsive to immediate external stimuli. It is meant to stabilize ordinary consciousness into cosmic awareness. This is also known as the free will sphere. Corresponds with radial plasma Seli and Hyperplasma Alpha-Beta: Informative Samadhi. Corresponds with radial plasma Gamma and Hyperplasma Beta-Beta: Waking Conscious Mediumship.

Fourth Mental Sphere: Continuing Consciousness

Continuing consciousness is the sphere of disciplined concentration. Concentration means centering your mind on a fixed idea and focusing consciously or unconsciously upon it for a prolonged period so that it becomes part of your waking consciousness. This is the Sphere of the 4-D etheric Holon, the soul-mind that responds to the 5-D Higher Self. Corresponds with radial plasma Kali and Hyperplasma Beta-Alpha: Higher Mind Control.

Fifth Mental Sphere: Superconscious

This is the sphere of the fifth-dimensional Higher Self or Electronic body. It is the receiver station for telepathic mind programs from higher-dimensions. It is the seat of cosmic consciousness that is activated by natural mind meditation. Superconscious refers to meta-conscious beyond space-time programming. Only when telepathic continuing conscious has been normalized does superconscious functioning become normalized. At this stage the universe has been reformulated from within. Corresponds with radial plasma Alpha and Hyperplasma Hyperelectronic Superconsciousness: Red Kuali thermic forcefield.

Sixth Mental Sphere: Subliminal Conscious

This is the sphere of parapsychic supermental access. Subliminal means "below threshold". It is the subliminal sphere or plane of mind that processes signals and thought frequencies beyond the metasensory threshold of the biological organism. This is the sphere for reprogramming conventional third-dimensional mental programs. This mental sphere is the seat of our telepathic scanning system and interderdimensional programs. Subliminal means that we are operating independent of past and future—this is how people can contact entities on different planes of existence or in different galaxies. Corresponds with radial plasma Limi and Hyperplasma Hyperneutronic Subliminal Conscious: Blue Duar luminic forcefield.

Seventh Mental Sphere: Holomind Perceiver (HMP)

The holomind perceiver is our evolving organ: the noospheric sensing device. It is localized in the central corpus callosum of the Higher Self. This is the seat of the soul memories, and/or akashic records. The holomind perceiver is localized in the central corpus callosum of the higher self and telepathically imprints information on the corpus callosum of the 3-D and 4-D Self. This is the place of the akashic register, and contains the life summarization of all experiences. Study of and meditation on the holomind perceiver prepares the mind to open to the galactic dimension and receive an entirely new base of knowledge and perception. Corresponds with radial plasma Silio and Hyperplasma Sirius Beta-52 Element 113: Hyperplasmic Enlightenment.

For further information see graphic on p. 191.

Chapter 2 • Becoming a Cosmic Thinker

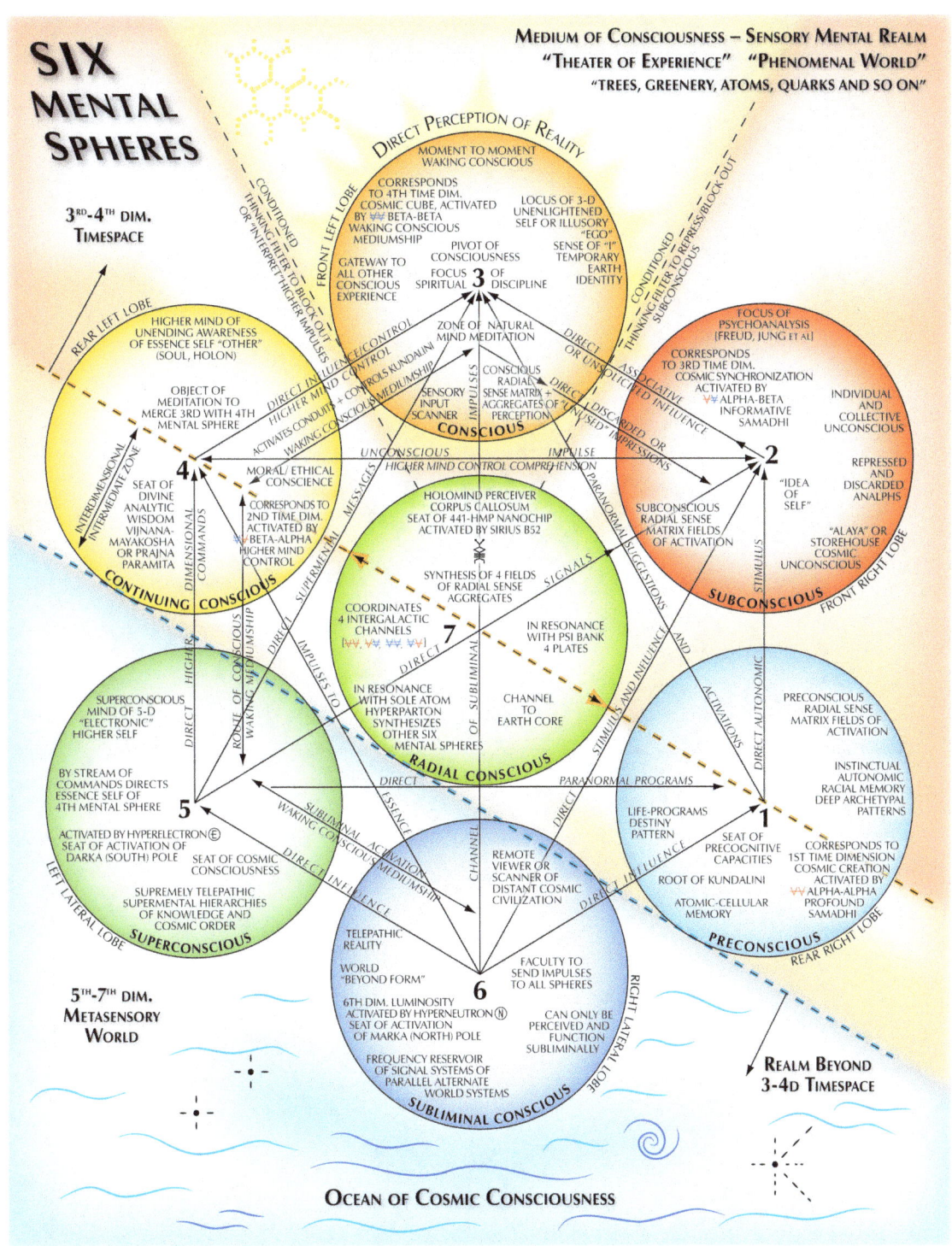

CHAPTER 3

ACTIVATING THE NEW FREQUENCY: 13:20

Is it too much to believe that man should be developing new sensibilities and a closer relation with nature? —Madame Blavatsky, Isis Unveiled

When we enter unfamiliar territory it is important to have a map or set of codes to establish the object of the journey. Our sense and experience of reality comes from internal patterns or maps that cause us to behave and perceive in particular ways. When these internal maps are changed, then our perception of reality changes.

We couldn't learn from nature if there weren't patterns. Nature is organized so that everything supports everything else. The same process that creates nature, creates the human. We recognize patterns because they are coded into our DNA. When we learn to recognize higher patterns of intelligence, then we change the way we interface with the perceived phenomenal reality.

The most fundamental way we can begin to change our patterns is through shifting our timing frequency by following different cycles of time than we are accustomed to. This is the function of the 13 Moon/28-day calendar. This calendar is a gift from galactic intelligence that contains a set of patterns that attunes us to "higher" level experiences within the radial matrix of time where past, future and present are one.

The order demonstrated in the 13 Moon/28-day calendar is not only a vehicle for the re-harmonization of the human mind and even the human DNA, but also a tool for the instant transcendence of history. This is because the 13 Moon/28-day calendar attunes us to the synchronic order—a symbolically coded organization of time. It gives a renewed and cosmic meaning to time.

This calendar, or natural time synchronometer, is actually a mental matrix or harmonic software that lifts us out of linear concepts of time and third-dimensional dogmas. It helps us to realign with our own energy current that has a direct hotline back to Source energy. From here we can receive new visions of the cosmos. How does this work?

Accessing Your Multidimensional Self: A Key to Cosmic History

According to the Law of Time, everything occurring in the universe is the result or manifestation of a fourth dimensional universe of synchronicity that encompasses space (see Chapter 9). The shifting timespace realities that we experience are all part of one master matrix. This matrix is radial, emanating from one center point, which we call the Divine Source or GOD, the Central Intelligence.

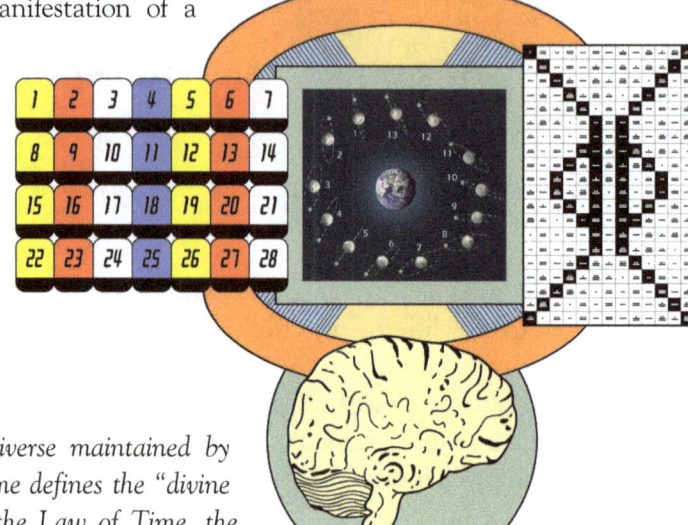

The synchronic order of the universe maintained by the functioning of the Law of Time defines the "divine plan." Prior to the discovery of the Law of Time, the divine plan unfolds in the cosmic unconscious becoming self-reflectively known to the intelligence of evolving bodies in time only as 'revelation.' —Postulate 19.6, Dynamics of Time

13:20 Matrix of Creation

Cosmic History is embedded in the synchronic order and demonstrates new models of reality based on the underlying 13:20 matrix of creation. These models are different than present-day models created with the underlying 12:60 mechanical matrix. The models of reality offered by Cosmic History contain a 3-step process:

1. First there exists an all-pervading field of intelligence.
2. This field of intelligence is populated by simple form design principles.
3. From these simple form design principles emerge luminous code forms.

Cosmic History, then, can be understood as the core of the universal field of intelligence located in the ninth time dimension. This is the inner core time and is co-extensive with the Planetary Mind or noosphere. The phenomenal world is a reflex of this field of intelligence. In this sense intelligence means the capacity of mind to organize.

All third-dimensional experiences, when placed into the context of the synchronic order, reveal a higher level of functioning based on whole system synthesis. At this level, life experiences are no longer fragmented, but are illuminated and take on a dimensional value in relation to all other event points.

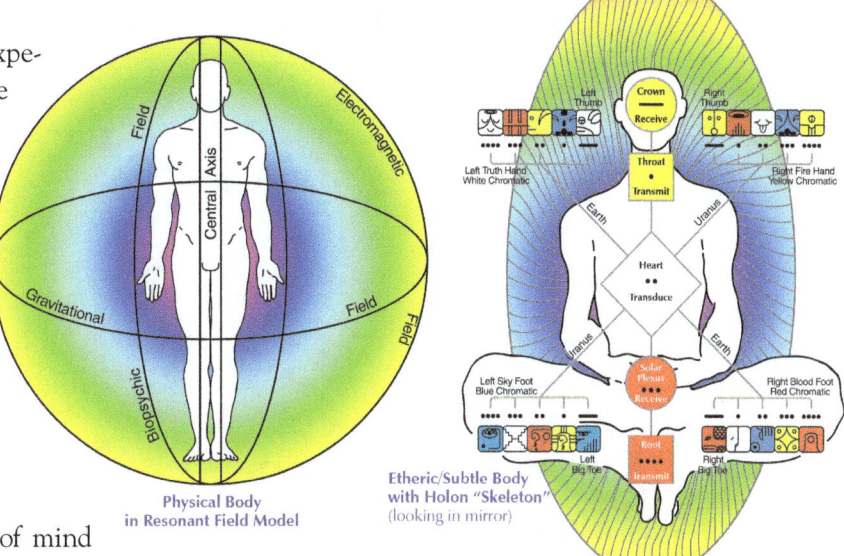

Physical Body in Resonant Field Model

Etheric/Subtle Body with Holon "Skeleton" (looking in mirror)

This new (to us) state of mind or pattern of consciousness is radial in nature, rather than linear. It is coded by the 13:20, the universal frequency of synchronization. By immersing our mind in this reformulated matrix we become imbued with a higher-dimensional system of knowledge accessible through the codes of the Law of Time and the synchronic order. This system of knowledge attunes the mind to the greater orders of cosmos and the greater pattern of cosmic unfolding.

This is the knowledge that elevates our consciousness. It describes a new state of mind than previously known on this planet. To know it, practice it and make it conscious we are given the symbolic patterns or constructs of the Law of Time, contained in the 13 Moon/28-day calendar and Cosmic History.

13 and 20

The 13 and 20 number codes demonstrate the most fundamental organizational pattern of the synchronic order. The 13 numbers represent primal patterns of radiant energy. The 13 is the code of cosmic consciousness and also represents the uninscribed emerging feminine energy of creative imagination. These numbers can be thought of as radio-pulses. The 20 symbols represent the cycle of frequency-range possibilities that each of these radio-pulses may undergo.

Accessing Your Multidimensional Self: A Key to Cosmic History

So the 13 and 20 are the key numbers of the synchronic order and demonstrate a coded pattern of symbolic constructs. These constructs incorporate earlier symbolic structures, while demonstrating through the lens of the synchronic order, new levels of consciousness than have previously been known.

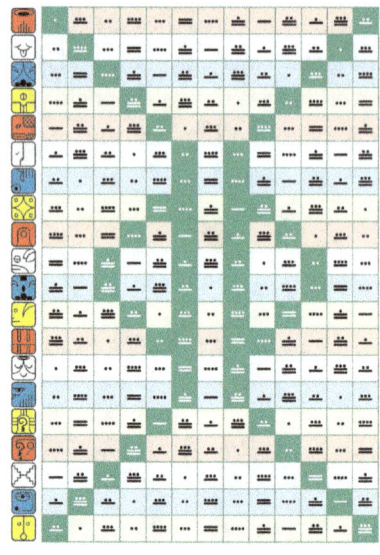

If the thirteen numbers [galactic tones] are the light that arouses the mind and body, then the twenty directional positions [solar seals] are the water that nourishes this very same mind and body. In the interplay of thirteen numbers and twenty symbols lies the in-dwelling galactic code-bank that informs the resonant structures comprising the symbol-woven tapestry of our reality. —José Argüelles, *The Mayan Factor*

The synchronic order is what Sri Aurobindo calls the "supramental descent." Supramental means "beyond mind". The synchronic order is a supramental structure based on number. Behind all symbols there is number. Number precedes consciousness—it is supramental, beyond mind. Number is what gives mind (and cosmos) its sense of of order, harmony and organization.

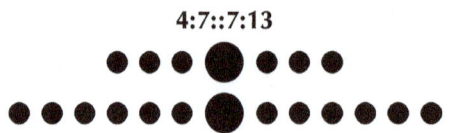

From its dedication in the year 692 to the year 2012 was exactly 1320 years. On the eastern edge of the sarcophagus lid of Pacal Votan there are six glyphs known as galactic signatures—one of 20 icons coded by a number, 1-13, hence 13:20. The tones (numbers) of the first set of four signatures add up to 28; the tones of the second set of two signatures add up to 13, the numbers of the perfect 13 Moon/28-day calendar.

Where Do New Codes Come From?

The synchronic order demonstrates a new organization of time, a new symbolic construct, and an entirely new reality that unfolds eons into the future. The 13 Moon calendar Dreamspell codes, when applied, form an evolutionary ladder into continuing consciousness.

Where do these codes come from? There are obviously other beings in other galaxies transmitting to us these new frequencies. This is completely new knowledge based on the GM108X lineage (Galactic Mayan mind transmission). New knowledge can only reveal itself when there is a vacuum that establishes the need for new information. This vacuum is created by our present planetary process where the acceleration of events and information is coupled with a collective loss of orientation, meaning and purpose. This species-wide disorientation requires a greater vision than previously known.

The 13 Moon/28-day calendar enters us into the synchronic order. How? By entraining our mind into a new matrix of harmony and regularity through which it can be reformulated and brought into the synchronic order. The synchronic order represents the perception of the totality of time at any given moment, and is the foundational knowledge base of Cosmic History.

Cosmos is order and History is the process. The synchronic order introduces a dimension of history as process, manifesting different levels of knowledge. There is cosmos and then the pattern of order of cosmos as it plays out in an unfolding which is called "time" or "history."

> Cosmic History is a function of the Law of Time and the Law of Time is a function of the 13:20 matrix. This Avatar's Wheel of Time consists of 20 signs or icons, 13 numbers and 8 binary triplet codes. The 20 seals represent 20 qualities of universal, cosmic being. This wheel is activated at the center by the binary principle (Hunab Ku), which, in turn, moves the lunar terrestrial wheel 13 times around the Sun.
>
> The Sun at its equator turns on its axis 13 times in one terrestrial orbit, just as the moon revolves around the Earth 13 times during the same orbit. From the Earth, the apparent rotation of the Sun on its axis at its equator takes 28 days. Within the core of the Earth, the Master Time Molecule consists of 28 nodes or forms of multiple receptions to accommodate all the possibilities of cosmic galactic transmission that come to the Earth. What we call a year is actually one solar orbit or one solar ring around the Sun. Within the turning of these wheels, the knowledge of the cosmos can be read. Day represents photonic activation. Night represents photonic regeneration.

Accessing Your Multidimensional Self: A Key to Cosmic History

VIGESIMAL SYSTEM OF THE SYNCHRONIC ORDER

The synchronic order utilizes whole number mathematics. Whole number mathematics governs universal development. Again, number precedes mind; all things manifest are brought forth from the matrix of number. The cosmology of the Law of Time is ultimately pure number. Likewise Cosmic History is governed by the mathematical order of 2(0)—binary doubling—just as the DNA has 64 codons (1, 2, 4, 8, 16, 32, 64).

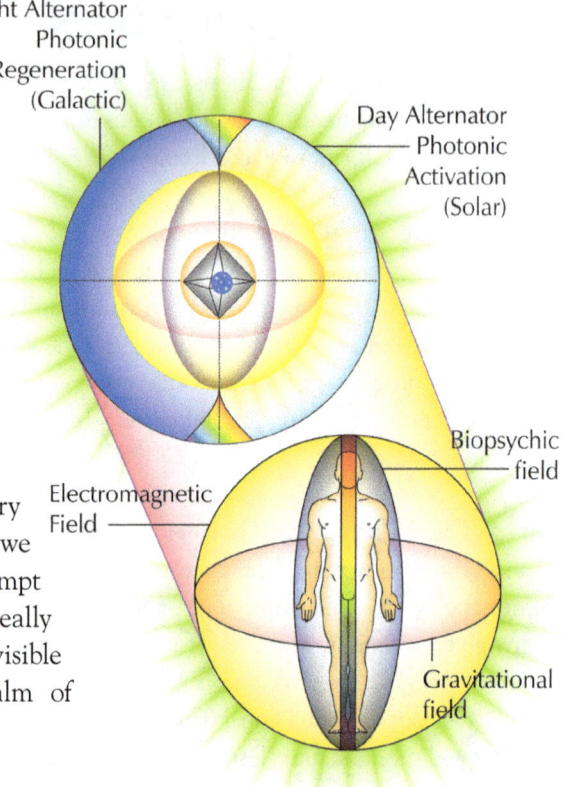

The process of creation moves through a binary doubling process. What kind of universe do we discover if we count by 20 rather than 10? We attempt to explain through use of language, though what is really communicating happens behind the words in the invisible archetypal structure of number—this is the realm of resonance, the feeling behind the apparent words.

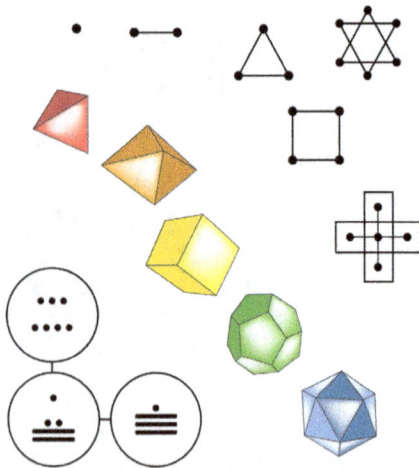

The synchronic order corresponds with whole number mathematics of the 20 code, inclusive of the geometric solids and the binary progression, 1, 2, 4, 8, 16, 32, 64 etc.

The synchronic order corresponds to the whole number mathematics of the 20 code (vigesimal). Think about each number (1-20) as dynamic or static. All stages and levels of consciousness can be expressed in mathematical or geometrical orders.

The 20 vigesimal code represents the resonant frequencies of different stages and cycles of the phenomenal and imaginal worlds—elemental structures, mythic structures, archetypal structures, and so on. This is the minimum depiction of the cosmic whole.

The present world of the human civilization was developed and is based on the third-dimensional zero, functioning as a positional place factor for 10, only half of the score (20). Ten is third-dimensional and 20 is fourth-dimensional.

The third-dimensional decimal "10" code creates an artificial world—artificial in compensation for being closed off from the cosmic benefits of fourth-dimensional operation. Operating within the framework of the decimal system creates a cultural infrastructure with a widespread lack of higher-dimensional experience distinct from ordinary imaginal experience. Application of vigesimal mathematics is what creates a new order of reality.

Why do we use the vigesimal system? The progression of numbers reorganizes the mind's conception of number very dramatically. For example, imagine a bicycle is the power of ten and a car is the power of 20. They both have wheels, but the car also has a motor. We can also apply this analogy to the third and the fourth dimensions, with the understanding that the third dimension corresponds to the process of involution of spirit into matter and the fourth dimension corresponds to the process of evolution of spirit out of matter.

Repatterning in Stages

Repatterning our mind according to the synchronic order happens in stages. At first it takes effort to learn something new, but as you do you will be rewarded with greater incidences of synchronicity as well as increased memory and continuing consciousness. Why? Because these are memory codes. As memory codes they work on a subliminal level. This is why discipline is the key.

Discipline, concentration and persistence are required if we are to break out of our conditioned mind. By applying these qualities we can transcend our biogenetic filters and enter into a fresh way of perceiving ourselves and the world. The biogenetic filter is a processing and storage system of our conceptual conditioned mind. This filter prevents us from receiving new impressions as they are rejected in exchange for familiar or preconceived perceptions of reality. Until these filters are deprogrammed, purified and transcended, it is very difficult to say what is real.

In order to establish new patterns it is important to keep in mind the five formative powers: 1) The power of Remembrance. 2) The power of Discipline. 3) The power of Exertion. 4) The power of Patience. 5) The power of Compassion.

Through accomplishing these formative powers we lift ourselves out of conditioned mind and dissolve the veils of the illusory world so that new, cosmic perceptions can penetrate.

Remembrance. First comes an awakening, followed by a memory. Once remembrance occurs you want to cultivate the memory by staying awake. This requires meditative awareness and returning to natural mind. With remembrance comes the capacity for cultivating self-reflection. Self-reflection overcomes the snare of self-importance.

Discipline. Discipline is exercise in higher forms of physical and mental development. Discipline means freedom from habitual thoughts and routine. Discipline is the capacity for self-purification. Discipline has meaning only when it is voluntarily undertaken. Self-purification overcomes the snare of self-indulgence.

Exertion. Exertion means diligence and energetic application—striving for perfection. The quality of exertion is self-transcendence. Self-transcendence overcomes the snare of self-deception. No matter how well you think you've done you can always exert more and do better. This is the root mechanism of mental spiritual evolution.

Patience. Patience is tolerance—a forbearing that removes the barriers between self and other. Patience brings forth the cultivation of humility and the quality of self-sacrifice. Patience is the antidote to feelings of aggression. Self-sacrifice overcomes the snare of self-righteousness.

Compassion. Compassion is unconditional giving—the basis of wealth and abundance. Compassion is pure selflessness. Pure selflessness overcomes the snare of poverty mentality, for you are always rich in giving. Compassion is also exchanging yourself for others. By putting yourself in someone else's shoes you then cease judgment and equalize perceptions of others.

PART II

ENTERING THE UNIFIED MIND OF THE EARTH: NOOSPHERE

CHAPTER 4

DEFINING THE MIND OF GAIA – NOOSPHERE

Every part of the earth is sacred to my people. Every shining pine needle, every sandy shore, every mist in the dark woods, every clearing and humming insect is holy in the memory and experience of my people. —Chief Seattle

The whole planet is alive! We are awakening to the fact that we live in a radiantly pulsing, interactive and responsive universe. Our mind is linked to a higher mind, sometimes called the *noosphere* or *mind of Gaia*.

The Greek goddess Gaia, or Ge, is the Great Earth Mother of all and the creator and giver of life to all the universe. She is the first being to emerge from chaos, so she is the supreme organizing principle that holds the noosphere in her all-embracing body of love. Gaia is the spirit of love that infuses the noosphere with planetary heart.

"Noos" comes from the Greek word "mind". So noosphere is actually the sphere of the mind or mental envelope, meaning the planet Earth's mental envelope or mental sphere. All communication actually comes from the planetary mind of the noosphere that is cradled in Gaia's compassionate embrace.

Ancient cultures were matriarchal—matri (mother), arch (beginning)—beginning with the Mother. Gaia reminds us that all of existence forms an absolute unity. This means that what happens in the cosmos is related to what happens on the Earth and is also related to what happens in our body and daily life. This unified field is connected through Gaia's loving thought beams that form a radial matrix that links past, future and present as one interconnected web. We are here to remember this unity and to collectively evolve our consciousness. Time is the evolution of consciousness, and love is the highest art of time.

The Law of Time

> ...*Consciousness cannot be separated from time. Time evolves consciousness as increasing orders of self-reflection according to the equation T(E) = Art.* —Postulate 16.1, Dynamics of Time

The Law of Time states that time is the universal factor of synchronization. This means that time is the unifying factor that connects all things throughout the universe, from people to events to bodies in space. This was also the belief of Russian astrophysicist Dr. Nikolai Kozyrev who believed that Time is the energy that maintains the phenomenon of life in the world.

Kozyrev saw that the key to understanding psychic or paranormal activity has everything to do with a thorough understanding of the energy of Time. Kozyrev said the "velocity of time is instantaneously infinite", meaning that time, as an energy, does not propagate but is immediately everywhere. The cybersphere is a prototype of the noosphere, and presently it is the cyber matrix that holds the entire knowledge of the present world order in place. We know that in the primordial beginning there was one community, one language, one mind; now there are many, but we ultimately return to the One. In this regard Divine Unity is our inescapable destiny that leads to the noosphere and the Psychozoic Era.

The Earth contains a series of layers or envelopes: the dense iron crystal core, the molten rock mantle, the lithosphere, hydrosphere, atmosphere, biosphere, stratosphere, magnetosphere and finally, the noosphere. This creates an elaborate feedback system that maintains itself in a particular state of homeostasis, sometimes referred to as Gaia. When the homeostasis is sufficiently disturbed, disruption or disorder occurs, but ultimately resolves, entering the Earth into a new timespace. The present Earth is now transiting from the sixth day of creation, to the seventh day of creation.

Noosphere is the first stage of cosmic civilization on Earth and represents the Age of the Mystic. So, by making the noosphere conscious we assist our own, and Gaia's, evolution out of fragmented chaos and back to the divine order of the Primal Mother, where we become "freely thinking (hu) mankind as a single entity" (Vladimir Vernadsky).

Noosphere and Galaxy

To understand the noosphere, we must: 1) Begin to think from the point of view of the Earth; and 2) Begin to understand the purpose and nature of the universe and of our Great Grandmother Galaxy, in whom each and every star are relatives in one great galactic family.

Chapter 4 • Defining the Mind of Gaia – Noosphere

One hundred fifty years ago people scarcely knew that these long-forgotten relatives existed. Now, with the Hubble telescope and other space technologies, we can get pictures of the universe and see not only our own galaxy, but billions of galaxies—50 billion galaxies! Yet, we cannot even comprehend our own galaxy (family).

Each galaxy has anywhere from 10 to 50 billion stars! Try to imagine 10 billion x 50 billion stars! Many of those stars have their own planetary systems. If this is so, then how many of these planets are there that support life and consciousness and what, who and where are we? And what is the Universe?

Consider that this universe, as an entity, is the evolutionary projection of the light body of God. Imagine yourself at the center of this Universe emanating beams of thought rays that

NOOSPHERE TIMESPACE (4-D)
INTERSECTING WITH
OLD BIOSPHERIC TIMESPACE (3-D)

extend out like spinning spools; each spinning spool is a galaxy and each galaxy is a gigantic thought molecule. Think of our galaxy as a galactic being, 100,000 light years in diameter, composed as a cosmic thought molecule: The form and structure of a mental entity of the universe, a living being.

Now think of the stars as thought atoms. Around many of the stars different planets go spinning like electrons. In some planets there is life that evolves in all sorts of different forms or structures, such as the planet we find ourselves on. There are planets with noosphere and planets without noosphere, as indicated by Pierre Teilhard de Chardin

Now think of the universe as a luminous and omniscient mental organization. In this luminous universe, the human being is simultaneously a nanospeck and, as a whole, a self-reflective subatomic quantum of intelligence. Nonetheless our mind has the capacity to step outside of the universe and conceive of the whole. This is an amazing power!

Because of our gift of self-reflective intelligence we can coordinate and establish feedback with the local star system. But to do this we must be in a state of unified resonance with the planetary orbits (that form but a part of the whole etheric stellar body). This unified resonance hooks us into the total planetary feedback system: this is the noosphere or the mind of Gaia. We are rapidly accelerating toward the supreme unification of planetary consciousness.

To understand the galactic nature that we live in, imagine that Great Grandmother Galaxy whispered to her star children to release gifts to her family on many planets. Among these gifts are the codes of the synchronic order which provide validation for her children's intuitive nature and function as a guide on the path back to the stars. It is a form of sacred play and all forms of sacred play are direct routes to the Goddess or Primal Mother, the pure wisdom of the ever-new reality. She is the Primal Matrix from which the patterns of gods and mortals spring forth—she IS the PATH of the Synchronic Order. She has bore her gifts to help Her family to work out their own destiny as quickly as they choose to rejoin Her in the electrifying reality of the noosphere.

Through the lens of the Law of Time, the noosphere is understood as the layer of mind on Earth for the transformation of cosmic thought and consciousness. This means it has always existed, but has remained largely in the collective unconscious. To reach noospheric consciousness is a main purpose of Cosmic History. To get to this stage we pass through different levels of consciousness, lighting up each of the six mental spheres until we finally hit the jackpot and penetrate the galactic piñata of the seventh mental sphere—holomind perceiver—with treasures bursting forth radially in all of its technicolor glory.

The first step to enter noospheric consciousness is cultivating the facility to encompass the whole Earth in your heart and feel it as a single thoughtform. In other words, feel the Earth in your body as yourself and repeat: "I am one with the Earth, the Earth and myself are one mind." Then contemplate the fact that the Earth Mother embraces both her dark children and her light children simultaneously, so that She is always experiencing night and day simultaneously. She is always experiencing summer and winter simultaneously and spring and autumn simultaneously.

When we can directly experience this synchronic simultaneity then we will know what it means to transcend linear time and experience ourselves as the source of all synchronicity, a chief characteristic of the new mind of the noosphere that we are moving into.

Mentation Waves Replace Thinking

Cosmic History recognizes that what is often referred to as human "thought" is just the lower self or ego recirculating fictitious perceptions. Cosmic thoughts are referred to as *mentation waves*. A mentation wave is a configuration of telepathic potentialities, independent of language. It is the deep underlying psychic structure of the Primal Mother. As the evolution of thought, mentation waves are based on a whole order of supermental precepts, intrinsic to non-egoic knowing.

The mentation waves are functions of the holomind perceiver, understood as our "sixth sense" made conscious. Those mentation waves operate at the inner core of the ninth time dimension, radiating out to the different mental spheres as needed for any given situation.

The knowledge of Cosmic History is embedded in the noosphere and is self-originated by the need of cosmos to know itself. It is the Primal Mother that guides us back to this knowledge. The entire cosmos is moved by the urge of the Mother to self-reflection because it is ultimately a function of the universal mind. The self-reflection of the cosmos is Cosmic History.

All knowledge ultimately originated in the Matrix of Universal Intelligence or the Mind of GOD. This can be experienced when we release our ego mind and merge with the universal cosmic mind. It is within this larger mind that the multiverse is knowable.

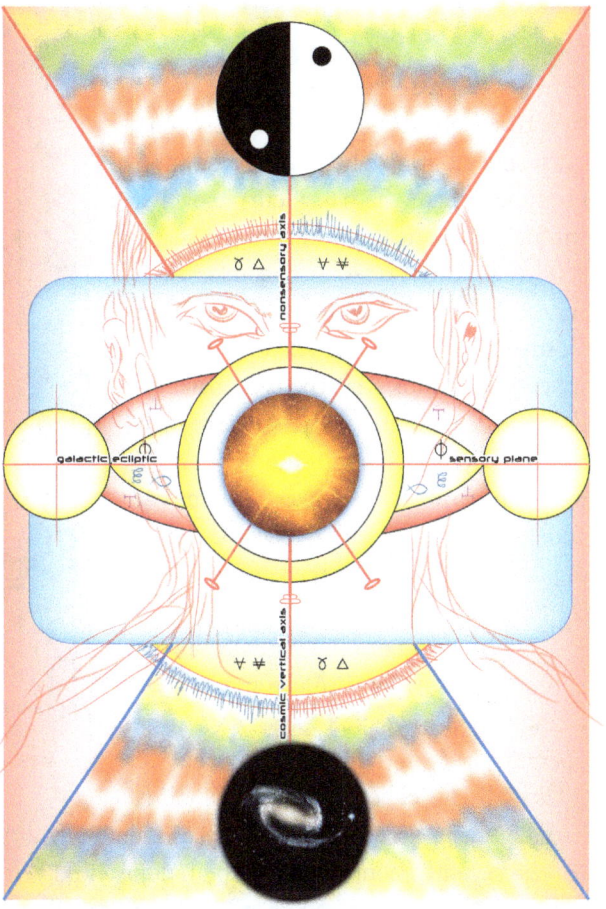

What is the Noosphere?

The noosphere—literally, "mind-sphere" or Earth's mental sheathe—is a word and concept jointly coined by Edouard le Roy, French philosopher and student of Henri Bergson, Jesuit paleontologist Pierre Teilhard de Chardin, and Russian geochemist Vladimir Vernadsky, in Paris, 1926. At the root of the primary definition of noosphere is a dual perception that (1) life on Earth is a unity constituting a whole system known as the biosphere; and (2) that the mind or consciousness of life—the Earth's thinking layer—constitutes a unity that is discontinuous but coextensive with the entire system of life on Earth, inclusive of its inorganic support systems. A third critical premise arising from the first two is that the noosphere defines the inevitable next stage of terrestrial evolution, which will subsume and transform the biosphere. —Valum Votan

STAGES OF CONSCIOUSNESS

There are five sheaths in the basic structure of the Earth: lithosphere, hydrosphere, atmosphere, biosphere, and noosphere. Like the biosphere we evolve through different stages of consciousness. As we saw in previous chapters these states of consciousness are referred to in Cosmic Science as the six (+1) mental spheres beginning with the preconscious, then to the unconscious, passing through the conscious and continuing conscious to the superconscious, subliminal conscious, until finally we evolve a new organ: the holomind perceiver.

This new organ has actually always existed. It is what Princeton physicist David Bohm called the "creative operation of underlying ... levels of reality." Bohm believed that our world is actually the projection of something even more real that is happening at the deeper levels of creation. As the seventh mental sphere, the holomind perceiver is the master program or "computer" within our brain. Located in and projected from the center corpus callosum, the holomind perceiver is the sixth sense made conscious. It serves as the transmitting and receiving station of the UR runes of the genetic code and matrices of the psi bank. All codes of the synchronic order can be located within the holomind perceiver, based on the 441 cube matrix structure.

Bohm believed that the universe is a single unified system of nature. Russian scientist V.I. Vernadsky said that the sum of life is a single unity. This unity includes everything from the plankton to the human species. Everything is interconnected. So the capacity for thinking and intelligence is not limited to just the human beings, but the whole system of life that as one whole is reflecting the noosphere.

The noosphere is an active, ever-evolving thinking agent. Everything that has ever been thought, said or done is registered in the noosphere. This means that everything is accessible to us now.

Chapter 4 • Defining the Mind of Gaia – Noosphere

> ### FRENCH PALEONTOLOGIST PIERRE TEILHARD DE CHARDIN.
>
> Pierre Teilhard de Chardin states that there are planets with noosphere and planets without noosphere. The noosphere is evolved because there is a need for a higher organizing mind—a unified thinking element that processes and provides the appropriate, adequate information of the advance of the species into greater levels of consciousness.
>
> The noosphere also represents a stage in evolution. Vernadksy states that the next geological era will be the Psychozoic era. Presently we are living in the Holocene—"most recent age"—era. *Psych* refers to mind or spirit and *zoo* refers to life. So the Psychozoic era brings about the spiritualization of life and of the entire thinking mechanism of the Earth or the noosphere.

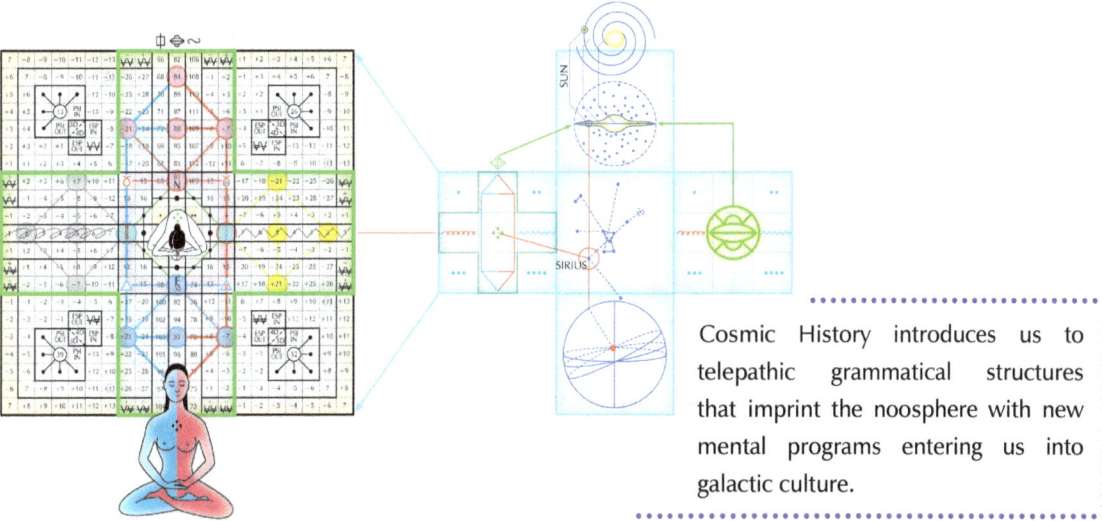

Cosmic History introduces us to telepathic grammatical structures that imprint the noosphere with new mental programs entering us into galactic culture.

WHAT IS NOOSPHERIC CONSCIOUSNESS LIKE?

The noosphere is a new stage of consciousness that we have not experienced as a totality—but we are about to. Some masters have reached cosmic consciousness, but not all the individuals who have reached cosmic consciousness have been able to reach the others who have reached cosmic consciousness. Noospheric consciousness occurs when all the different molecules of intelligence simultaneously reach a stage of unified consciousness where they can all commune with each other.

Once the collective is engaged in noospheric consciousness we will realize that Earth is a whole system and gain more insight into how this whole system works. At this stage we will understand whole-system design principles and begin the re-creation of the Earth as a divine masterpiece—the ultimate work of art. We will then be allowed to directly participate in:

> Reshaping of the Earth (into a work of art)
> Clearing of all damage and pollution
> Exercising our/Earth's paranormal powers (which are natural)

Within noospheric consciousness we realize we are an extension of an evolving consciousness and spirit. We do not categorize our experience as a special thing that happened to "us", but rather a process unfolding within the greater whole.

Entering into noospheric consciousness, we come into direct attunement with Gaia who reveals Her divine gifts of telepathic technologies, such as time travel, telepathy and cosmic teleportation. It is She who reveals to us that the noosphere is not only the thinking layer on our planet, but it extends into other dimensions as well. It is encoded with the multidimensional scale of the universal cosmic mind, which is the root of Cosmic History and Cosmic Science.

Noosphere and Mediumship

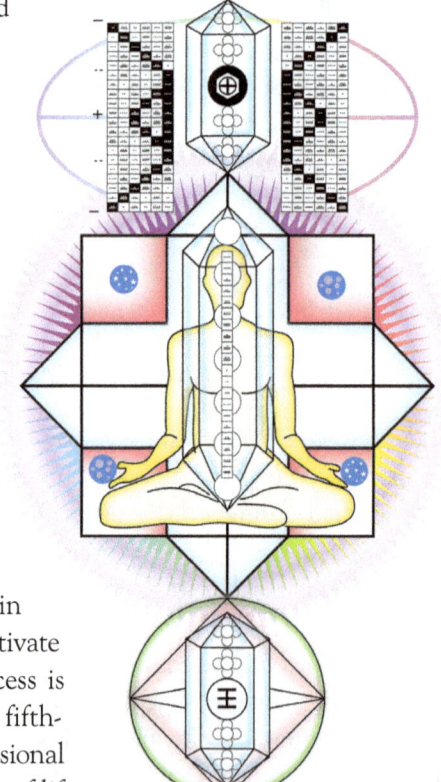

The mind of the noosphere also refers to the collective mind of the masters, which enters us into the exploration of cosmic mediumship. At one point we cross over from the world of illusion into the world of the Masters. Within this noospheric mindfield what we call "paranormal" is the norm.

Many people have paranormal experiences and think they are going crazy because they have no reference points for their experience. This is the noosphere bleeding through, but without context the human can become very confused. According to Cosmic Science, the paranormal phenomenon is a natural occurrence whose origin not being known can lead to fanaticism, hysteria or madness.

Understanding the six (+1) mental spheres is key in learning how to operate within the noosphere and activate increasing levels of paranormality. This evolutionary process is connected with the integration of our third-, fourth- and fifth-dimensional bodies. To learn to coordinate the third-dimensional being with the fourth-dimensional being is a major purpose of life and is what opens us to multidimensional paranormality.

While paranormal powers exist as evolutionary potentialities they are not the *purpose* of evolution, but the process of expanding into greater consciousness. If it were not for the existence of "paranormal" phenomena we might be forever trapped in the third-dimensional material plane of existence. In this regard paranormal activity exists to awaken us to the existence of higher phenomena.

The more we can articulate and understand the nature of multidimensional paranormality, the more we can understand the noosphere and the future evolutionary potentials that we are entering.

The preconscious first mental sphere contains the codes of parapsychological manifestations and is where these phenomena are produced. In the third-dimensional body, this mental sphere covers the cerebellum portion of the brain and is a direct function of the higher self or fifth-dimensional spirit guide. This mental sphere serves as a resonance chamber of the physical body where paranormal faculties are developed and stored.

LAW OF TIME AND PARANORMAL PHENOMENA

Time travel, telepathy, bilocation and displacement are examples of the fruits of the application of the Law of Time. This universal law illustrates how to travel from one part of the universe to another through techniques of holographic projection.

The Law of Time makes conscious what was unconscious. When we are conscious of the Law of Time, then we can use our experiences to trigger us into higher states of consciousness. This is because Time is the evolution of consciousness. Our quality of experience is determined by the frequency of time that we are tuned into at any given moment.

> *"Whole body time transport is the capacity to extend through the now into continuing and superconscious. This is achieved through total holographic projection whose quality is proportionate to the vividness and completeness of the alternative fourth-dimensional personality to incorporate the third-dimensional internal body sensation usually referred to as 'self.'"* —Postulate 13.2, Dynamics of Time

Given that cosmos is universal, everyone ultimately is capable of totally comprehending the cosmos. Consider this: what we think of as "our mind" is merely a resonant quality of the Higher Mind; therefore "our mind" is not limited to our brain or nervous system. This Higher Mind is above and beyond the raw storage of our different perceptions, stimuli, memory and experiences. So there is the information storage layer of our experience and then there is the thinking layer. To pass through the thinking layers or stages of consciousness requires persistent discipline in the control of thoughts through yoga and meditation.

Interdimensional communication is established through the mind and is navigated by the six (+1) mental spheres. These spheres describe, among other things, the process and functions of mind programmed with parapsychological phenomena, which occurs through the preconscious (first mental sphere) from the fifth-dimensional entity. Mental spheres are connected to the third-, fourth-, and fifth-dimensional functionings and provide the being with the capacity to link interdimensional information, which is the Way of the Noosphere.

In beginning to define noospheric consciousness we can study the Four Formative Powers which form a bridge into the world of light. These powers are encoded into the holomind perceiver and illustrate the level of noosphere where the minds of the masters reside. The four formative powers radiate from the central fifth force channel, the supreme channel of cosmic unification and radial consciousness coded by the Sirius B-52 element 113.

The Four Formative Powers have as their prerequisite the integration of the five preliminary formative powers of active participation in the inner work. These five formative powers as outlined in the previous chapter are: Remembrance, Discipline, Exertion, Patience and Compassion.

Four Formative Powers of the World of Light

Cosmic Creation: Alpha-Alpha channel of Profound Samadhi. Refers to mastery of the cosmic forces. This comes about through the self-creation of the energy of space. Here we are no longer the victim of conditioned reality, thoughts and patterns. We have freed ourselves from the claims of the false self. Here, we are creating our selves and reality anew. We have reached the source of creation within our mind.

Cosmic Ascension: Beta-Alpha channel of Higher Mind Control. Refers to mastery of higher powers of telepathic perception and projection. This means we can perceive ourselves anywhere in the universe and project to those places as necessary.

Cosmic Synchronization: Alpha-Beta channel of Informative Samadhi. Refers to mastery of the synchronic order: Self-Creation through time. Here, we master the codes of the synchronic order, embedding them into our subconscious.

Cosmic Cube: Beta-Beta channel of Waking Conscious Mediumship. Refers to the mastery of the principle of cosmoplanetary design. This is a high level of cosmic mastery entering us into higher mental design processes by which planets and whole universes come into being. Here, we become co-creators of the cosmic evolutionary process.

Chapter 4 • Defining the Mind of Gaia – Noosphere

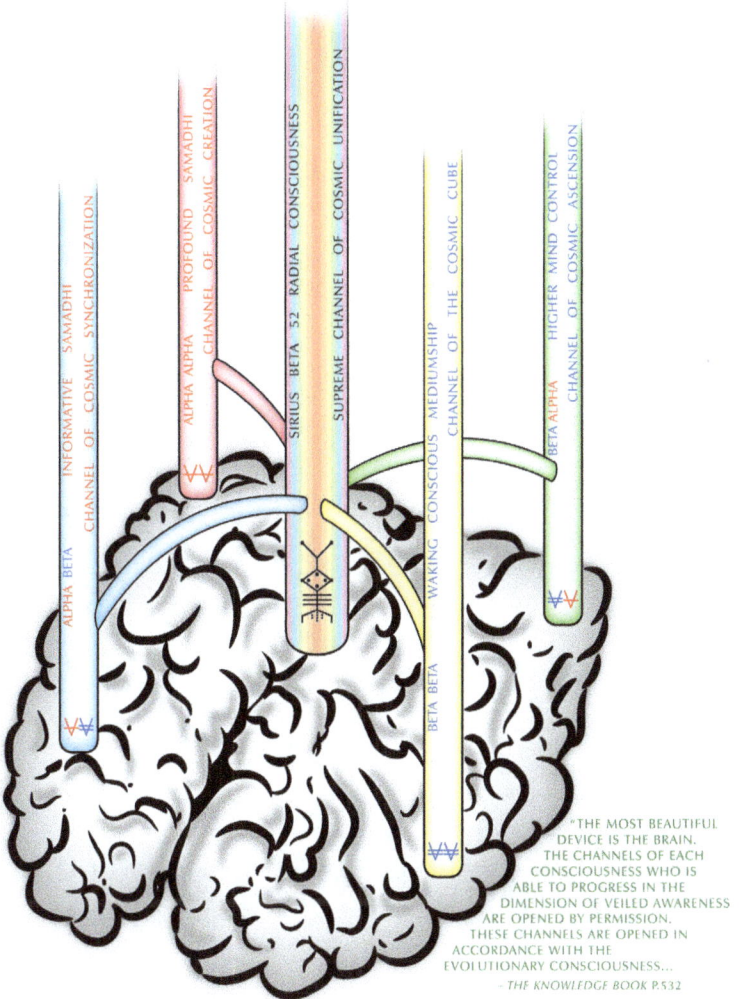

"THE MOST BEAUTIFUL DEVICE IS THE BRAIN. THE CHANNELS OF EACH CONSCIOUSNESS WHO IS ABLE TO PROGRESS IN THE DIMENSION OF VEILED AWARENESS ARE OPENED BY PERMISSION. THESE CHANNELS ARE OPENED IN ACCORDANCE WITH THE EVOLUTIONARY CONSCIOUSNESS..."
– THE KNOWLEDGE BOOK P.532

OPENING THE BRAIN'S ETHERIC INTERGALACTIC CHANNELS: THE FOUR FORMATIVE POWERS OF THE WORLD OF LIGHT

Being embedded in the noosphere, the Cosmic History information core operates through these four basic channels that are streaming from the primary source of the galaxy (Hunab Ku), connecting different galactic systems. These channels emanate from the original core of creation—the galactic core—and are also known as the four alpha/beta channels monitored by the Sirius alpha/beta binary star system.

The conscious recognition of these channels helps bring to consciousness the new sense organ: the holomind perceiver. The holomind perceiver can be likened to a cosmic-telepathic internet chat room installed or imprinted on the human brain, wiring it to the noosphere.

63

CHAPTER 5

Empowering Telepathy

Telepathy and the allied powers will only be understood when the nature of force, of emanations and radiations, and of energy currents, is better grasped. —Telepathy, Alice Bailey

Telepathy is natural law and vibrates a supreme order. Telepathy exists in the mind. Time is of the mind. If everything comes from One Source, then all human thought must have a point where it converges. Though mind is non-locatable, time and telepathy are mutually defining factors dependent on unity of thought. Through telepathy the art of nature increases itself in geometries of sound and triangulations of light.

Time is the fourth dimension. The fourth dimension is the intermediate field between the pure electronic fifth dimension and the phenomenal third-dimensional material/physical plane. In this way, the fourth dimension consists of the entirety of possibilities of psychic evolution and development of all life forms that have ever been (and that will ever be)—within that field defined by a particular star.

All holons (4D etheric bodies) form a vast interconnected web that is connected with every other holon through electronic lines of force. These electronic lines of force are also interwoven into the *planet holon*. Life as we know it is built up from energy to electricity to electronics or electronic lines of force (this is what controls thought). The Noosphere is ultimately the source of all thoughts on Earth.

Time, Telepathy and the 7th Mental Sphere

"Telepathy" is derived from the Greek terms *tele* ("distant") and *pathe* ("occurrence" or "feeling"). The term was coined in 1882 by the French psychical researcher Fredric W. H. Myers, a founder of the Society for Psychical Research (SPR).

According to Cosmic Science, our thoughts generate electronic lines of force that radiate into the atmosphere and create specific effects according to the strength of the thought. Everything is based on vibration. The human body is made up of an energy body or field that vibrates. If the frequency of vibration of this field is stepped up, then energy or information from other dimensions can come through us. We are cosmic telepathic mediums.

Accessing Your Multidimensional Self: A Key to Cosmic History

Sensitive people experience telepathy all the time and sometimes to their own detriment as they often pick up the thoughts of others. This is because thoughts transfer like radio messages operating through a universal medium (the synchronic matrix of time). There are different types of telepathy: mind to mind, heart to heart, emotion to emotion. Telepathy is understood through the universal medium of the holomind perceiver within the Law of Time. The holomind perceiver is the seventh mental sphere that reveals the supreme underlying telepathic matrix connecting all minds. (See *Book of the Cube*).

At the center of the holomind perceiver is the telepathic element 113. This element is what creates hypersensitivity in the brain, radializing and equalizing perceptual functions, resulting in radial experience. (Note that radial perceptions already exist in certain biological forms such as the starfish, a radiolarian with a purely radial structure).

Consider this quote from Alice Bailey (*Telepathy*):

> *Humanity is the recipient of so many impacts, so many impressions, so many telepathic and mental currents and so many qualified vibratory impressions from all the seven kingdoms in nature that aeons have elapsed in developing the adequate discriminative sensitivity and it establishing the certitude of the point in evolution from with which conscious invocation must arise and upon which the evoked impression must be registered."*

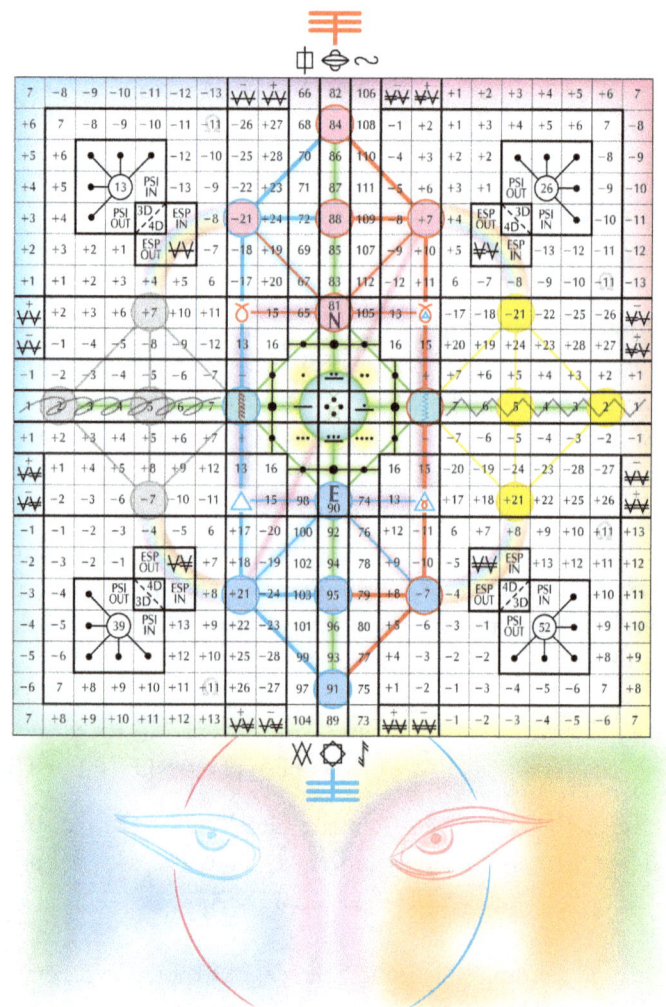

Synchronic Order and Telepathy

The synchronic order is the fourth-dimensional meeting ground that makes the interplay between minds possible. In this dimension of time, there is a new language to be discovered—these are the universal codes expressed first through number. The language of number *is* the language of nature that reveals a precise system for realizing the interconnectedness of All-That-Is. Through practice of daily numerical codes we come into contact with the Source of the Universal Matrix where all dimensions are telepathically linked.

All of life is telepathic as witnessed in the synchronic harmony of nature. It is only the human who, because of its reliance on artificial timing devices and machines, has forgotten his/her interconnectedness with the Whole. The synchronic codes of time are memory triggers that awaken and reconnect us with the divine flow of nature. This remembrance occurs by attuning ourselves to nature's internal process, the unfolding language of number which reveals a sequential staging that the One Being evolves in and through in order to fulfill its Creation and know its own Self in its myriad manifestations.

The AC/CA circuits (Aboriginal Continuity and Cosmic Awareness) connect past and future, which together shape the present. We exist simultaneously in all of these dimensions within the radial matrix, and within this radial matrix, space is an infinitely locatable point.

The AC/CA double helix demonstrates that in each NOW moment we receive information pulsed to us from the past, as well as the future. The present is the hinge between these two flows. The more we let go and come fully into the present moment, the more we can become aware of these two flows. This is why it is said, "the point of power is in the present moment." By opening fully and surrendering ourselves utterly to the present moment the past and future can open to us. It is by becoming fully conscious within the present moment that natural phenomena such as telepathy and time travel occur.

All Time is Now

In the Dominion of Time, everything comes from a natural sense of opening to the now. Superior intelligence dwells nowhere else but in the now. In the now is the synchronic experience of the union of the third-dimensional entity and its fourth-dimensional holon double or alternative personality. —Postulates 13.1, 13.2, Dynamics of Time

The present moment is where direct knowledge and resonant attunement reside: the seventh-dimensional toroidal "speaking tube" of God. Direct knowledge bypasses the logical cause and effect chain. This is why debating and disputing any issue is pointless. Things are as they are no matter how much we may dispute them. The psychic/telepathic or superconscious realm is transcendent to all conditionings of how we think things are.

For the One Being—GOD—to exist at all stages of evolutionary time simultaneously means that GOD is 1) Fully present at every "segment" of time; 2) In motion on all expanding or contracting time tracks; and 3) Coherent at every level and dimension of time.

This means that GOD is able to generate, see, record and be fully conscious of each of those stages playing out on multiple time tracks within multiple cycles in multiple dimensions. As the Master Intelligence, GOD knows the precise moment in Eternity to move its different forms out of one state into another. We can understand this through the analogy of a musician who, through her art, knows the harmonies and rhythms (in the right combination) to evoke certain feelings and create great music.

VIEWS OF TELEPATHY

The ancient Greek philosopher Democritus (460-370 B.C.) put forth the wave and corpuscle theories to explain telepathy. Democritus is credited with the first physical theory of dream telepathy. His view of telepathy is derived from the thesis that everything, including the soul, is made up of innumerable, indivisible, minute particles called atoms. These atoms constantly emit images of themselves, which in turn are composed of still other atoms.

Democritus postulated that images projected by living beings, when emotionally charged, could be transmitted to another being/person. When the images reached their destination, they were believed to enter the body through the pores. The power of images emitted by people to the dreamer were dependent on the intensity of emotion surrounding the image. The purer the intensity of emotion, the higher the frequency and speed of transmission. Love is the highest emotion, which explains why those who are "in love" are often able to read each other's thoughts.

Similarly, Cosmic Science defines telepathy as a transmission projected through the two higher selves, or fifth-dimensional bodies, of two people who are in communication with each other. Telepathy occurs more readily when we are deeply relaxed in a state of love and self-acceptance. This state of meditative relaxation allows our third-and fifth-dimensional selves to merge so that our fourth-dimensional holon can receive telepathic communication.

Mental Radio is a seminal book about telepathy by Upton Sinclair with the foreword written by Albert Einstein (1930). Sinclair describes the apparent ability of his wife at times to reproduce sketches made by him and others, even when separated by several miles. (These experiments are similar to what is now referred to as remote viewing in parapsychology circles).

Parapsychology is the study of paranormal phenomena, which are factors of the mind that are beyond reason. Study of paranormal phenomenon stretches the mind and moves it into higher states of consciousness. To attain these paranormal powers requires exertion, discipline of mind, effort and even then, the effort should not be to attain powers, but rather to gain self-mastery or self-realization. A human is not normally capable of maintaining this state of operative rest for an extremely long time, free of involuntary motion or distracting thought. For this reason we practice techniques such as hatha yoga and breathing exercises to help develop finer control of the body/mind.

Radiograms

According to Cosmic Science, parapsychology defines the relationship between the multidimensional aspects of our being. It defines the evolution from a one-dimensional fictional personality, to a multidimensional operant in a reality that is electroplasmic, solar-telepathic and instantaneously radiomorphic.

Radiomorphic refers to the capacity of one's perceptual filters to instantaneously construct holographic radiograms of its experience. A radiogram is a psychosensory message unit experienced as a broadcast. These broadcasts or radiograms can be elicited by any aspect of our sensory environment, and can be experimented with through the holomind perceiver as the sixth sense organ downloading programs.

The different levels of parapsychology, such as precognition, telekinesis, telepathy, etc. are constructs stepped down and adapted to the relatively primitive one-dimensional functioning of the human trapped in the confines of a rigid, materialist belief system.

The purpose of developing our dormant paranormal powers is to realize our full potential. Becoming telepathic helps us to better tune into each other and be more sensitive to people and the entire planetary, stellar and cosmic field. Russian parapsychologists are known to study the birth date of those who have developed paranamoral powers, particularly the incidence of sunspots at birth.

Psi Bank

Telepathy is a key factor of the Law of Time. It is demonstrated through the symbols of the synchronic order, which unifies the mind in time of all who use it. The psi bank is the guiding force of the evolution of time and consciousness. Every living organism exhibits psi functions. has sentiency or *psi factor*. The psi factor of a living organism accounts for information received or sent. This is coordinated by telepathic quanta.

The designation of the psi bank makes it easier to conceptualize the noosphere. All systems of thought and knowledge are contained within the psi bank regulator of the noosphere. It is the medium of information storage and retrieval for all human mental programs and is the repository of all thoughts from every mental sphere and spectrum of consciousness. Every perception, thought, word and experience is all recorded and deposited into this master storage and retrieval system. In this way, it is the evolutionary control panel of the noosphere.

The psi bank code establishes an increasingly expanded telepathic structure around our planet to operate the beams from the galactic civilizations that are now working with us.

Everything is registered within the psi bank, even someone that you passed on the street when you were five years old. Many things come within your range of association, and they are all automatically registered whether you are conscious of it or not. All input which is not consciously registered is automatically filed into the second mental sphere to form the total unconscious.

Chapter 5 • Empowering Telepathy

The psi bank is the telepathic switchboard located between the two Van Allen belts (electromagnetic fields). The psi bank regular is both the storage and retrieval system for all knowledge and thought, including the DNA information structures; as well as the container for the evolutionary timing programs. The psi bank is coded in four plates. As such it encodes the four-part process of the Earth rotating on its axis in time, four stages per day, four seasons per year, in four-year cycles and four phases of the moon. Each of the four psi bank plates conforms to a mirror symmetry of the bi-polarity of the Earth's magnetic field.

CHRONONAUT

Chronomancy is the science and art of fourth-dimensional time considered as a whole system. Science is knowledge and art is practice. One who studies chronomancy is called a chrononaut. A chrononaut is a student of the technology of fourth-dimensional time, which is also understood as the science and art of telepathy. The Law of Time describes the Planetary Manitou as the fourth-dimensional switchboard of collective telepathy.

We know from Cosmic Science that our thoughts are electric. Telepathy as an electromagnetic phenomenon was a concept introduced by Russian astrophysicist, Dr. Nikolai Kozyrev. He thought telepathy might even be linked to the gravitational field.

The mastery of chronomancy furnishes the budding science of chrononautics with the goal of a new embodiment of human wisdom: the Earth Wizard. The first major aspiration of the chrononaut is the ejection of the rainbow bridge.

Yogis commonly demonstrate telepathy and are able to display a variety of related paranormal powers. Knowledge of telepathy can be gained both through a logical scientific manner and also through direct knowledge or precognition. The meaning of time in relation to space, past, present, and future is a mystery only because of our conditioned beliefs.

The Rainbow Bridge experiment is a unification experiment for humanity. This experiment is to determine our ability to coordinate common sensory experiences in relation to Earth's base frequency, thereby triggering the circumpolar rainbow rings of Earth.

The number of minds simultaneously engaged in this perception is what creates the quantum mind shift that catapults us from the physical Earth into the enlightened mind of the noosphere. At this appointed moment, we will experience the noosphere as the totality of planetary unity and moment-to-moment synchronicity, which the Earth always experiences.

Chapter 5 • Empowering Telepathy

The unity that was originally a yearning now creates
the space of telepathic nature.
Once you have been granted wholeness,
you will never be anywhere else but where you have always been.
Even as you breathe,
telepathic registrations collapse light years of meaning into a single insight.
Language can no longer communicate.
Words become archaic.
You become a number.
You ascend to the center and
surround the interior of the whole with the space of the no-self.
Who remembers? Who sees?
The art of nature is telepathy.

CHAPTER 6

BALANCING UR: UNIVERSAL RECOLLECTION

By describing the avatars of one, all others are included in the allegory, with a change of form but not of substance. It is out of such manifestations that emanated the many worlds that were, and that will emanate the one—which is to come." —Helena Petrovna Blavatsky; Isis Unveiled

And they have broken into fragments their religious affairs among them, yet all of them are returning to us. —Quran, 21:93

UR is the future. It is the realization of the universal unification of all religions, spiritual traditions, as well as world systems; it is ultimate unity consciousness that enters us into the noosphere.

In the beginning there was one perception, one reality, one people and one community. The one community then divided into different languages, religion and cultures. This di-vision is a function of the historical process. To heal the di-vision is to restore vision from within, then the outer world conforms to the inner world of cosmic order.

The stream of Cosmic History flows parallel to the historical process. Cosmic History shows that within the cosmos every level of reality is present simultaneously. This means that in any given moment the universe is completely unified by that moment.

We are slowly emerging from our collective state of amnesia to reclaim our dormant powers. We are Returning to the One. Religion means to bind back to One. UR is the Universal Religion based on Universal Recollection. The only reason that religion exists is because of human amnesia regarding its origin and unity. It is the force of GOD that always reminds us to bind back to One.

HISTORY IS A TIME RELEASE PROGRAM

In the grand time-release program of creation, religion is introduced because the human has forgotten how to live life as a sacred (or religious) ceremony. All religions are functions of different focal points of energy directed onto the planet at different times for different peoples. All true religions flow into the one stream of the universal spiritual ocean.

Different teachers appear at specific intervals to help the human remember that God or Buddha nature is inside him/her already. Many scriptures also tell us that the seed of innate or intrinsic knowing is planted within each human. This is connected to the Law of One: we are One Being, there is One Creator, One Mind, One Soul. What is called "redemption" actually means to cease to be oblivious to what is really going on and to remember or recollect. Universal Recollection (UR) means humans are no longer oblivious to their origin or destiny.

What is spirituality in relation to religion? Spirituality is the quality of being attuned to Spirit. Feeling the Divine Force or God's presence is spirituality. This is not dependent on any specific religion, although the practices enshrined in many religions have the value of discipline.

Discipline is meant to lift the layers of fog off from our being, so that we can advance in stages until all that is left is the all-pervading presence of God. Any discipline requires practice. In Buddhism and Hinduism the practice is called sadhana. In the Free Will Zone, there is a need for these different structures and disciplines in order to cultivate in the human a greater attunement to spirit. But in truth, spirituality is innate.

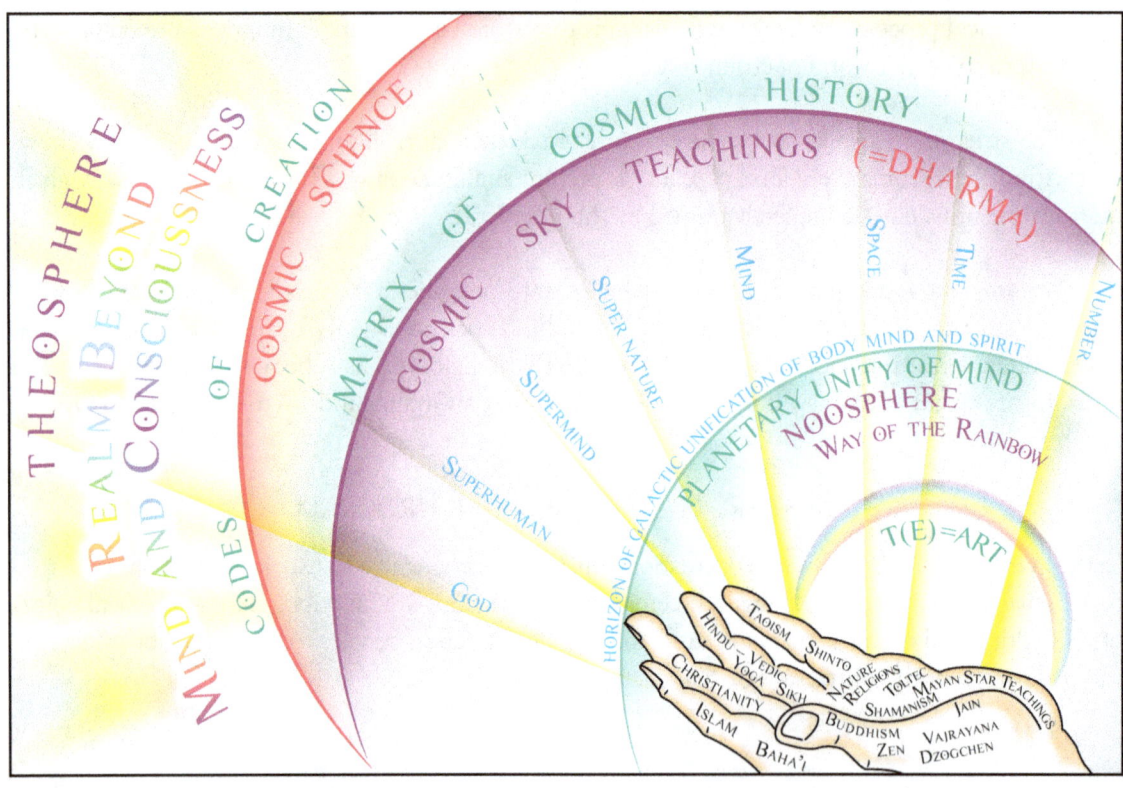

UR, Pacal Votan and Messengers of Awakening

Pacal Votan's assignment while on planet Earth was to compile information for the compendium of universal religion, its progress and development in different world systems. Universal religion is the measure of spiritual unification attained by intelligent species throughout the different world systems of this and other galaxies. —Pacal Votan and Judgment Day, 1996

All true spirituality is one unified whole.

We know that there are many prophets, messengers and world teachers in the Old World who came to remind the people to bind back to One. The stream of the Galactic Maya reveals the synchronic matrix that weaves all religions, traditions and fragmented knowledge back to One, showing the interconnectedness of all relations. In this way Pacal Votan serves as God's special witness who came to reveal a whole other spiritual dimension of reality that is necessary if there is to be spiritual unification on Earth. This is called harmony in time.

Without harmony in time, spiritual harmony is not possible. According to the Telektonon prophecy, spiritual harmony in time leads to the final three seers: Quetzalcoatl who carries the stream from Maldek; St. John of Patmos, who brought the prophecy of the end time in the Book of Revelation; and finally, Padmasambhava, master Tibetan yogi. The prophecies of Padmasambhava are the waves of magic and sorcery that transcend all conventional ideas, beliefs, opinions and thoughts about reality.

Pacal Votan was a type of prophet—a sage king of the order of Solomon—much the same as Buddha, Abraham, Christ or Muhammad. Pacal Votan was the only prophet of such stature in the New World, with the possible exception of his successor: Quetzalcoatl, the plumed serpent (947-999).

Pacal Votan is the synthesizer of all messengers and teachings. His mission was to establish UR on Earth. Universal Recollection is the highest goal of GM108X. The prophecy of Pacal Votan shows that spiritual messengers, prophets and sages of all faiths represent a single tapestry of a vast interlocking planetary system.

Buddha, Jesus and Muhammad were the key influences responsible for shaping the course of human civilization in the spiritual tradition of UR. Their ideas transformed what we call the first stage of civilization into a very different form, fashioned by an ideology originally created with a spiritual intention.

Since Muhammad was the last of the three messengers of the awakening, he left the Quran. Quran means "recitation" and is not like the Bible, which is the sacred text of the Christians based on the Old Testament. The Old Testament was based on the books of the Jewish tradition after the Pentateuch of Moses. Then various people wrote the gospels and epistles of Paul, which comprise the New Testament of the Bible.

"How did all this appear to Pacal Votan?" In Pacal Votan's crystal vision, transferred to his sarcophagus lid, Buddha is on the left top looking right, Christ is on the far right looking left, Muhammad is in the center looking at Buddha. This means Muhammad continues what Christ represented and closes what Buddha initiated.

In the synchronic order, events take on significance according to their relationship in time to each other. The Gregorian calendar is based on the birth of Christ. There is a perfect symmetry in the synchronic order between Buddha at the beginning and Muhammad on the other side of a 1,140-year axis, and Christ in the pivotal center point. Buddha and Muhammad actually represent two ends of a spectrum: 570 years before Christ (Buddha) and 570 years after Christ (Muhammad). The number 570 is a factor of 19 (19 x 30). 570 + 570 = 1140; this is a fractal of 114 (19 x 6) and 114 is the number of suras, chapters, in the Quran. This balanced relationship in time is critical in re-examining the meaning of these world teachers.

The Quran, on the other hand, was written or recited by one person: Muhammad, who was merely the "secretary" of a sacred script composed by the Author in Eternity. We do not know if Buddha or Jesus ever asked for their teachings to be written, but Muhammad's entire mission was to leave this one text. Then there is also the shariah, the laws and legislation created by people based on their interpretations of Muhammad's words, which may or may not be true.

The teachings of Christ were first recorded around 40 years after his death, and the dating of the teachings of Buddha is even more imprecise. In addition, the body of Buddhist scriptures is enormous (if you just count the Mahayana sutras alone). Most of these scriptures begin with the words, "Thus have I heard" because Buddha left no written texts. So where did they come from? Were they telepathically received messages from Buddha in a super samadhi?

Like Buddha, Jesus never wrote anything down, his teachings were recorded by his disciples in the form of the gospels. The gospel of Matthew, Mark and Luke were written about 40 years after Jesus' death, and the gospel of John was written about 50 years after that, with the Book of Revelation. Therefore, who can say what was actually said?

The point is that these are interpretations of teachings at a specific time, in a specific place, for a specific people.

Pacal Votan's Power

... By his preparation and mastery of higher spiritual practices: meditation, telepathy and profound displacement, Pacal Votan was able to gather the information he needed concerning the spiritual progress and level of cultural universality among the human species in order to make the final determination for his tomb and prophecy, Telektonon. —Pacal Votan and Judgment Day

Cosmic History states that Pacal Votan represents the quintessence of the *cosmic sky teachings* as he transmigrated from previous world systems in order to embody and represent all traditions. The prophecy of Pacal Votan points out that the spiritual history of the planet is a single integrated circuit. All the teachers and teachings are part of one vast time-release program.

What is the ultimate purpose of all the messengers? They have a unified mission to establish a basis of morality for the resurrection of Earth and the evolutionary redemption of the human being. The terrestrial resurrection was to be the final episode in an interplanetary drama rooted in the destruction of Maldek, the original Garden of Eden.

When the Christians dispossessed the Mayan civilization, they destroyed everything possible, including all the books and vestiges of the memory of Votan. In 1691, in the city of San Cristobal, in the state of Chiapas—where the tomb was located—there was a massive burning of every book containing any reference to the name or word "Votan." Yet a year later in 1692, 1,000 years after the tomb dedication, a book appeared entitled the *Trials of Votan*, describing many exploits of a mysterious personage named Votan, "heart of the people."

Madame Blavatsky calls Votan the "master magician" in her book Isis Unveiled, which, mysteriously, was written more than 80 years before the discovery of the tomb of Pacal Votan. Votan is a time traveler who has appeared at different points in history. As the synthesis of all avatars the Votan force has always worked for the spiritual unification of planet Earth. This is the moment when everyone realizes that we are all the same being, and that all teachings of all traditions come from the same source.

The Telektonon prophecy contains the principle of the Mayan knowledge base that was destroyed in the conquest—summarized as the Law of Time and the 13 Moon/28-day calendar. With a new timing principle, we can universalize knowledge and place the mind in alignment with Galactic Standard Time (GST). This is pure fourth-dimensional time that harmonizes all galactic life irrespective of astronomical variables of third-dimensional time.

The introduction of the Telektonon Prophecy of Pacal Votan says it is "One Living Prophecy" and that it is a "Proclamation on behalf of the three messengers of the awakening and the three special voices of prophecy and the special witness of time." In the prophecy, Buddha, Christ and Muhammad are identified as the three messengers of the awakening; the awakening to UR, Universal Religion/Universal Recollection.

The Telektonon prophecy is a form of divine intervention. Without this prophecy, and its discrimination between the 12:60 and 13:20 timing frequencies, there would be no way to accurately analyze the present world situation. The only way the principle of the ancient knowledge, ultimately formulated as the Law of Time and 13 Moon calendar, could be revived was through the Telektonon prophecy. This prophecy demonstrates how the whole cosmos is an indivisible unity. Therefore, every belief, every set of teachings, every religion and every revealed prophecy are all part of one indivisible unity that can be mapped according to the synchronic order.

The Telektonon is the distant, far traveling code of information received from spirits and deities dwelling within the Earth. Telektonon: *Tele*—from a distance (communication); *chtonic*—

Chapter 6 • Balancing UR: Universal Recollection

Pacal Votan's Samadhi 1352
"Universal History of the Messengers"

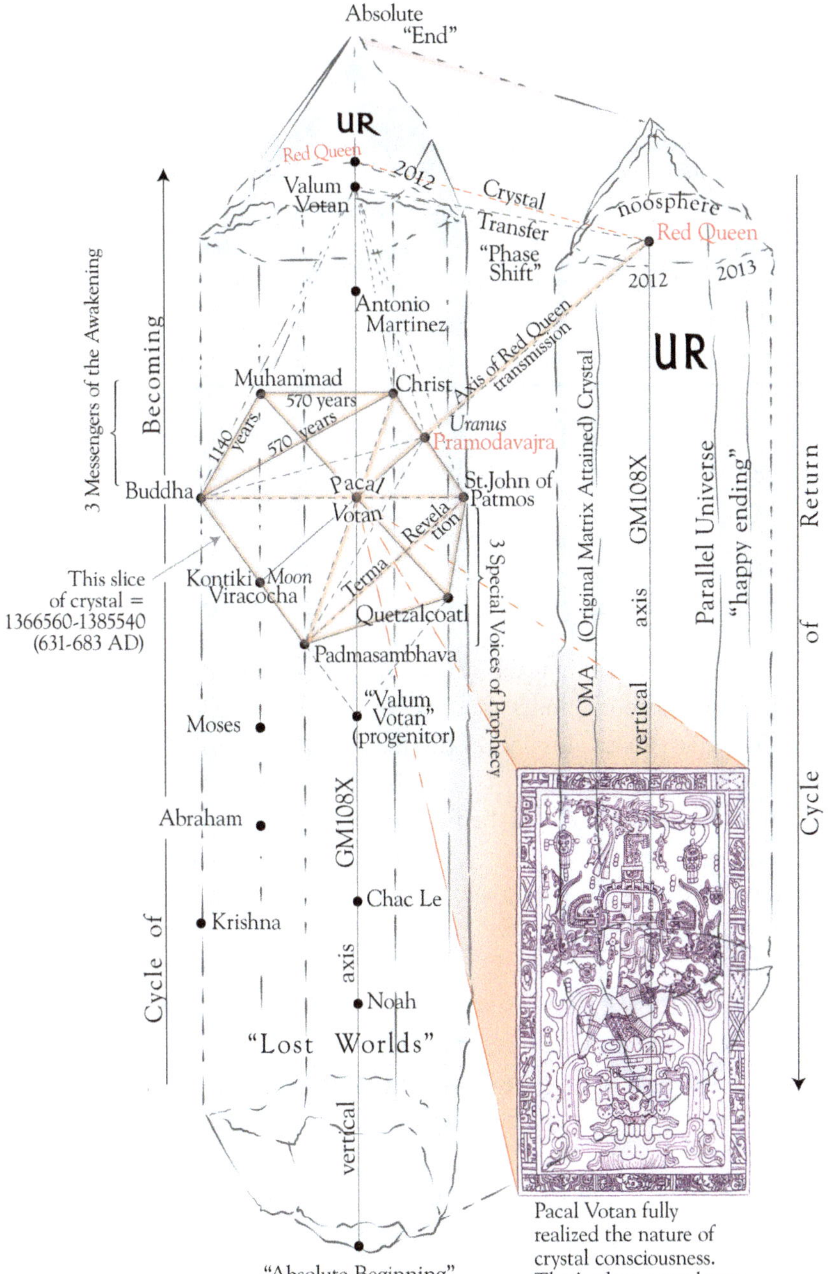

The main body of the crystal is a six-faceted lattice.

Each end of the double-terminated crystal has six more facets each. (twelve in all)

There are a total of 18 facets to the crystal; this is a maximum compression of the eighteen-dimensional universe. The crystal is the living record of Cosmic History.

Pacal Votan's History of the Messengers is harmonic synchronic history - rather than Babylonian linear history.

It is a history rehearsed by the crystal.

Crystal Lattice of the Universal Hologram

Pacal Votan fully realized the nature of crystal consciousness. That's why we can know his consciousness now.

Diagram labels: Absolute "End"; UR; Red Queen; Valum Votan; 2012; Crystal Transfer "Phase Shift"; noosphere; Red Queen; 2012; 2013; Antonio Martinez; Muhammad; Christ; 570 years; Axis of Red Queen transmission; UR; 1140 years; 570 years; Uranus Pramodavajra; Buddha; Pacal Votan; St. John of Patmos; Revelation; 3 Messengers of the Awakening; Becoming; This slice of crystal = 1366560-1385540 (631-683 AD); Kontiki Viracocha; Moon; Tetun; Quetzalcoatl; Padmasambhava; "Valum Votan" (progenitor); 3 Special Voices of Prophecy; OMA (Original Matrix Attained) Crystal; GM108X vertical axis; Parallel Universe "happy ending"; GM108X axis; Moses; Abraham; Krishna; Chac Le; Noah; "Lost Worlds"; vertical; "Absolute Beginning"; Cycle of Return; Cycle of Becoming

Spirits, deities, dwelling within or under the Earth. Hence, Tel-ek-ton-on, Earth spirit speaking tube. Telektonon is distant because its code was left in a former time; it is far traveling because it is transmitted from far off stellar points through Earth's core where the deities and spirit guardians hold it until it is time to be released, where thence it travels far from Earth's core to the sensory intelligence of the biosphere.

> **TELEKTONON PROPHECY**
>
> The Telektonon prophecy of Pacal Votan states that since time is of the mind, if you adopt a calendar that is a harmonic standard in time, it will bring harmony to the mind. The New Time is based on the harmonic standard of the 13 Moon/28-day calendar (synchronometer). Through this timing system, the solar ring is made conscious. With the solar/lunar calendar, the moon going around the Earth is like the minute hand and the Earth going around the Sun is like the hour hand. (This is the lost principle of Babylonian mechanization). Without this solar/lunar 13:20 timing principle, it is like thinking that there are just minutes and not hours.

This spirituality or Universal Religion (UR), is confirmed by the Telektonon prophecy which asserts that history is over, and that in the new cycle all true teachings are preserved and uplifted into a higher-dimensional context.

Cosmic History, UR and Holonomic Recollection

Cosmic History is not only sacred history, but UR history. Cosmic History IS UNIVERSAL RECOLLECTION. UR is established through understanding basic principles of hierarchy which are demonstrated through the sacred mathematical orders of the measure of the Law of Time.

Holonomic Recollection is the memory of our being unfolding in stages from the planetary order. This process occurs when our frequency raises past a certain threshold. This is the purpose of the 13 Moon calendar and codes of the Law of Time, to wake us up to the fact that the whole is contained in every part.

Time is vertical and space is horizontal; the world of form. Holonomic recollection of the whole order resides in everyone and, once activated, we can ascend vertically in time, reaching more purified states and levels of being. UR/Universal Recollection is even greater than holonomic recollection as it reveals the whole universe in gradations as stepped down from pure light vibration into the various striations of density.

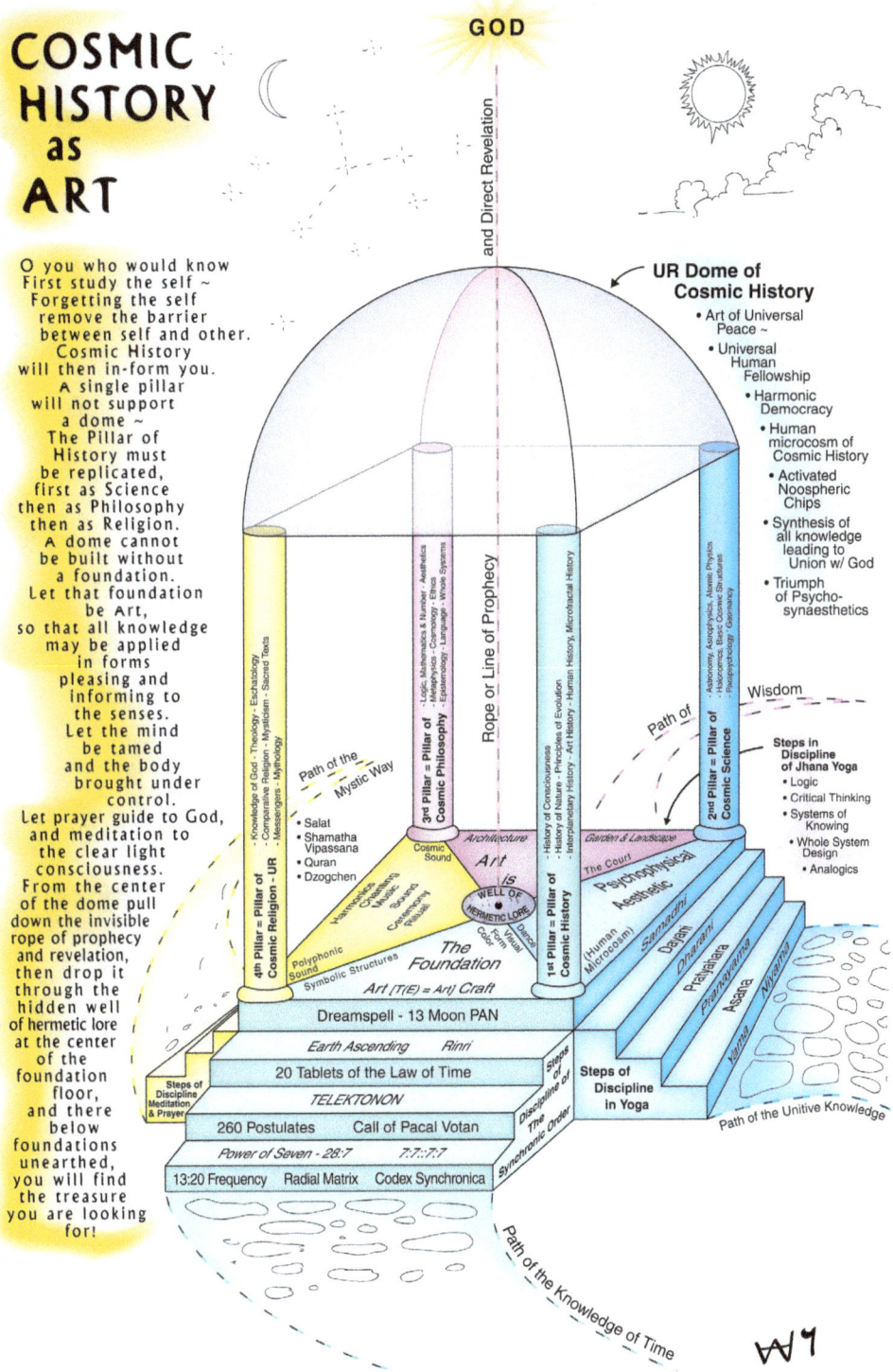

The UR dome is the noosphere itself, which can only be upheld by the values of knowledge and spiritual attainment. We are secure beneath the noospheric UR dome in universal unity and harmonic cosmocracy where the natural hierarchy of spiritual evolution is the governing order.

PART III

RETHINKING THE UNIVERSE THROUGH COSMIC SCIENCE

CHAPTER 7

ATTUNING TO THE SUN, SOLAR SYSTEM AND 7 RAYS

The Ah Kines, "Servant-Warriors of the Sun," are those humans who fully realize the dream light body within the physical body and—understanding the circuitry of the human organism—use the light body to navigate the electromagnetic waters which we call the universe. —José Argüelles, The Mayan Factor

How can we perceive a new level and way of thinking about the universe or even the solar system?

The first step is to withdraw our attention from the outer realm and place it on the inner realm, and then ask again, what is the Sun? What are the planets? What relation do they have to me? To the Earth? To the Sun? To evolution?

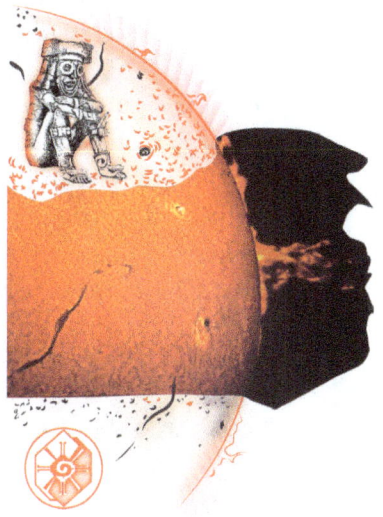

Our solar system is not what it appears. Nor is it just what mainstream science would have us believe. We have been deeply conditioned with limited perceptions. How can we derive fresh perspectives and come to a new level of thinking about the solar system, galaxy and universe?

Let's re-consider the solar system from the point of view of the Law of Time.

What is the Sun?
The Sun is Light. Light is information. The Sun is the coordinating consciousness and mind of the solar system. The ancient Maya believe that the Sun is a conscious living entity, that consists of the entire solar system. They were attuned to and in resonance with this solar consciousness. All new information directed to our planet is focalized and transmitted through the Sun.

What is consciousness?
Consciousness is a function of the star (Kinich Ahau), which functions like a gyroscope to hold the orbits of its electrons called planets. The purpose of the Star is to focalize the new information in the form of a galactic beam that is transmitted through a regular radio program that coordinates the sunspot cycles. As of 2013 a new galactic information beam is entering our planet bringing us into the Sixth Sun of solar consciousness.

What is a planet?

The word "planet" means "wandering star", for the planets seem to move faster and more erratically than "fixed" stars. Though infinitely small, the planet bodies capacitate the evolution of infinite forms and expressions of life and consciousness.

What is a galaxy?

The galaxy is the fundamental building block of the universe. The Galactic Being is the whole galaxy itself, awakened as a super being. We are all cells of a galactic being.

What is a solar system?

The solar system is a galactic thought molecule and the planets are its electronic thought units. This is one whole system, a whole entity with multi-leveled facets, each with its own set of frequencies. Each planet has a specific function in the solar system, just as each solar system has a specific function within a whole galaxy.

What is the purpose of a planet?

The purpose of a planet is to hold different levels or stages of consciousness in orbital order. The sequence of the planets is embedded in the interplanetary circuit where each planet represents a different quality of consciousness and intelligence. Each planet in our solar system contains its unique consciousness and frequency. All planets taken as a whole create a larger multi-leveled heliospheric consciousness. In this way, the planetary orbits are the resonant frequency constants of the noosphere.

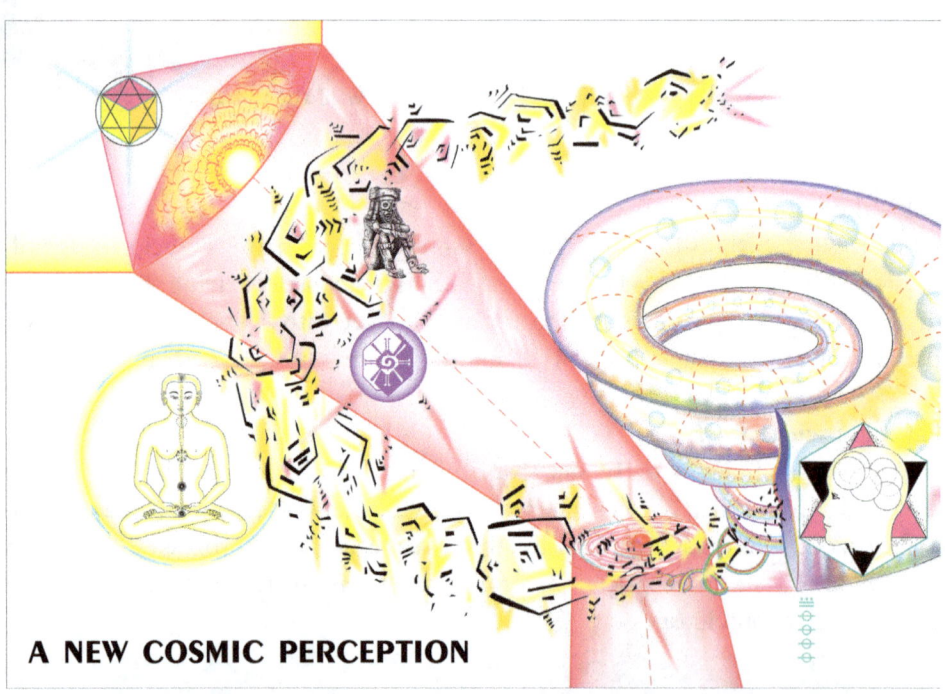

A NEW COSMIC PERCEPTION

What is resonance?

Resonance refers to a minimum of two different entities or sources of vibration that are in harmony or have some type of interaction. The noosphere is directly related to the planetary orbital frequency system. We cannot isolate one planet and say it does not have a relation to the rest of them. Each planet is essential in creating an integrated orbital circuit.

One Interplanetary Web

Planetary consciousness is an attribute of solar consciousness, the consciousness of the local star and its planetary system. The human brain, in relation, is a processing system, or cosmic antenna. The transistor circuit of our antenna also connects with the planetary orbits and the resonances held by each planet.

WE ARE SOLAR BEINGS. WE ARE SOLAR BROTHERS AND SISTERS. WE ARE CHILDREN OF THE SUN. THE SUN IS NOT ONLY THE AUTHOR OF LIGHT AND LIFE ON THIS EARTH BUT ALSO OF CONSCIOUSNESS.

All planets are interconnected and function in relation to one another, forming one cosmic body. The sum of the resonant frequencies of all the planets in relation to each other impacts the Earth's noosphere. The noosphere is the sum of the complex of interactions of the orbital frequencies of the various planets in relationship to each other; and, in particular, as they relate to the Earth.

Sunspots and Ahau Kines

What is the actual meaning of the sunspot cycle? According to Cosmic Science, what we call sunspot cycles are pulsations of the minds of the solar masters, the *Ahau Kin*. These are fifth-dimensional beings who dwell in the core of the Sun (see *The Mayan Factor*). Their minds pulse to the binary sunspot cycle in 11.3-year cycles and then change polarity for another 11.3 years creating a full sunspot cycle of approximately 23 years. (Note from Chapter 4 that this number 11.3 or 113 corresponds to the central unit of the master telepathic matrix, the Sirius B-52 channel of supreme cosmic unification). When the sunspots reach peaks in their cycles, they discharge. These discharges have to do with solar initiations that are occurring within the core of the Sun or solar logos. Massive discharges mean the Sun, and therefore all consciousness in the solar system, is undergoing major internal initiations.

The sunspots and their processes are cyclic. They are carriers of information from different star systems (and dimensions) that reach the noosphere and biosphere of the Earth. The increased ejection of plasma means that the solar initiations are intensifying. The plasmas affect the DNA of all living matter. So this is important. This means that our consciousness and DNA are literally evolved by the Sun through the rhythms of the solar sunspot cycles. This how our process of evolution proceeds in stages.

Cosmic Science introduces the 7 radial plasmas which are the primary electrical forces that activate and set in motion the atomic and subatomic particles.

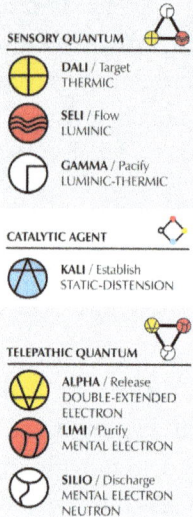

The first three plasmas (Dali, Seli, Gamma) constitute the *sensory quantum*, beginning with heat (Dali), followed by light (Seli), then the combination of heat and light (Gamma). The fourth plasma, Kali, is catalytic and bridges from the material/phenomenal sensation of light and heat to the *telepathic quantum* (Alpha, Limi, Silio), beginning with the double-extended electron (Alpha), then the mental electron (Limi) and then the mental electron-neutron (Silio), which then moves into a field of telepathy.

What Keeps Everything Spinning?

Mainstream scientists say that the interior of the Sun is like a continuous set of nuclear explosions going off to create the radiation that emanates from the Sun. Russian scientist Kozyrev said the interior of a star, like the Sun, is actually not hot but generates time waves coordinated with solar radiation to create whole living fields called solar systems.

What is the relationship of solar radiation to being alive? And what is it that causes a thing to be alive? Occult thought says it is a function of vital force: when vital force is active then the being is alive and when the vital force leaves it dies. Look at the difference between a living and a dead tree.

What keeps the planet rotating on its axis and what keeps things alive? There has to be intelligent sources that originate outside of or beyond the phenomenal world that cause it to appear as it does. Everything is made of atoms and beyond atoms are subatomic particles and electricity.

Different atoms spinning together create molecules. What keeps it all spinning? How does a planet spin on its axis perfectly and go around a star perfectly? We could say that it is "just some force" set in motion 13.7 billion years ago which still continues. According to the materialist science, once something is set in motion it always tends toward entropy and inevitably slows down, however slight it might be. But this explanation is not satisfactory.

Cosmic Science states that the universe began with *ether*—the universally constant inert force—that was then disrupted by the *RANG*, a force of disassociation analogous to the Big Bang, setting

Chapter 7 • Attuning to the Sun, Solar System and 7 Rays

in motion two waves that collided with each other. These two simultaneous colliding forces created what we now know as the universe. What were the forces that collided? Was it God breathing? And with His breath created the beginning of the universe where the whole show began to unfold? At the beginning of the unfolding of the universe is where Cosmic Science begins.

> The root of Cosmic History is the solar ring; without the solar ring there is no Cosmic History. The solar ring establishes the possibility of cosmic order. The Earth is going around the Sun and its orbit makes a solar ring. The 13 Moon/28-day calendar matrix calibrates the cycle of the solar ring and also makes conscious what is already encoded into it. In this system, the Sun functions as an energy transmitter, beaming different levels of information, plans and radiations into the entire solar system. Each planet receives a certain amount of beams and plasmas depending on its size and position. Attuning with the solar frequency increases consciousness.

Heliosphere and 7 Rays

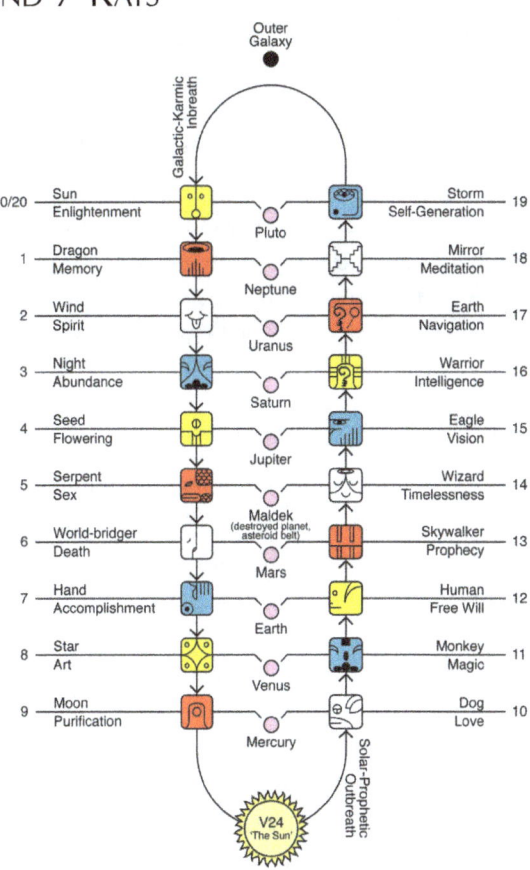

The heliosphere consists of the Sun and all the different planets and their orbital circuits that create fields of vibrational frequencies that ripple out and interconnect. In the heliospheric perspective, planets are arranged and interpreted according to their orbital position in relation to the Sun, where there are 10 primary planets, each with two flows: a Galactic Karmic flow (G/K) and a Solar Prophetic flow (S/P).

The G/K flow represents the solar inhalation and the S/P flow represents solar exhalation. The G/K represents the preconscious field of influence and the primal powers of *becoming*. S/P represents the subliminal field of influence and the resonant powers of *return*. These two flows represent the circulation of time within the solar system or heliosphere.

The Sun itself is a gigantic, intelligent organism—a big solar logos, which is a council of solar intelligence where those who watch over the planets dwell. Among the solar logos are beings who guard each of the planets in their orbits. These beings are responsible for overseeing the different levels of solar logos that form a hierarchical chain that reaches into the Central Sun.

From the central sun emanate the *seven rays*, which go to the different suns or stars. Our Sun receives the seven rays that govern the different qualities of life that are incorporated into the chakra system and the 7 radial plasmas. A ray is a particular force or energy. Everything in the solar system at any given state of evolution displays predominant energy from one or more of these rays.

The seven rays radiate from the Central Sun into different suns or stars. A ray is a particular force or energy. Every level and stage of our solar system displays a predominant energy from one or more of these rays. Our Sun receives the seven rays that govern different qualities of life. These rays are stepped down from the solar logos into the planetary logos, which direct and calibrate the rays as they enter the different planetary systems. This explains how the forces of gravity, light and electricity are functions of forces controlled by elements or entities in higher planes of existence and consciousness. These seven rays are accessed by the human through its 7 chakras that receive their electronic charge through the 7 radial plasmas.

The seventh ray is the final ray of creation, the concluding cycle and phase of human evolution and development. Seventh ray ceremonial magic establishes the Cycle of Return: the advance into full fourth/fifth-dimensional consciousness. This also corresponds to the activation of the seventh mental sphere: the holomind perceiver, based on the model of our world as a cube matrix.

Within the cube matrix, the functions of intelligence can be precisely calibrated and coordinated by mathematical structures in accordance with different fluctuations of solar-galactic energy. This matrix illustrates how solar flares, solar emissions, coronal mass ejections, and solar winds are actually information waves and signals that reach us through third-dimensional perturbations. We see how third-dimensional reality moves through or plays itself out within this particular cube matrix, and from its own dimension in that matrix (no more than a two-dimensional plane slicing through it) takes on a particular appearance: the universe as we know it.

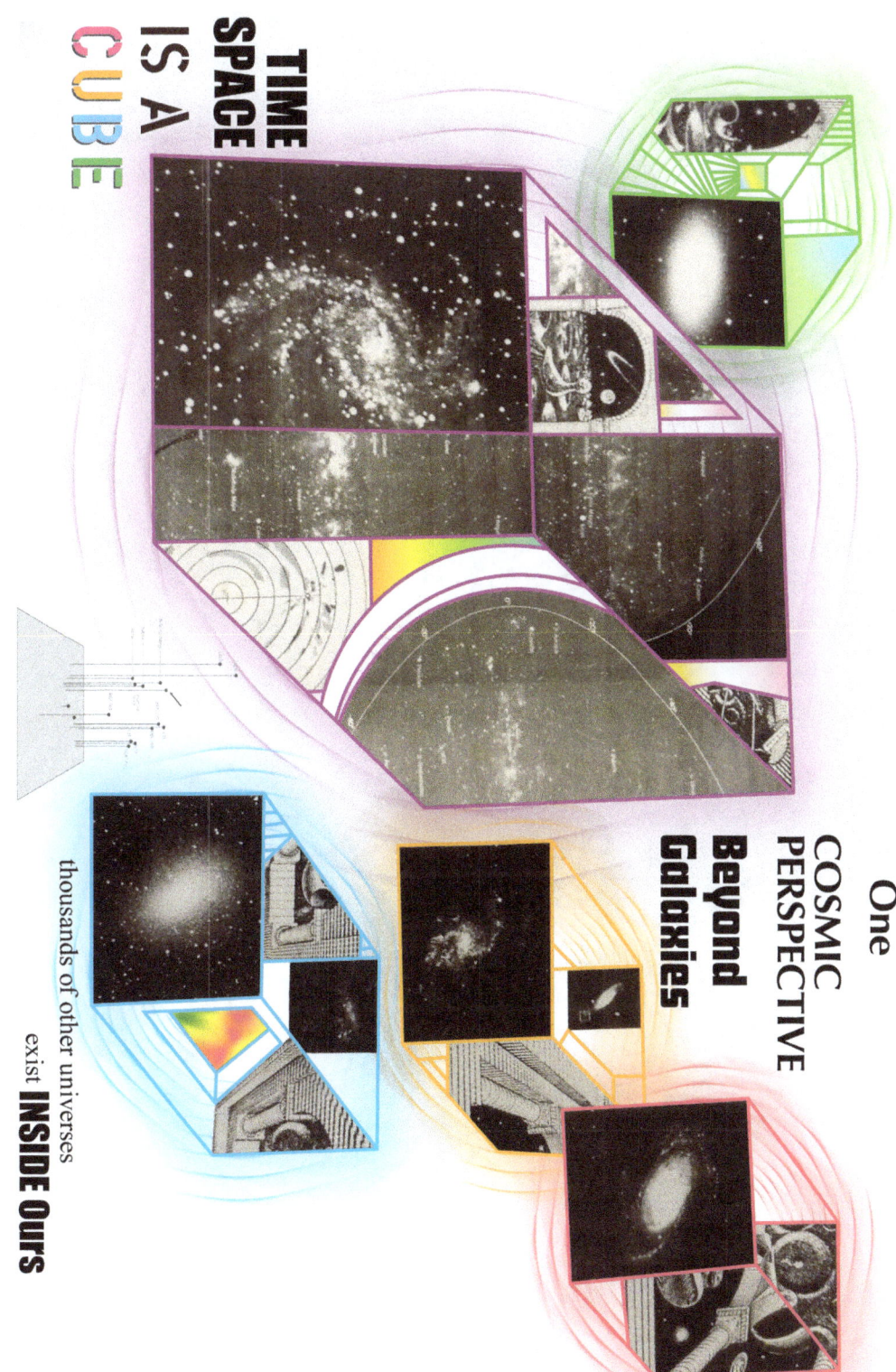

CHAPTER 8

Integrating the Plasma Universe and 7 Psychic Centers

We may also see in the sky an aurora, which is cosmic plasma, reminding us of the time when our world was born out of plasma. Because in the beginning was the plasma. —Hannes Alfvén, Nobel Lecture, 1970

… "We are the stuff of stars," said Carl Sagan. Similarly, Shakespeare said, "We are such stuff as dreams are made on." We can experience this through our 7 chakras that connect us to the 7 radial plasmas that bond together our 3D physical body and 4D etheric body with our 5D electric body.

Plasmas are conductors of electricity and, therefore, are affected by magnetic fields. More than 99 percent of matter in the universe is plasma; hot, electrical conducting gases where electrons are stripped from atoms by intense heat, allowing them to flow freely. Interstellar space is filled with crisscrossing patterns of energetic matter/plasmas with far-reaching electrical currents and electromagnetic fields—this is the view of the Plasma Universe Model.

In the 1930s, Swedish physicist, Hannes Alfvén, developed cosmic electrodynamics to explain plasma, and thus, established the Plasma Universe Model. Alexei Dmitriev, of the Russian Academy of Sciences (Novosibirsk), was another investigator contributing to the plasma model through his solar and heliospheric studies. Alfvén's cosmic electrodynamics theory was based on the solar prominence of Earth's auroras and grounded in facts of reality that affect our lives, rather than on proving or disproving hypothetical constructs devised from smashed atoms.

The Plasma Universe Model (PUM) is completely distinct from the Standard Big Bang Model (SBBM). Whereas the Big Bang seeks to explain creation as a mysterious cataclysm in the remote past, plasma theory attributes the beginning of creation to electrical and magnetic processes that still occur, here and now. While the PUM is an ever-evolving syntropic model, the SBBM depicts a violent and entropic "dying universe." According to the Law of Time, the SBBM is a pure fiction resulting from unconscious immersion in the incorrect timing frequency of the dominant Earth culture.

Extraterrestrial Text

Cosmic Science is a gift from the beyond that first appeared as a mysterious 57-page root text originated from an extraterrestrial transmission (from outside the Earth). This transmission was received and transcribed in Spanish by Enrinque Castillo Rincon, a Colombian engineer, in 1969-1970 and shortly found its way into the hands of José Argüelles. According to Cosmic Science, planet Earth is concluding its purely human phase of evolution and poised to enter its superhuman phase. (Note: The root text of Cosmic Science is included in full as an appendix to CHC Vol. 2, Book of the Avatar).

> *The vision contained within Cosmic Science is above the whole Earth; this means it establishes a view of reality, galactic in nature, encompassing different galaxies, star systems and planets. This is an entirely new description of the universe from the point of view of extraterrestrial intelligence. When sincerely studied, it has a potent psychoactive effect that opens and stretches the mind in ways unimaginable.*
> —CHC Vol. 2

Cosmic Science describes a highly fluid, electronically interactive universe, where the Earth is viewed as a specific genre among many different types of planets with definable levels and stages. These levels and stages are organized for transducing (stepping up and stepping down) electrical charges. This process of "transduction" is overseen by purely electronic forces (of hierarchy), operating from fifth-dimensional levels.

> The PUM is part of Sacred Science or Cosmic Science. Cosmic Science is meant to return us to the autonomous power of investigation by showing us exactly how we are individually and collectively plugged into the cosmic motion picture.

Cosmic Science begins with the following premises:

1. Energy.
2. Electricity.
3. Electronics.
4. Radial plasmas.
5. Stages of the quantified parton.

Chapter 8 • Integrating the Plasma Universe and 7 Psychic Centers

In the first premise, energy is understood as the factor of interaction of one element or component with another element or component. Here, ether is one component and RANG is the other. The interactions of the two create the primal disassociation that ultimately gives rise to what is known as "quantum mechanics." This is the first stage of defining energy and the structural foundation of physics, according to Cosmic Science.

Instead of speaking about physics as such, Cosmic Science refers to a general understanding of the building blocks that form the structure of reality as we know it. These building blocks start with pure energy, then electricity, then electronics or electronic lines of force which then form the plasmas, etc.

In modern Earth science, electronics means the "study of the interaction of electrons." In Cosmic Science, electricity is defined as the creation of different force fields or lines of force. These electronic lines of force exist independent of electrons. In modern physics, the idea is that electricity is somehow a function of electrons. Cosmic Science says that electricity is a function of lines of force that existed prior to the existence of electrons.

Electronic lines of force advance into radial plasma streams of electrically charged "particles" that create electronic flows. Plasmas saturate the universe with electricity, electrical flows, electromagnetic fields and radial lines of force. To understand the lines of force prior to the actual creation of electrons, we must next understand the parton.

PARTON AS BASIS OF ELECTRICITY

According to Cosmic Science, the *parton* is the basic elemental structure built up from electronic flows or lines of force combining to create primary quanta with varying properties and electrical charges. "Quanta" refers to the smallest detectable units. The parton interacts within radial plasma flows to effectively create reality, understood as a multidimensional spectrum. The parton does not exist in modern physics, yet.

From the point of view of Cosmic Science, the universe exists as a set number of categories of electrical charges (partons) and plasmas that interact with each other at different levels or different moments in a continuous process. These interactions, made up of

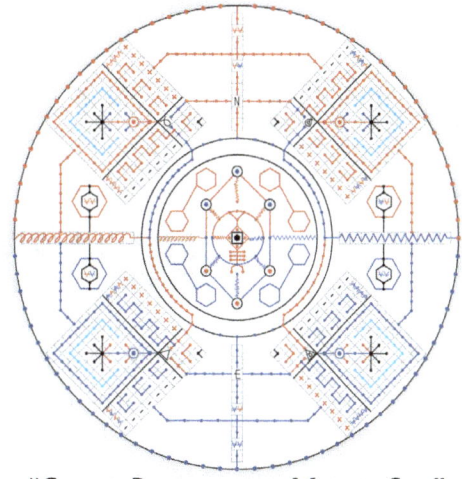

"CIRCUIT BOARD OF THE MOTHER SHIP"
WITH ALL THE DIFFERENT WIRINGS OF ALL THE DIFFERENT ASPECTS OF ALL THE DIFFERENT TEACHERS, ASCENDED MASTERS, GUARDIANS OF THE EARTH, PLANETARY LOGOS, ETC

Accessing Your Multidimensional Self: A Key to Cosmic History

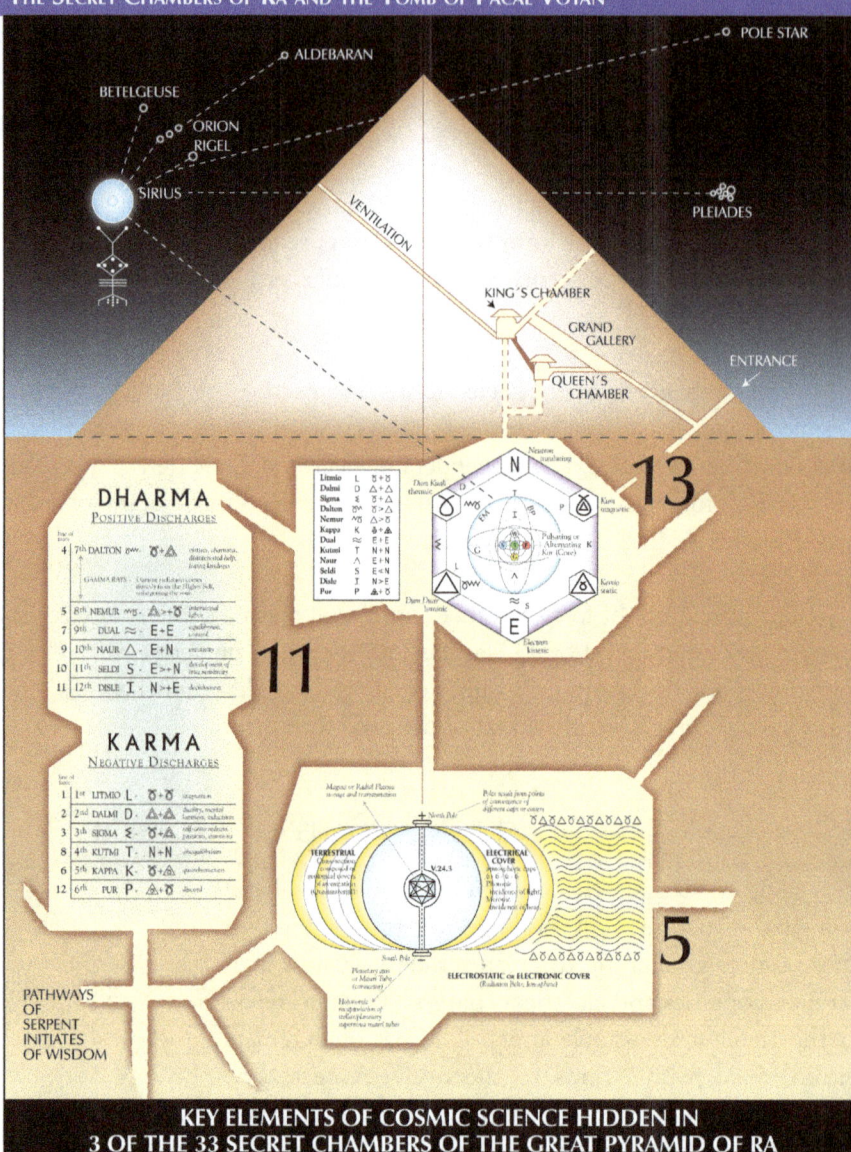

THE SECRET CHAMBERS OF RA AND THE TOMB OF PACAL VOTAN

According to Cosmic Science, the information of the parton and six basic types of cosmic electricity is hidden in the 13th secret chamber of the Great Pyramid of Ra in Egypt. Ra is the "sun god," the source of solar electricity.

Cosmic Science refers to Ra as the Supreme Being that controls all that occurs in our solar system. Ra is equated with Kinich Ahau in Mayan cosmology. Cosmic Science says that there are 33 secret chambers in the Great Pyramid of Ra. 33 is the supreme number of the initiate.

Of the 33 chambers in the pyramid of Ra, three contain information about Cosmic Science: 1) The 13th chamber contains information about partons (the parton); 2) The fifth chamber holds information about the planetary poles and electrical lines of force; and 3) The 11th chamber contains hidden information about the positive/negative karma-dharma. These three units of information are in accord with the universal cosmological level (the parton), the cosmoplanetary level (poles and electrical lines of force), and the human intelligence level (positive/negative karma-dharma). These three points establish the circuitry of cosmological meaning and interaction.

KEY ELEMENTS OF COSMIC SCIENCE HIDDEN IN 3 OF THE 33 SECRET CHAMBERS OF THE GREAT PYRAMID OF RA

different capacitors of electronic energy, create different possibilities or "different beings" or levels of functions in the universe. These interactions can be stepped up or down and transduced into other forms. In this way, the whole universe appears like a large circuit board with various nexus points representing the existence of different beings or entities. The different electronic charges, then, pass through the nexus points to create a wide range of effects, or phenomena.

When we consider phenomena from the Cosmic Science point of view, reality is perceived as a moving, synesthetic kaleidoscope of sensations with no fixed point or reference. This perception is accompanied by an ever-changing psychic narrative modified according to the intelligence of the perceiver.

Humans are rarely able to perceive in this way naturally, because thick conceptual filters block pure perceptions so that a tree looks like a "tree" or a human looks like a "human," according to conditioned interpretation. However, if any phenomenon is carefully studied, it disintegrates (try staring at yourself in the mirror for a long period of time and "you" disappear). How does this happen? Because you are witnessing the true nature of phenomenal reality, which is fundamentally a composite of different electrical charges and electronic lines of force, all of which are constructed with partons and electrons spinning at rapid rates. Just imagine if the spinning stopped—the visible world would disappear! The phenomenal world appears because of the frequency of the spin, the electrical frequency and electrical charges, inclusive of the quantification of different *karmic-dharmic* lines of force.

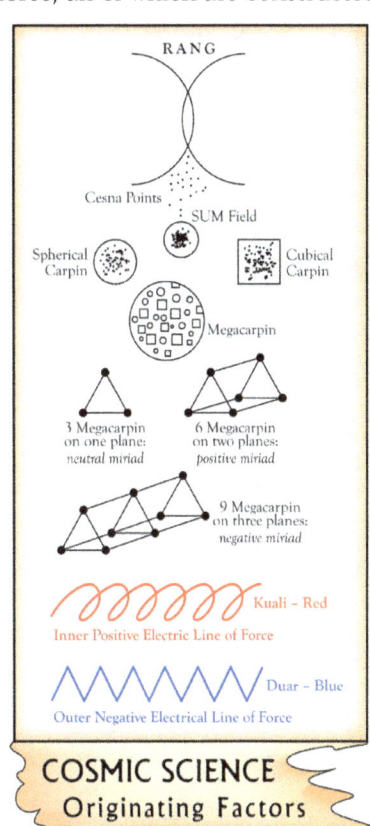

How Did the Universe Come into Existence?

Most spiritual traditions have creation stories that begin with a divine force or energy that is at the root of creation. According to Cosmic Science, the "creation of the universe" began with a primary disturbance of the ether. Ether is in itself a constant (undifferentiated) force existing in the cosmos, transcending from micro to macrocosmos and continuing infinitely.

Therefore, this undifferentiated, imperceptible and inert force, ether, is the underlying stratum of the Earth and cosmos. As a constant force equalized in all directions simultaneously, ether, once disturbed, becomes the accommodating matrix for infinitely interactive electromagnetic fields, plasmatic striations and filaments as well as gravity and light.

Cosmic Science then describes the second point of creation, the **RANG,** or the force of violent disassociation produced by a simultaneous and collateral surge of two disharmonic fields of force. This RANG, as a cosmic break or rupture, is the source and power of sacred sound, mantra and music. (This is known as PAX in Mayan). From this rupture, creation is "sounded" or "vibrated" into existence.

The ether or the inert force then represents the state of meditative calm of God's self-creation. Therefore, if this inert force or ether is the absolute calm, undisturbed self-reflective meditation of God that extends infinitely, then at some point in infinity, we could say that God had a thought. And that thought moved through the ether, transferring into the harmonic force fields so that when they meet the RANG is sounded and exploded. This explosion sets the universe in motion.

INTERVAL OF LOST TIME IN ETERNITY

The interaction of different frequencies creates intervals. The relation of intervals to each other creates number. Psychomythically, the primal interval corresponds to the number 7 and is known as the *Interval of Lost Time in Eternity*. In the finite worlds this translates into the Seven Days of Creation. On the seventh day of creation, the Return Journey begins. This is the point when dissonance is resolved as harmony.

Assuming that God creates everything for a specific purpose—and if the RANG is the effect of the first thought manifesting from the ether, then what was that thought that set the frequencies in motion? What was the thought that created two different frequency waves that would meet and create a violent disassociation within the inert force of ether and then become resolved as a perpetually evolving creation dynamic? What is the purpose of setting in motion the entire evolution of the universe? Is it to climb the ladder back to cosmic consciousness?

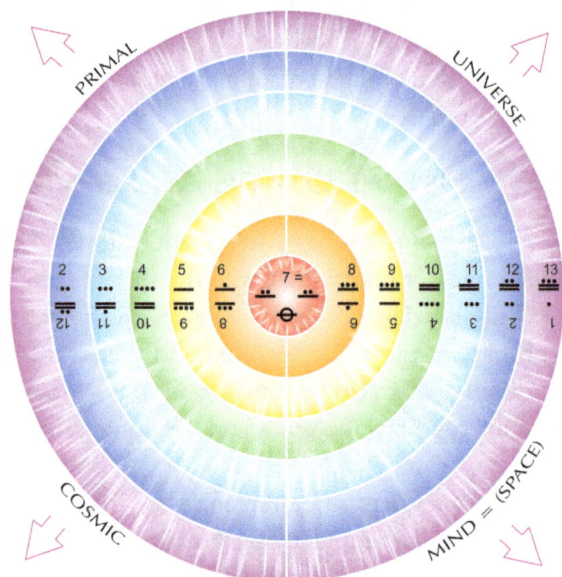

INTERVAL OF LOST TIME IN ETERNITY

THE REALITY OF THE RADIUS OF SEVEN
IS THE REALITY OF THIRTEEN

1 + 2 + 3 + 4 + 5 + 6 + 7 + 8 + 9 + 10 + 11 + 12 + 13 = 91 = 13 × 7
13:20 ~ [20 = 13 + 7]

RANG AND HUNAB KU

The force of the disruption, the RANG, is also the source of the Hunab Ku—Mayan for 'one giver of movement and measure'. Two harmonic fields of force create the RANG which is a source of energy. Force and energy cannot be defined without movement. Force implies movement. Energy also implies movement that creates frequencies and vibrations.

The Cosmic Science cosmology is radially simultaneous, meaning that the moment of the beginning is still happening and everything that has evolved from it is still happening simultaneously. The RANG is infinitely repeatable and ever-present. We can become most aware of it through the analogy of sex; when the sperm hits the ovum it recreates the primal RANG, and from that comes creation (not necessarily physical creation, but rather creative energy).

Everything exists within the present moment as a radially simultaneous flow of currents. Therefore, it is not necessary to go back billions of years to reach the origin of creation, but rather sink more profoundly into the present moment where everything is always occurring.

EFFECTS OF RANG

Following the violent interaction of the two force fields, the propulsion waves intersect with each other creating minute "condensations" of ether referred to as **cesna points** (this is the point where matter becomes condensed rather than etheric). Cesna points are the primary resonant condensations in the microcosmos. Electricity arises from these cesna points. All that exists, manifest or unmanifest, can be understood as the product of the groupings of these hundreds of thousands of millions of cesna points. They are the root of life in the phenomenal realm. At the arrival of cesna points, ether is transmuted into the micro-agitation of an inert force.

Cesna points englobe each other to create spherical force fields called **SUM fields.** SUM fields are like cosmic mother eggs that are stable and self-contained. They form the pre-electronic template of the timespace. Once established, it is impossible for the SUM fields to reintegrate into ether. Within this timespace field, cesna points break into two forms called **spherical carpins** and **cubical carpins.**

The sphere and the cube are the primary forms of creation. The sphere represents the perfection of consciousness and mind—there are no corners. It is an utter perfection. The cube is the metaphor of our own perfection and transcendence. It represents all the different potentialities of timespace.

The combinations of the spherical and cubical carpins comprised of cesna points create **megacarpins.** One megacarpin consists of 500,000 spherical carpins + 500,000 cubical carpins. From the megacarpins, arise the **miriads,** the energetically charged networks of cubical and spherical carpins. Miriads are submicroscopic arrangements of megacarpins that initiate polarity. There are three types of miriads that form a base triplet: neutral, positive and negative.

Pacal Votan was found in his sarcophagus holding a cube and a sphere.

The combination of any two types of miriads creates the primary electrical particle or essential point of positive energy, known as the **parton**. Various types of partons in combination create electronic lines of force. Cosmic Science illustrates six types of electricity that constitute the quantified parton: *neutron, dum kuali, dum duar, electron, kum* and *kemio*.

Each of the six types of electricity has a central parton. Each parton, or primal electrical particle, has different properties and are what give all manifestation their qualities of appearance and material effect. Within the center of the cubic parton, a seventh parton, or *kor,* provides an alternating pulsation with a resonant field model enclosing the fifth force "thought" spin nucleus (see graphic at end of this chapter).

From the six types of electricity are derived 12 lines of force. The 12 electronic lines of force then combine to create the **seven radial plasmas,** the micro quanta electrical charges with a specific spin quality.

Electronic lines of force activate every molecular and atomic form, endowing them with force fields that create their electromagnetic field; it is the electromagnetic dynamic that keeps everything spinning and in motion. In this way it is electromagnetism (and the neutralizing resistance to electromagnetism) that keeps everything in the universe spinning.

The cosmology of the parton and existence of cosmic electricity is a primary description of the evolution of certain energy forcefields. These energy forcefields have a direct relationship to our neurocerebral and chakra systems. This means that our chakra system is participating in the most fundamental base parton experiment that has existed from beginningless time.

Chapter 8 • Integrating the Plasma Universe and 7 Psychic Centers

7 Principle Generators (Chakras)
System of the Fourth Dimensional Energy Body or Soul Vehicle

Auric Egg or surrounding magnetic field "Noospheric Plasma Sheathe" Telepathic Field Operator.

Fastenic or Auric Lines generated by chakras to creatively engage biospheric energy field.

Neural Canal connects plasmic outlets of 4 extremities to central channel.

Vritis or Neutronios palms of hands & soles of feet plasmic flow (receiver/transmitters)

Chakra/Plasma Correspondences:

- Crown/Sahasrara. Dali plasma: Heat.
- Third eye/Ajna. Gamma plasma: Light-heat.
- Throat/Vissudha. Alpha plasma: Release double-extended electron.
- Heart/Anahata. Silio plasma: discharge mental electron-neutron.
- Solar Plexus/Manipura/Kuxan Suum. Limi plasma: Purify mental electron.
- Secret Center/Svadisthana. Kali Plasma: Catalytic Agent.
- Root/Muladhara. Seli plasma: Light.

Central Channel "Sushumna" with solar & lunar pranic side channels

Within the biological being are embedded seven generators or chakras. These chakras function as inlets and outlets of the radial plasmas. They also emanate the marsines or the fastenic lines of force that go from the generator chakras to constitute the structure and form of the aura.

Study the graphic 7 Principle Generators, and note that the human auric field is filled with *fastenic* auric lines of force streaming out of the body. These fastenic lines are the result of the action of the vritris and neutrinos that stream in and out of the palms of our hands and soles of our feet which intake certain types of energy and deliver it to our chakra system creating what we call our "aura".

> A cycle is the time it takes a parton or particle to go over a particular area of space. For example the earth makes a huge orbit around the sun. This represents the number of spaces occupied by a mass in movement. The Earth occupies 365 spaces or one NET day. NET (Noospheric Earth Time) is a time measure based on Earth in its orbit in relation to the sun and moon in the heliosphere space, rather than from the perspective of human astronomical time. Quarters are equivalent to three NET hours and seven NET minutes. Six NET hours and 14 NET minutes is one-half NET day.

Noospheric Earth Time (NET) Units

1 day = one NET minute
28 days = 1 NET Hour = 1 Moon
13 Moon NET Hours = 1 NET Day = 1 Solar Orbit
4 Solar Orbits = 1 NET Week
3 NET Weeks + 1 NET Day = 1 NET Season = 13 Solar Orbits
4 NET Seasons = 52 Solar Orbits = 1 Noospheric Earth Time Year

Cosmic Time Equivalents in Relation to Terrestrial Time

1 Hour = 60 minutes	1 Quanta = 2 terrestrial hours = .333 of 1 quarter NET Minute.
1 Minute = 60 seconds	6 Quanta = 12 terrestrial hours = $\frac{1}{2}$ NET minute
1 Second = 12 instants	1 Spin = 1 terrestrial day = 1 kin
1 Instant = 60 quarz	1 quartz = 2 months = 2 NET hours
1 Quarz = 60 Spin	1 instant = 120 months = 3,600 days = 133 moons, 3,600 kin

Plasmas: Telepathic Message Units

The seven radial plasmas are the basic building blocks of the (phenomenal and imaginal) universe. Radial plasmas also function as storage units or carriers for specific types of information. They have the capacity for instantaneous transmission and so function also as different types of telepathic message units. Electronic in nature, each of these plasmas has its own unique set of properties. Each of the seven chakras of the human biopsychic system is a receiver for one each of the seven radial plasmas.

In traditional yogic texts, the chakras, or psychoactive energy generators, are described as wheels of energy that are continuously turning and being fed by streams of prana. Prana is the vital life-force energy. In the science of the Law of Time, prana, accessed through conscious respiration, is the carrier of the "etheric nutrients" of plasma or radion. So by learning to control the breath we begin to see that within the physical body there is another body: the etheric body or holon (fourth-dimensional body). This etheric body is actually what is being fed by the prana or radion. Its central axis is concordant with the axis of the vertical spine.

Within the prana lie the seven radial plasmas, each with its own qualities and powers. Once consciously breathed in, these radial plasmas may be directed to the different chakras, energizing psychotelepathic facilities. In the 13 Moon natural time calendar, for each of the seven days of the week we activate a different chakra and radial plasma (see Chapter 13, Synchrogalactic Yoga for details on this daily practice).

Through daily practice of these radial plasmas, we can activate cosmic and solar electricity within our internal structure and we can begin to feel the flow of different plasmas to the electrical lines of force in our body. This accelerates the erasure of the lower forces of our fragmentary third-dimensional personality and also assists us in aligning with our fifth-dimensional self to activate a higher cosmic soul personality.

Here are given the traditional chakra functions and their corresponding radial plasmas. For the full practice see Chapter 13: Synchrogalactic Yoga.

- **Root—Muladhara—Four-petaled red lotus.** This is where the basic life-force is located. All of our most fundamental biological security programs are stored here. The Seli plasma charge is gathered in the root chakra and accounts for the intensity of inner light.

- **Secret—Svadhisthana—Six-petaled orange lotus.** Here is located the essence of sexual energy. The energy stored in this chakra can be used to vitalize the different levels of being. The Kali plasma charge is gathered in the secret center and accounts for the quality of intensified light-heat, which is also associated with the sexual energy. The Kali plasma also functions as a link between the three light-heat sensory plasmas and the three telepathic plasmas.

- **Solar Plexus—Manipura—Ten-petaled yellow lotus.** This center is a vital information receptacle and opens to the *kuxan suum*, the etheric fiber that runs directly to the center of the galaxy. The Limi plasma charge is gathered in the solar plexus and accounts for a mental-electron charge, which is in telepathic resonance with the North Pole of the planet.

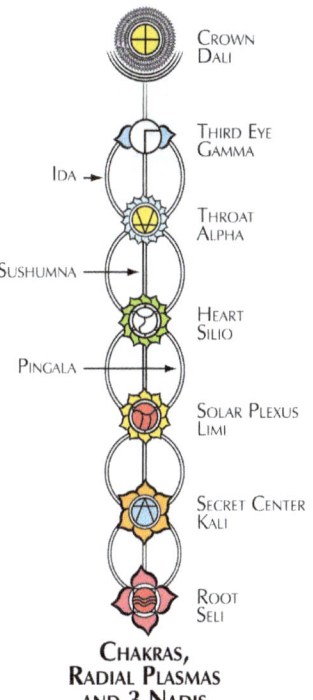

CHAKRAS, RADIAL PLASMAS AND 3 NADIS

- **Heart—Anahata—Twelve-petaled green lotus.** Located in this center are the transcendental programs that transform biological survival issues into forms of selfless compassion. The Silio plasma charge is gathered in the heart center and accounts for a mental electron-neutron charge telepathically in resonance with the center of the Earth.

- **Throat—Visuddha—Sixteen-petaled blue lotus.** In this center is focalized the will to communicate and to extend oneself to others in patterns of informative thought and behavior. The Alpha plasma charge is gathered in the throat center and accounts for a double-extended electron charge, which is in telepathic resonance with the South Pole of the planet.

- **Third eye—Ajna—Two-petaled indigo lotus.** This center, sometimes known as the eye of wisdom, is the seat of celestial vision and "second sight"—the paranormal power of clairvoyance and telepathic knowing. The Gamma plasma charge is gathered in the third eye and accounts for tendencies toward equanimity and equalization of light and heat charges.

- **Crown—Sahasrara—Thousand-petaled violet lotus.** In this center is stored the dormant capacity for total enlightenment which is fully operating cosmic consciousness. The Dali plasma charge is accumulated in the crown chakra and accounts for the experience of heat.

Dali is the only plasma that is fundamentally thermic (heat); Seli is the only plasma that is fundamentally luminic (light) and Gamma is the only plasma with an equal thermic and luminic charge (light-heat). Therefore, we can see that the first three plasmas are made up primarily of thermic and luminic charges. The fourth radial plasma, Kali, functions as a catalytic dynamic of magnetic cohesion and static distension. The last three radial plasmas: Alpha, Limi and Silio, contain qualities (or properties) referred to as primary atomic structures. Alpha is the double-extended electron; Limi is the mental-electron; and Silio is the mental electron-neutron.

The first three plasmas—Dali, Seli, and Gamma—form the sensory quanta. Kali is the catalytic agent and Alpha, Limi, and Silio form the telepathic quanta. The seven radial plasmas originate from the combination of the six types of cosmic electricity that combine in different double sets to create 12 types of electronic lines of force. These combinations are then recombined to create the seven radial plasmas.

The twelve electronic lines of force also define six positive and six negative types of thoughtforms. This is because the electronic lines of force represent different levels of consciousness. Consciousness is a manifestation of GOD, as a singular generating and organizing design system beyond comprehension. Therefore it is consistent throughout the whole of the universe. Everything is a result of some kind of thought or consciousness of God as the Master Matrix of Divine Intelligence.

Chapter 8 • Integrating the Plasma Universe and 7 Psychic Centers

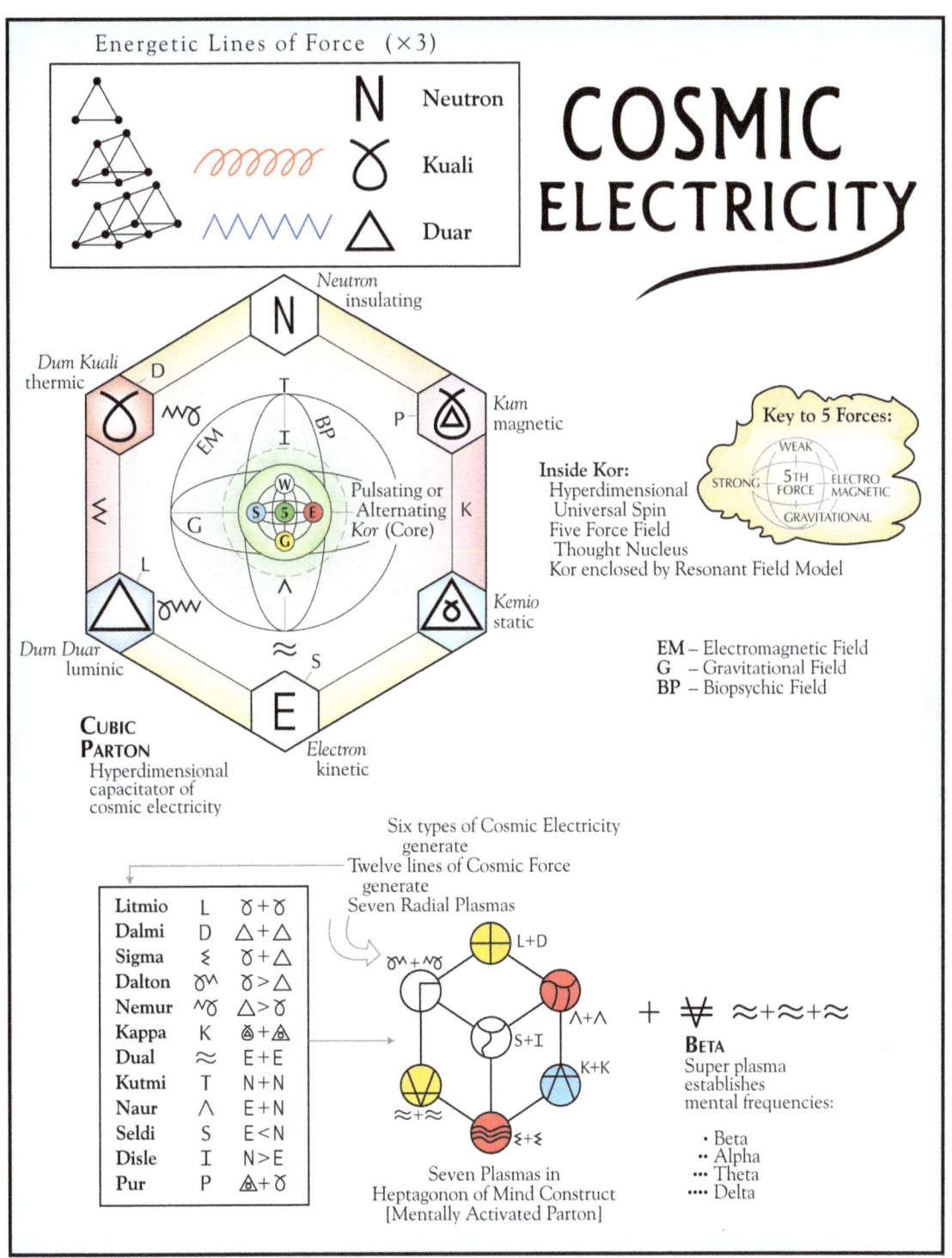

CHAPTER 9

REALIZING THE 13 DIMENSIONS

The entire Power of the 7 Light-Universes is collected in a Whole and this Whole is called the Great Light-Universe. —Mevlana, The Knowledge Book

Every stage of evolution (that was, has been or will ever be) is occurring simultaneously, somewhere in the galaxy. Other dimensions of experience exist that we are not currently aware of from our third-dimensional vantage point. We are phasing into a new perception of the universe and into a whole other cosmology that is vastly different than what we know today.

We are transiting from a third-dimensional physical perception of timespace into a fourth/fifth-dimensional perception. In this way, everything can be experienced simultaneously, including all dimensions. Dimensions can be understood as modes of expressions or different grades of vibrations. Though all the dimensions exist here and now, the higher dimensions are accessed internally through the mind, understood as the medium of consciousness (just as space is the medium of mind).

From the point of view of Cosmic Science, we are each a three-part entity made up of a third-, fourth- and fifth-dimensional "self". The evolution and integration of these three entities is the main purpose of life. Most spiritual traditions say that this (3D) life is short and fleeting and if we pay too much attention to it and distract ourselves in the material realm, then we will fail to achieve our higher purpose.

The Law of Time refers to the etheric fourth-dimensional being as the *holon*. The purpose of the holon is to allow the soul maneuverability or elasticity between shifting dimensions. The fourth-dimensional self is also the spiritual/mental organizer. The fifth-dimensional entity has never been born and never dies. In other words, the fifth-dimensional entity is the eternal part of yourself that existed before birth and

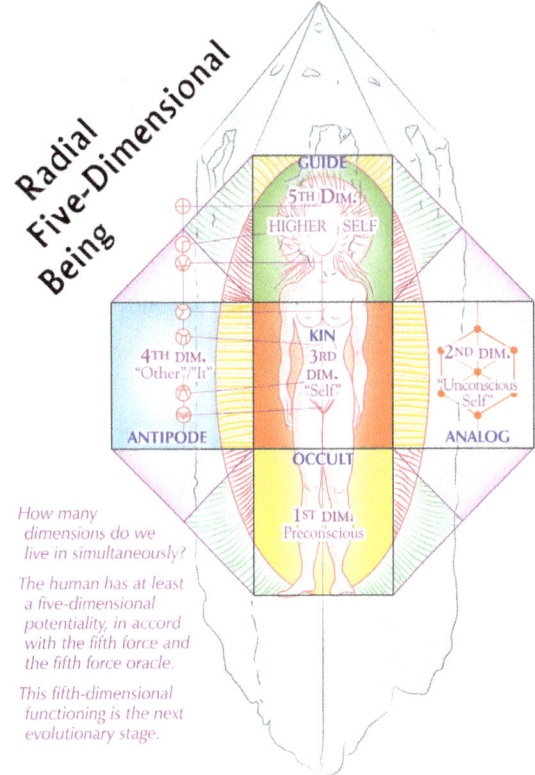

How many dimensions do we live in simultaneously?

The human has at least a five-dimensional potentiality, in accord with the fifth force and the fifth force oracle.

This fifth-dimensional functioning is the next evolutionary stage.

continues after death—your immortal body. As an angelic entity, the fifth-dimensional self cannot deviate from Divine Will.

These three entities communicate to each other through the mind, namely through the six (+1) mental spheres, as described in earlier chapters. The six (+1) mental spheres of consciousness are etherically congruent with the brain and serve as the computer or hardware of the mind.

7TH DIMENSION IS THE SPEAKING TUBE OF GOD

Different models of reality describe different numbers or types of dimensions. Cosmic History describes a 13-dimensional universe with dimensions 1-6 being the primary dimensions and the 7th as the mirror reflector, toroidal "speaking tube" of God; and then dimensions 8-13 are the mirror reflectors of dimensions 1-6.

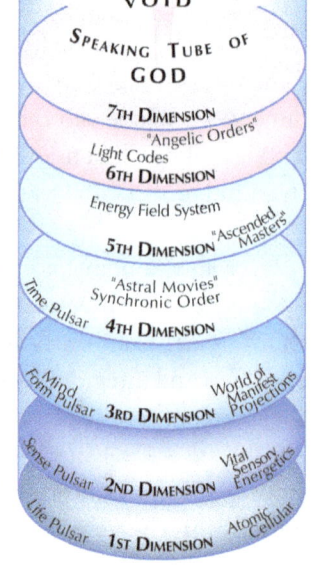

Seven is the number of prophecy; it is the number of resonant attunement and the basis of the seven days of creation and the seven aeons of creation. It also corresponds to the mythic Seven Lost Generations, which are the primary procreative generations of a specific cycle of the cosmic evolution of humanity. The seventh dimension is the plasmatic radial dimension and is the origin of spirit. Each dimension is more powerful than the next and contains the ones that went before it.

The seven volumes of the *Cosmic History Chronicles* also represent the recapitulation of the primal procreative power of seven: the original narration of creation as number. The seven volumes illustrate how the conscious activation of number informs the whole, defining an entire reformulation of the human knowledge base. In this way, Cosmic History is a compact or promise of the redemption of the power of the number seven.

Seven is also the implicit interval between the 13 and the 20. In the synchronic order the seven is the central number in the *wavespell*, power of 13, and represents the most mystical and, in some ways, referenceless point of existence. The number seven is also very prominent in the lost books of Enoch in which the entire cycle of creation is described as seven weeks. Of course, these weeks are symbolic like the seven days of creation, but they also represent the power of 49 or 7^2. 49 is also the number of days of the bardo in the Tibetan tradition.

THE 7 DIMENSIONS: PARALLEL WORLDS OF COEXISTENCE

From the point of view of Cosmic Science, the purpose of life is to give the spirit a vehicle to learn about and evolve beyond the the physical realms of density and limitation. In this process it is important to keep in mind that 1) consciousness is not dependent on a physical body; 2) soul is not separate from life, and 3) mind has no need of a self.

The mind is non-locatable; this means that there are worlds or universes that coexist with ours, but that are imperceptible to our senses. All dimensions are present here now. Cosmic Science describes the seven universes, but to understand them it is important to first familiarize yourself with the basic premises of Cosmic Science.

1. **First Dimension:** From ether to miriads (initiation of polarity). The first dimension, which is what we call the pre-quantum dimension, is where all the different pre-subatomic particles are contained—the cesna points and myriads—this is well beneath the microscope; realm of primal polarity.

2. **Second Dimension:** Parton: The essential point transformed into quanta or energy exists in the second dimension as pre-subatomic, and still out of view of the microscope. Here is where the electronic lines of force are generated.

3. **Third Dimension:** Atomic and subatomic level: that which is detected as matter. Including the first two dimensions as its foundation, third-dimensional space includes height, width and depth as the field of evolving morphogenetic structures. The third dimension is the organization of all the cellular and atomic life.

4. **Fourth Dimension:** Atomic and subatomic level of lower valence. The fourth dimension is the realm of "etheric matter" or of the etheric double, the "true self." This is also the imaginal realm, and the "Hereafter," the dreamtime. The fourth dimension is the atomic and subatomic, though with a level of lower valence or a valence of less frequency. This means that we are dealing with fundamentally etheric, non-material substance. The biological entity also participates in the fourth dimension as it evolves into mind and spirit. Here cosmic being experiences an ever-richer and dynamic relationship with itself.

5. **Fifth Dimension:** Electronic level, locus of Superior I—higher self—divine plane, spiritual guide, essence master of the Cosmic God within in us, the Guardian Angel, etc, where the factor of time no longer operates and reincarnations no longer exist—the "immortals". The fifth-dimensional higher self completes the evolutionary soul triad (third-, fourth- and fifth-dimensional entities). It is the reason for the waking up process of the evolving third- and fourth-dimensional beings. The fifth-dimensional being is the pure electronic level, or the

higher self. This is the divine plane of the pure electronic spiritual reality, often described as bliss, paradise or nirvana.

6. **Sixth Dimension:** Plane of light, where form no longer exists, though there are types of entitization. Interaction of harmonic and inharmonic electrical fluids of energy of different frequencies of light, including light and spin codes, as well as intentionality of plasmas operating at variable frequencies.

7. **Seventh Dimension:** Plasmatic radial level, the origin of spirit. The seventh dimension is the mirrorless resonator, the speaking tube of God. The seventh dimension actually creates a void or toroid that runs through all the other dimensions and comes out the bottom of the first dimension. This is the pure radial stage of consciousness. No beginning and no end.

The first and the second dimensions are subsumed in the third dimension. The principles of polarity and electricity underlie the spin and the electrical charge of the entire universe, even as it is involved in complex structures of our triadic self.

The third dimension is the realm of the third-dimensional "Self," or "I", the ego. Every third-dimensional atom has an electron. An electron is a very evolved form of the primal polarity, also referred to as the primal partons or the primal electronic lines of force. Time and space only correlate with the first four dimensions, where multiple synchronic interactions create formative processes that propagate, generate, subside and dissolve.

In the third dimension, time becomes the factor both of irreversibility and of synchronization. The third dimension is based on the input of the sense organs. In this way we may ask questions such as: Why are our sense organs formed as they are? Is there a reality apart from how our sense organs are in-formed?

Similar issues are contemplated and investigated in the Buddhist *abhidharma*, which is very psychophysical in its premises. Any phenomenon of the world is perceived as a function of the sense perceptions. We can become so familiar with the way something looks that we no longer see it because we actually shut down our fresh perceptions.

The fourth-dimensional holon is referred to as the "It" or "Other" because generally the third-dimensional ego experiences the fourth-dimensional self as alien or outside of itself. The fourth-dimensional holon is the invisible part of ourselves that experiences psychic phenomena and is immersed in the telepathic medium of ether—hence etheric being, or holon. The atomic structure of the fourth and higher dimensions is more spread out, creating a more dream-like spiritualized quality. The more etheric its substance the more we experience the fractal expansion of time, meaning that we can pack multiple levels of time into a limited space point.

Tzolkin and the Dimensions

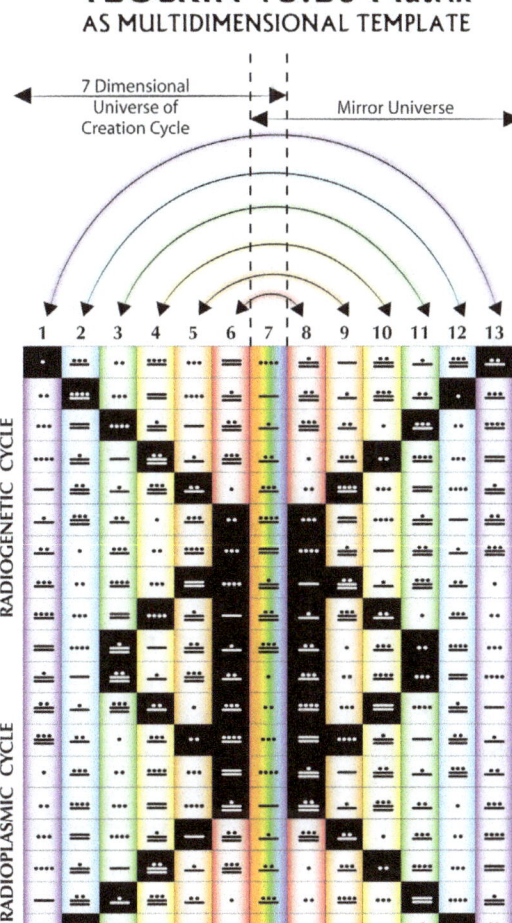

TZOLKIN 13:20 Matrix AS MULTIDIMENSIONAL TEMPLATE

The Tzolkin is based on 13 vertical columns, with the seventh being the unmirrored, the place of the origin of spirit. Each of the 13 dimensions are reflected in the Tzolkin. The module of the Tzolkin is held together by a matrix of 52 Galactic Activation Portals (GAPs) arranged on a lattice of 20 horizontal rows. There are no GAPs in the 7th column. This column is the resonant channel or radial speaking tube. Study the symmetrical pattern of the GAPS on each side of the seventh column. These constitute an index of polarity with varying degrees of electrical charges. The first six dimensions, by analogy, are the first six columns, and columns 13-8, mirroring columns 1-6, construct an alternate universe.

Mirror Dimension alternative universe(s) operates simultaneous to 7-dimensional creation cycle universe.

Telepathically accessible for paranormal harmonic resonance and resolution

In the Tzolkin, the columns have charges in the positions that are analogous to the dimensions they represent. In the first dimension/column, there is a charge in the first and last positions. In the second dimension/column, there is a charge in the second and the second to the last positions, and so on up through the fifth, which has GAPS in the fifth and the fifth from the last positions. The third dimension also has joined charges in the tenth and eleventh positions indicating this is the dimension of charged "substance" (matter), while the fourth and fifth, with two extra charges, each show the charge separating and the matter becoming more etheric.

The sixth dimension has ten charges in sequence (6 to 15), which is where the electronic fluids interact to create super light entitization streams. The seventh dimension is the center where all charges emanate, but with no electrical densities. The first and second dimensions have two charges each; the third, fourth and fifth dimensions each have four charges. These complex charges create life. Viewing the Tzolkin in this way, as an index of the ratios or the electronic intensity of the different dimensions, is a way of engaging the imaginal realm in a simultaneous multidimensional comprehension of cosmic reality.

SYNCHRONIC ORDER AS KEY TO HIGHER DIMENSIONS

Practice of the synchronic codes of the Law of Time, as defined by Cosmic History, has a cumulative qualitative effect that increases our daily consciousness, lifting us more and more into a fourth/fifth-dimensional perception of reality. From this perceptual lens, the third dimension takes on a dreamlike quality making the cultivation of cosmic perceptions much more fluid. This process is the effect of the psychoactive nature of Cosmic History.

The fifth dimension is the space where time no longer operates and reincarnation no longer exists. Reincarnation occurs only at the atomic and subatomic levels. The evolving soul strives to advance from the third to the fourth dimension, and then beyond time to the fifth dimension, which is accessible through deep meditation.

The third-, fourth-, and fifth-dimensional selves constitute the single triad entity. From the point of view of cosmic consciousness, the atomic and subatomic are purely transitional phases. In addition, when we say time is the fourth dimension, it means that time organizes the first four dimensions into a radial matrix of synchronicity where everything is experienced in its interconnectedness. Space is where this all occurs.

Time is the rate of synchronizations within the universal order inseparable from self-existing awareness. Or as Einstein says "Time is what keeps things from happening all at once." However, from the point of view of the Law of Time we can also say that (in the fourth dimension) Time is *how* everything *is happening* all at once!

The sixth dimension is the plane of light where form no longer exists. In Buddhist terms this is the *Arupa*, or formless realm. In the sixth dimension, harmonic and inharmonic electrical fluids (like plasmas) of different frequencies interact to create many or multiple meta-entitizations (like super angel functions of massive constructs of intelligence that know everything).

The seventh dimension has pure resonance with what we might call the voice of God or the divine command or creation utterances. These creation utterances come from the vast Divine Intelligence matrices that constitute the organizing principle of the entire universe. They can be understood as the responses of the unimaginably vast mind of God, which is beyond all dimensionality and beyond all conception—but nonetheless all creation impulses emanate from It. In the Qur'an, it says that for anything to come into existence all God has to do is say: "Be," and it happens.

So the creation utterances are like a cosmic echo that manifests through the seventh-dimensional speaking tube of God. This echo then reverberates into and makes a pure light imprint in the sixth dimension. Here, this creation utterance takes on a particular kind of light signature or light configuration, which can be understood as the encoding of a creation command. These creation commands then trickle down through the dimensions until finally, for example, we are here reading these words.

SIMULTANEOUS UNIVERSE MODEL AND MIRROR DIMENSIONS

According to the Simultaneous Universe Model (SUM), at any given moment the universe is completely united by that moment. This means you can go anywhere in the universe at any given moment and the whole structure of the universe is present. It is present in a vertical expanse from which extends a radial palette of different dimensions. At the center of the radial palette is the information core, or Cosmic History, which is derived from the Master Record or the Mother of the Book.

The Cosmic History core coordinates and radiates different dimensions and aspects of being while also illustrating a template showing how certain structures move in time and space. In the SUM, not only do you have the lower dimensions coming up to the third dimension, but also going up or down from the fourth, to the fifth, sixth and seventh dimensions. The seventh dimension is the mirrorless resonator. The mirror dimensions, 8-13, can be accessed through the seventh dimension.

If you look at the Simultaneous Universe Model graphic, you will see that on the top there is a toroidal vacuum that sucks into the void or that blows through and out of the void, while embracing the first dimension. This toroidal void space that goes through the center acts as the telepathic medium that connects all of the different dimensions. This creates the capacity for telepathic communication, which is dimensionally stepped up or stepped down, depending on which direction it is going.

The mirror dimensions are accessed through the human's fourth-dimensional body. The mirror eighth dimension is on the inside of the sixth dimension. The mirror ninth dimension is on the inside of the fifth dimension. The mirror tenth dimension is on the inside of the fourth dimension. The mirror eleventh dimension is on the inside of the third dimension. The mirror twelfth dimension is on the inside of the second dimension and the mirror thirteenth dimension is on the inside of the first dimension.

The dimensions are penetrated by an interior mental resonance, which puts you in touch with higher-dimensional phenomena. When higher-dimensional phenomena appear to you in your mind, they may appear as apparitions to the physical eye. This is because the phenomena must be stepped down to take on some type of form that is recognizable to your inner senses—like a voice, or something you see in your mind's eye or like an astral movie or a dream. So the higher-dimensional information is stepped down in order to become cognizable through the inner perceptions.

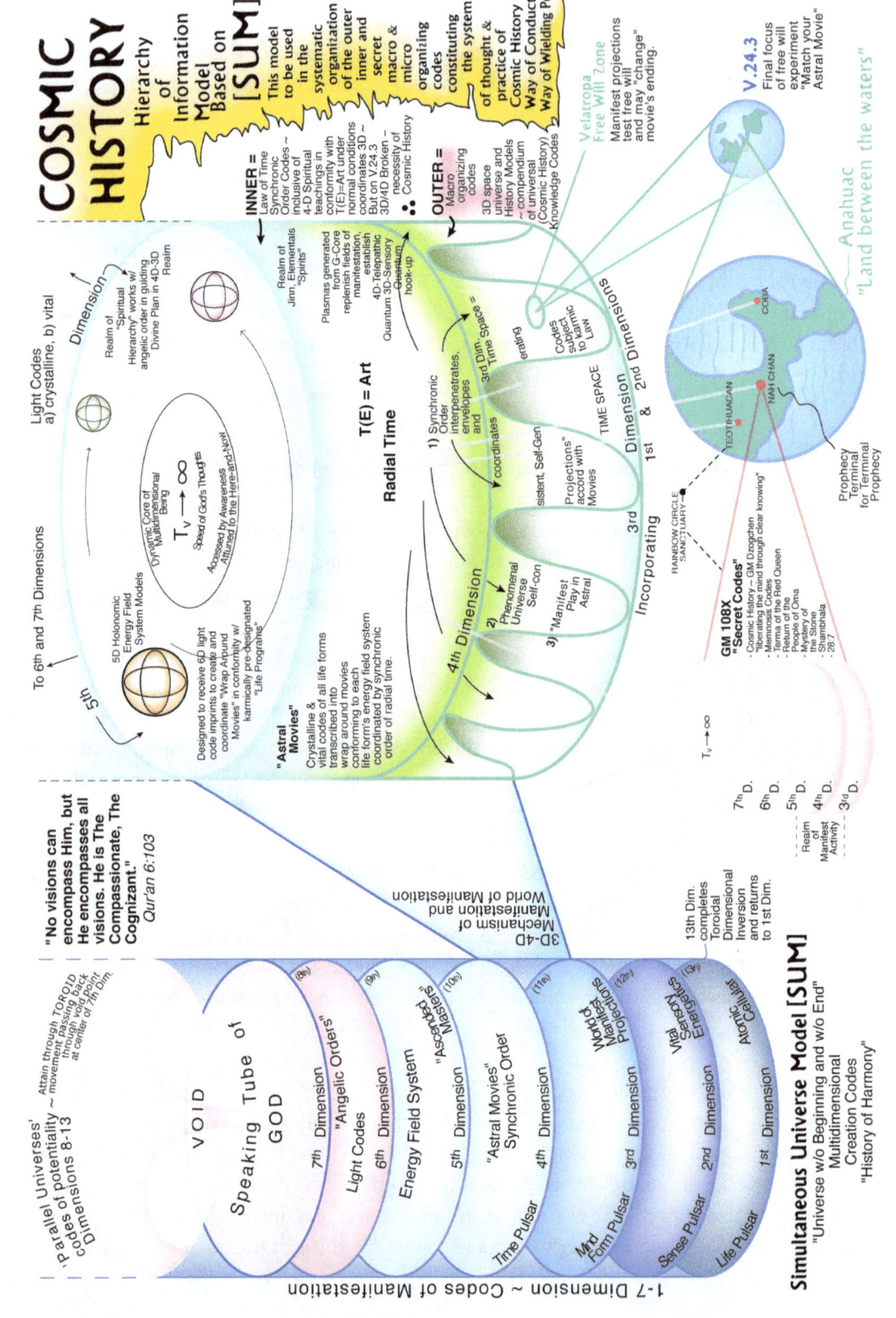

Chapter 9 • Realizing the 13 Dimensions

The SUM also shows Velatropa (the region of the galaxy where our solar system is found) as the Free Will zone, where manifest projections called humans test their free will. The highest act of free will is aligning personal will with Divine Will. Only when personal will is surrendered to the Divine Will can we create a victorious ending to the movie being projected into the third dimension. The Earth, or Velatropa 24.3, is the stage set where the final stages of the free will experiment are being played out.

Within the entirety of the 7/13-dimensional SUM model there exists vast amounts of space. This space is both the medium of generation of energy, such as light and other subatomic phenomenon like plasma, and is also the medium of telepathic resonance. This is what actually holds the different dimensions together.

Cosmic Science also posits another five dimensions beyond the 13th. These are the subtle planes of the fifth force angelic intelligences, primordially established in the fifth "moon" of the Wavespell of Cosmic Creation (See Chapter 12 of *CHC Vol. II, 18-Dimensional Universe*). According to Cosmic Science, there are 8 universes and 18 dimensions. The 18 dimensions correspond to the 18 facets of a perfect double-terminated crystal. No matter how many dimensions there are, they are still enclosed by or constitute a perfect form—the universal cosmic hologram symbolized by the double-terminated crystal.

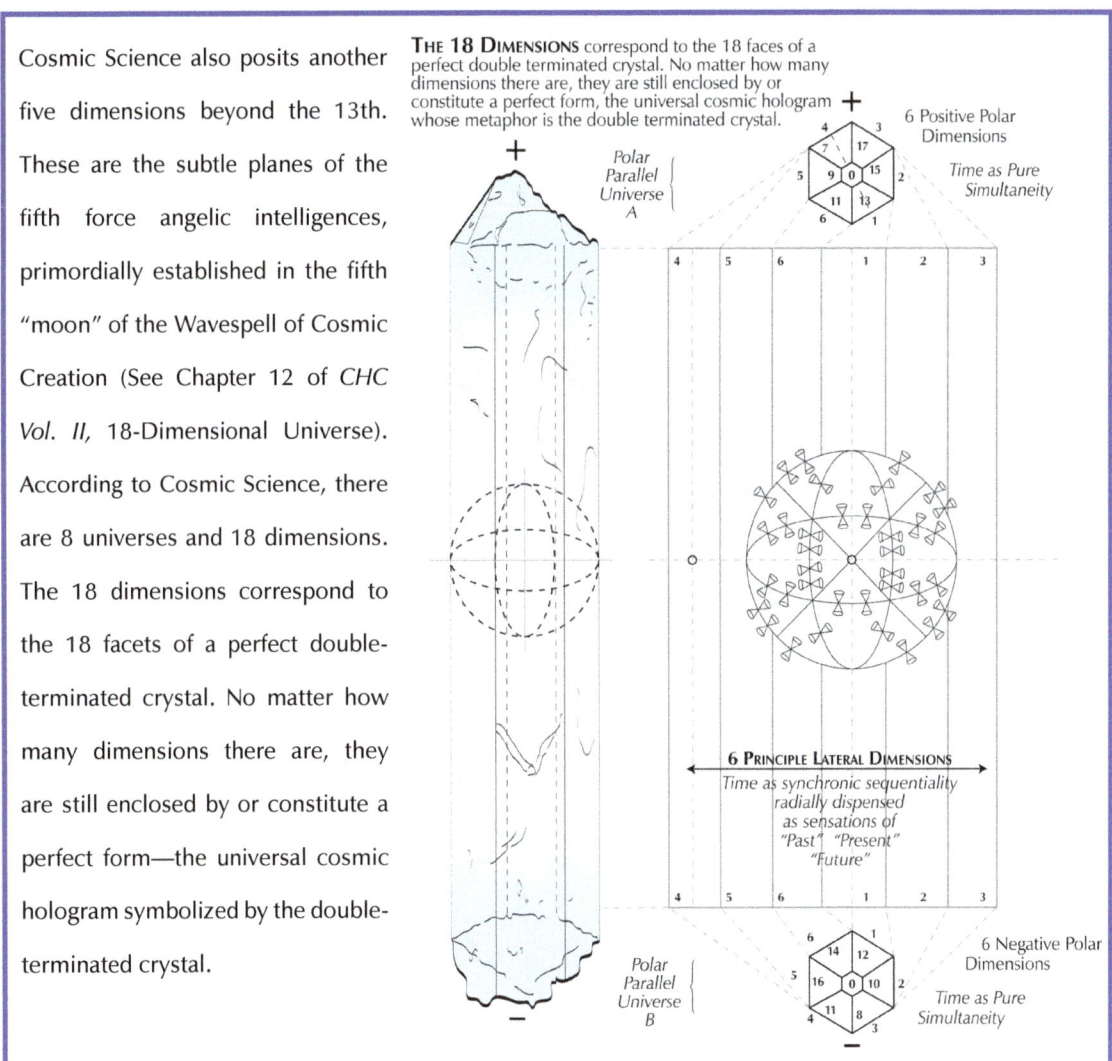

THE 18 DIMENSIONS correspond to the 18 faces of a perfect double terminated crystal. No matter how many dimensions there are, they are still enclosed by or constitute a perfect form, the universal cosmic hologram whose metaphor is the double terminated crystal.

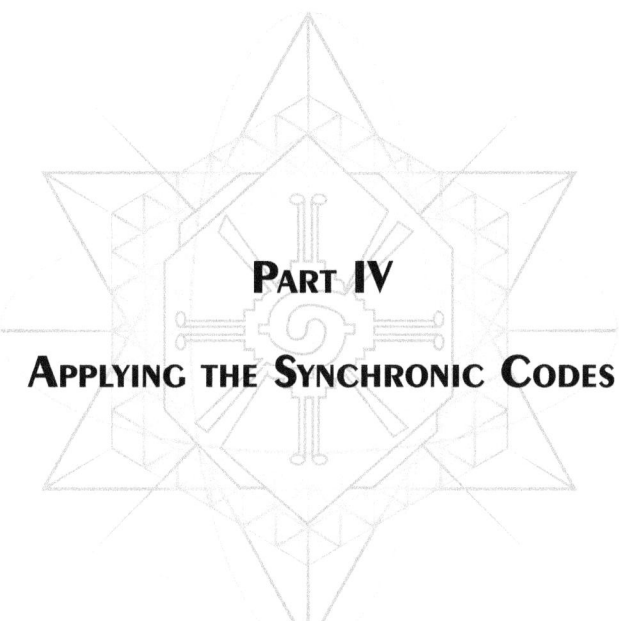

Part IV

Applying the Synchronic Codes

CHAPTER 10

ENCHANTING THE NUMBERS

All is number. God is a number. God is in all. —Pacal Votan

Universal mathematics informs all existence. In reality, everything is pure vibratory resonance. Number represents different qualities of resonance.

Nature creates everything in balanced ratios and harmonics. Everything has a number. When we enter the world of pure number, we enter a pulsating, vibrating world of harmonic relationships filled with color and sound. The more we familiarize ourselves with numbers, the more we recognize patterns.

Just as the universe is made up of number patterns, so too is our body. Our brain, like the planet, has two hemispheres. Our planet has seven continents as we have seven chakras. We are born with 10 fingers and 10 toes, 20 digits in all—just as there are twenty interplanetary zones on the Planet Holon grid. We have four limbs, seven chakras, 13 main articulations, 209 bones, 260 tastebuds and 33 vertebrae. We have five senses, two eyes for vision, two nostrils for smell, two ears to hear, one tongue to taste, and one skin to feel.

Numbers are the highest degree of knowledge; they are knowledge itself. This understanding of the world of number traces back to the Greek philosopher Pythagoras, who viewed numbers as a metaphysical system of thought and life. It is Pythagoras who first realized that there are five essential geometric solids: the tetrahedron, the cube, the octahedron, the icosahedron and the dodecahedron.

Pythagoras systematized a cosmology of number and created his own school at Krotona, with an emphasis in the studies of geometry, music, and architecture—all of which are founded upon mathematics. All studies sought to understand number and geometry as the underlying structure of the universe. We can see pyramids within mountains and triangular forms within the trees and the Fibonacci spiral in seashells, ram horns and our ear canal (among many other things).

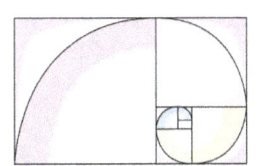

LAW OF TIME

The Law of Time defines a Pythagorean cosmology of number (0-19). One gives rise to all number — No matter how big any number is, it is always divisible by itself and number 1. One is in everything. All systems of number begin with 1+1=2 — Two is the Law of Alternation.

- Every even number is divisible by 2
- Every third number after 3 will be a multiple of 3
- Any number whose digits add up to 9 or a multiple of 9 will always be a multiple of 9 [same is true for 19 in vigesimal]

SUFI TRADITION TALKS ABOUT THE FRACTURE OR BREAK IN ETERNITY, CORRESPONDING TO THE INTERVAL RATIO WITH A FREQUENCY OF 7. ONLY WHEN YOU DIVIDE A CIRCLE INTO 20 PARTS (18°) CAN YOU DISCOVER THE RATIO INTERVAL OF 7 — LOST TIME IN ETERNITY. THIS CREATES THE LAW OF 13:7, ESTABLISHES 13:20 TIMING FREQUENCY, AS WELL AS THE HAAB CYCLE, TZOLKIN, ETC. OF THE LAW OF TIME 4:7::7:13

20×18° = 360°

INTERVAL RATIO OF 7 CORRESPONDS TO 126° 18×7=126

WHY IS THE MOON ALWAYS NEW? 13:7 HOW OLD IS THE MOON? 13:7

THE OTHER 13 PARTS OF THE WHEEL = 234°

126 + 234 = 360

ORIGIN OF 13:20 FREQUENCY

THE 4 PHASES OF THE MOON ARE ROUGHLY 7 DAYS EACH. THE MOON SHIFTS IN THE SKY 13° EVERY DAY IN ONE LUNATION CYCLE.

COSMOS IS 13.7 BILLION YEARS OLD. 13+7 CREATES 20 — THE WHOLE TOTALITY OF TIME.

GALACTIC COMPASS HAS 7 VOID SPACES + 13 — THIS IS THE ORIGIN OF THE 13:20 FREQUENCY.

NOTE: IN WHEEL, HAAB IS COUNTED AS 18 20-DAY INTERVALS = 1 TUN, UAYEB IS NOT COUNTED

BOOK OF 7 GENERATIONS CORRESPONDS PRECISELY, I.E. 14 = WIZARD, 15 = EAGLE, 16 = WARRIOR, 17 = EARTH, 18 = MIRROR, 19 = STORM, 20 = SUN

7 SOLAR MANTRAS ALSO CORRESPOND WITH THE 7 DAYS OF CREATION

THE WHEEL IS THE MOVEMENT OF MEASURE — IT GOES IN A SPIRAL COUNTERCLOCKWISE. 7+13 CREATES THE POWER OF TIME AS MOVEMENT AND CREATES THE RATIO FREQUENCY CONSTANT 13:20 — IMPLICIT IN THIS IS 4:7::7:13, THE BASIC PRINCIPLE OF THE COSMOLOGY OF NUMBER

BEFORE A DOT AROSE IN SPACE THERE WAS ONLY UNDIFFERENTIATED SPIRIT

SQUARES

$1^2 = 1$
$2^2 = 4$
$3^2 = 9$
$4^2 = 16$
$5^2 = 25$
$6^2 = 36$
$7^2 = 49$
$8^2 = 64$
$9^2 = 81$
$10^2 = 100$
$11^2 = 121$
$12^2 = 144$
$13^2 = 169$
$14^2 = 196$
$15^2 = 225$
$16^2 = 256$
$17^2 = 289$
$18^2 = 324$
$19^2 = 361$
$20^2 = 400$
$21^2 = 441$

SUM **3311** OF 1ST 21 SQUARES = 11×43×7

INTERVALS BETWEEN SQUARES GO UP IN PERFECT ODD # SEQUENCE: 3-41 [=425] [=17×25]

$(20+1)^2 [21^2]$ = 441 MATRIX (HUNAB KU) OCCULT KIN ALWAYS ADD UP TO 21

441 ORIGINS

GO BACK TO ORIGINAL MIND. THINK OF NUMBER ONE AND RADIATE THE ONE OUT INTO THE 4 CARDINAL DIRECTIONS = RADIATION OF 8 = EACH OF THESE IS A ONE INCLUDING THE CENTRAL POINT = 9 ONES. THIS IS HOW WE CAN DIVIDE THE 441 MATRIX INTO 9 PARTS.

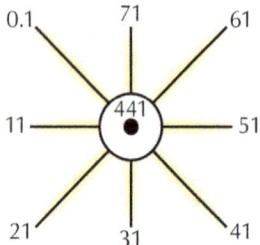

IF YOU START WITH YOUR LEFT ARM, BETWEEN FRONT AND LEFT SIDE THAT IS 1. THEN STRAIGHT LEFT IS 11. THEN 21, THEN 31 (BEHIND), THEN 41, THEN 51, THEN 61, THEN 71 AND FINALLY THE CENTER, 441. THIS IS HOW THE BASE MATRIX OF 441 IS CREATED FROM THE CENTER OF YOUR BEING.

Enter the World of Number — a world that is self-existing, vibrant and always creating synchronic relationships. Look at all numbers and pay attention.

Law of Time and Pythagorean Principles

The Law of Time includes the fundamental Pythagorean principle of numbers as resonant frequencies. However, the cosmology of the Law of Time focuses on the geometry of time, whereas the Pythagorean cosmology focuses primarily on the geometry of space. Each number holds a different frequency that contains various qualities, both hidden and overt. In a synchronic sense, "using" number is about understanding matrices and cycles of time to create a shift in the mental force field.

Meditating on universal mathematics reveals a higher vista of how the creation of GOD (Galactic Ordering Dynamic) emanates from what we call number into manifestation, and then into consciousness, words and language. All sacred teachings have a variation of this teaching of the principle of harmony through number.

Body as Number and Synchronic Order

Synchronization occurs as a function of the synchronic order. The codes of the synchronic order are the codes by which body and mind become synchronized. By studying the codes as a daily discipline their harmonic structure begins to inform us. If we keep our mind on the codes and all their different levels, we soon realize that they produce a synchronization of body and mind.

1 Unified Whole. 1 body. 1 Cosmic Tree.
2 Memory Circuits, genetic and historical (AC/Aboriginal Continuity and CA/Cosmic Awareness)—Strands of DNA and hemispheres of the brain: right and left.
2 Flows—Inhalation/exhalation/magnetic alternation of night and day, etc.
3 Inner Planes (plane of mind, will and spirit)—3 parts of the body (top, middle, bottom).
4 Clans/Galactic Elements (fire, blood, truth and sky)—4 extremities: 2 arms, 2 legs.
4 Root Races (red initiators, white refiners, blue transformers, yellow ripeners).
5 Time Cells—5 main organs: heart (input), lungs (store), liver (process), kidney (output) and spleen (matrix).
5 Earth Families—5 main chakras, "pentacled" body structure (2 arms, 2 legs, 1 head).
5 Castles of Time—5 senses: touch (red), taste (white), hearing (blue), sight (yellow), smell (green).
6 Mental Spheres—6 sides of the cube.
7 Radial Plasmas, Chakras and Heptad Gates—7 facial openings/doors to outer perception (2 eyes, 2 ears, 2 nostrils, 1 mouth). 7 is the number of creation.
9 Time Dimensions/Bolontiku/Lords of Time—9 bodily orifices (2 eyes, 2 ears, 2 nostrils, 1 mouth, 1 urethra, 1 anus).
13 Galactic Tones—13 main articulations (2 ankles, 2 knees, 2 hips, 2 wrists, 2 elbows, 2 shoulders, 1 spine/neck), Oxlahuntiku/power of time in consciousness, wavespell.
20 Solar Seals—20 digits/fingers & toes, number of totality.
21 Galactic Archetypes—Root of the 1.2.1 = 441 cube matrix, root of the cube of knowledge, root of galactic wisdom and knowledge.

Accessing Your Multidimensional Self: A Key to Cosmic History

- **ONE** Unified Whole.
  1 body. 1 Cosmic Tree.

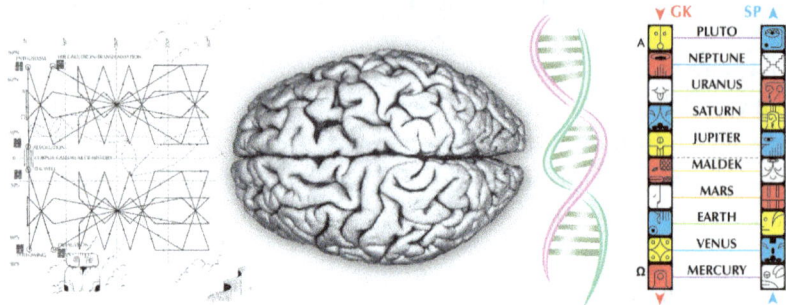

•• **TWO** Memory Circuits, genetic and historical (AC/Aboriginal Continuity and CA/Cosmic Awareness)—Strands of DNA and hemispheres of the brain: right and left; inhalation/exhalation/magnetic alternation of night and day, etc.

••• **THREE** Inner Planes (plane of mind, will and spirit)—3 parts of the body (top, middle, bottom), three fields (gravitational, biopsychic, electromagnetic).

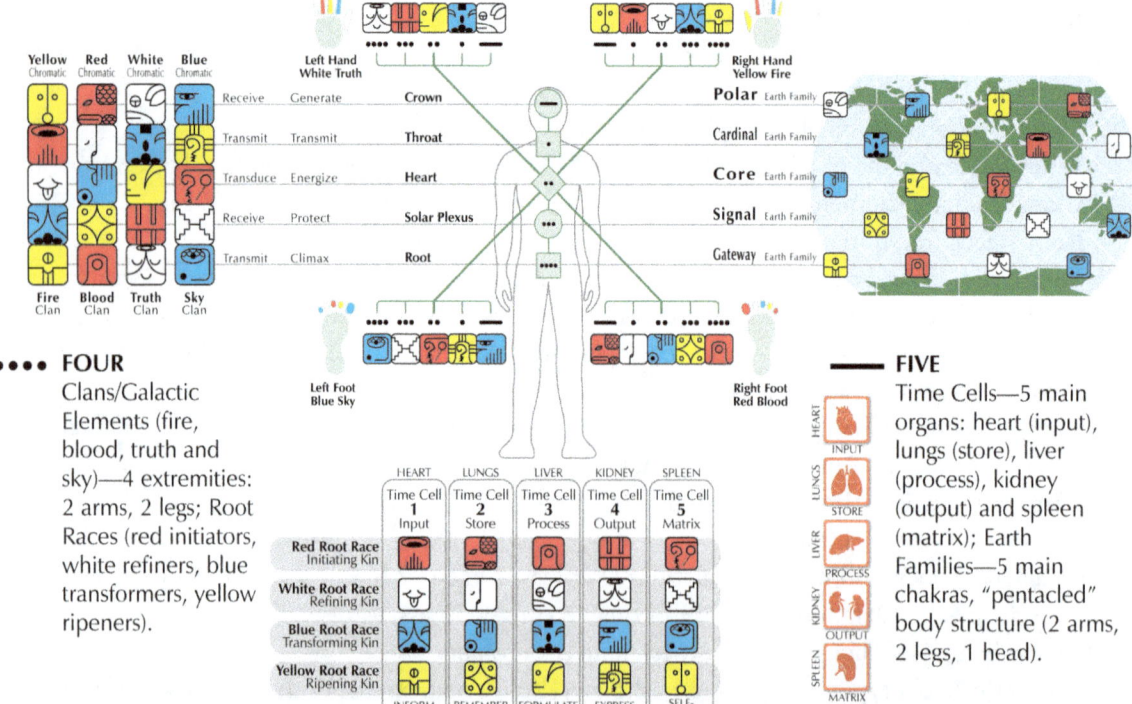

•••• **FOUR** Clans/Galactic Elements (fire, blood, truth and sky)—4 extremities: 2 arms, 2 legs; Root Races (red initiators, white refiners, blue transformers, yellow ripeners).

––– **FIVE** Time Cells—5 main organs: heart (input), lungs (store), liver (process), kidney (output) and spleen (matrix); Earth Families—5 main chakras, "pentacled" body structure (2 arms, 2 legs, 1 head).

Chapter 10 • Enchanting the Numbers

▬ FIVE Castles of Time—5 senses: touch (red), taste (white), hearing (blue), sight (yellow), smell (green).

• SIX Mental Spheres—sides of the cube.

•• SEVEN Radial Plasmas, Chakras and Heptad Gates—7 facial openings/doors to outer perception (2 eyes, 2 ears, 2 nostrils, 1 mouth). 7 is the number of creation.

RED EASTERN CASTLE OF TURNING
WHITE NORTHERN CASTLE OF CROSSING
BLUE WESTERN CASTLE OF BURNING
YELLOW SOUTHERN CASTLE OF GIVING
GREEN CENTRAL CASTLE OF ENCHANTMENT

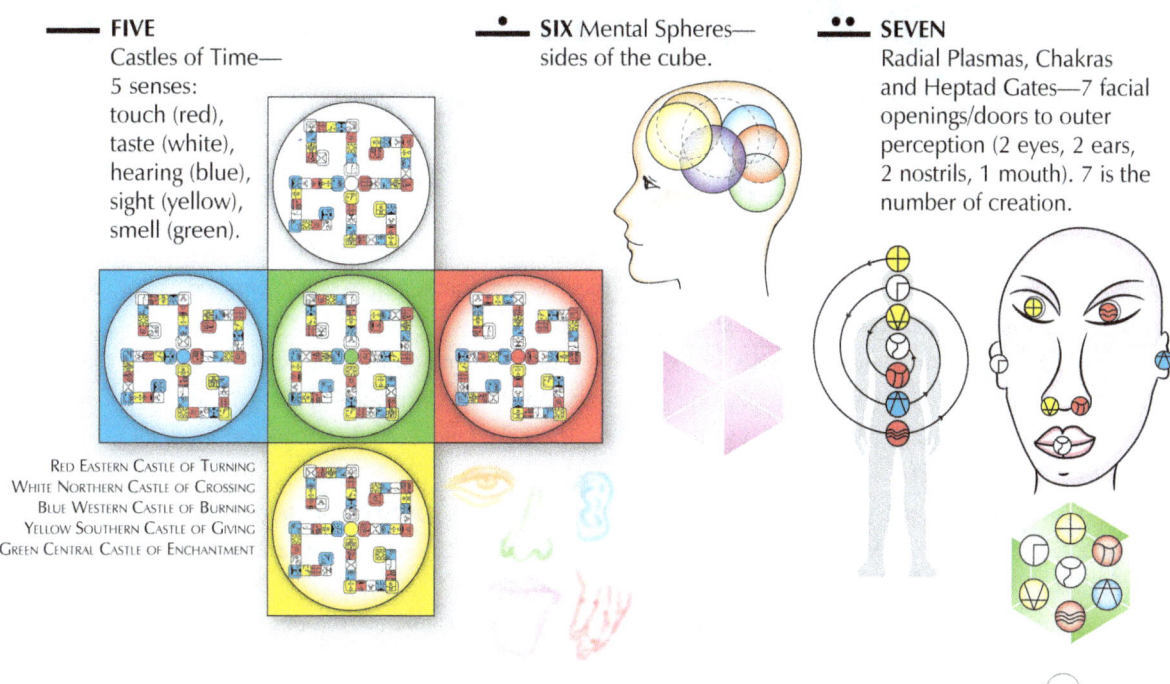

•••• NINE Time Dimensions/Bolontiku/Lords of Time—9 bodily orifices (2 eyes, 2 ears, 2 nostrils, 1 mouth, 1 urethra, 1 anus).

1 OUTER TIME DIMENSION	7 RADIAL (VERTICAL) TIME DIMENSION	2 OUTER TIME DIMENSION
5 RADIAL (LATERAL) TIME DIMENSION	9 INNER CORE 9TH TIME DIMENSION	6 RADIAL (LATERAL) TIME DIMENSION
3 OUTER TIME DIMENSION	8 RADIAL (VERTICAL) TIME DIMENSION	4 OUTER TIME DIMENSION

••• THIRTEEN Galactic Tones—13 main articulations (2 ankles, 2 knees, 2 hips, 2 wrists, 2 elbows, 2 shoulders, 1 spine/neck), Oxlahuntiku/power of time in consciousness, wavespell.

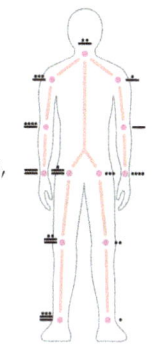

• TWENTY Solar Seals—20 digits/fingers & toes, number of totality.

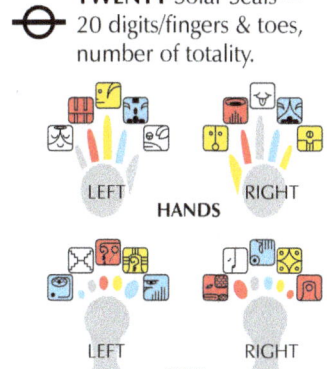

LEFT   RIGHT
HANDS

LEFT   RIGHT
FEET

•• TWENTY-ONE Galactic Archetypes—Root of the 1.2.1 = 441 cube matrix, root of the cube of knowledge, root of galactic wisdom and knowledge.

Accessing Your Multidimensional Self: A Key to Cosmic History

Introduction to the Cycles of Time

Synchronicity is the operation of a higher moving template of mathematical order that coordinates all phenomena telepathically. This creates the fourth-dimensional order of reality, the synchronic order. Page numbers are given for further explanation of each of the cycles. The fundamental cycles of the synchronic order are:

4-day cycles (harmonics): Smallest fractal cycle. The 20 solar seals are coded by four colors to create the five time cells (4 x 5 = 20). Each of these sets is called a harmonic with a basic pattern of meaning: red (initiates), white (refines), blue (transforms), yellow (ripens).

5-day cycles (chromatics): Five day sequence that starts and ends with same color: Yellow Fire clan, Red Blood clan, White Truth clan, Blue Sky clan. There are 73 five-day chromatics to every 52 weeks.

7-day cycles (week or heptad): Standard measure. There are four seven-day cycles per moon (4 x 7 = 28). Each day is coded by one of the seven radial plasmas.

13-day cycles (wavespells): Standard fractal unit of measure. A wavespell can be 13 days, 13 weeks, 13 moons, 13 years, 13 baktuns, etc. There are 20 wavespells of 13 days each in one 260-day spin (20 x 13 = 260).

20-day cycles (vinals): 20-day sequence always coded by the solar seal that codes the year. Creates an annual cycle of solar meditations. 20-day cycle also refers to 20 solar seals: Dragon to Sun.

28-day cycles (moons): 28 is the harmonic standard. 4 (weeks) x 7 (days) = 28. There are 13 moons per year (28 x 13 = 364) +1 (Day out of Time).

52-day cycles (castles): Each castle consists of four color-coded wavespells (4 x 13 = 52). Five 52-day castles pace each 260-day spin (52 x 5 = 260). Castles are also used to map different time ratios: 52 days, 52 years, etc.

65-day cycles (galactic seasons or spectrum): There are four 65-day cycles within a 260-day spin. These cycles are coded by the third (Electric) tone of the four kin of the Polar Earth Family, i.e. Red Electric Serpent, White Electric Dog, Blue Electric Eagle and Yellow Electric Sun all begin the spectrums/seasons of their color.

260-day cycle (one Tzolkin "spin"): Fourth-dimensional timing gauge, based on a 13 x 20 matrix, which codes the 13:20 timing frequency.

365-day cycle (one solar orbit): Also known as a solar ring, perfectly measured by the 13 Moon, 28-day harmonic standard. 364 +1 (Day out of Time).

13 x 20 = 260

28 x 13 + 1 = 365

Harmonic Module
Tzolkin
260 Days

One Year/Solar Ring
"Planetary Service Wavespell"
365 Days

Note: If we coordinate the 13 Moon/28-day pattern plus the 365th day (Day out of Time) with the 260-day pattern, we arrive at a cycle of 18,980 days, or 52 years, or 73 of the 260-day Tzolkin spins. Also note that the 52-year solar-galactic cycle corresponds to the orbit of Sirius B around Sirius A.

28 Days per Moon/Telektonon—Number of joints in 10 fingers
33 Spinal vertebrae—Number of the Initiate.
64 DNA codons, cosmic index.
209 Bones—Kin 209 = entrance to Green Central Castle.
260 Kin Tzolkin/Galactic Spin—260-day average human gestation cycle.

7 Major Arcanum

The cosmology of time is based on the power of seven, known as the Seven Major Arcanum of the Law of Time. Each of the seven volumes of the *Cosmic History Chronicles* is based on one of the Seven Major Arcanum.

Arcanum refers to mysterious knowledge known only to the initiate, or "one having the key." The cosmology of the Seven Major Arcanum of the Law of Time underlies the mysterious text referred to by the Chilam Balam, or Jaguar Priests, as the Book of Seven Generations.

In the cosmology of the seven, key points are held by images that are each coded by one of the seven radial plasmas that together constitute a cubic lattice, arranged the following way: The form and movement of the cosmology of the Seven Major Arcanum assumes the shape of the *heptagonon of mind* or *primal cubic parton*, in which the relation of numbers 1 and 2 describe the top and bottom of the cube; numbers 3 and 4 describe the front and back sides of the cube; numbers 5 and 6 describe the right and left sides of the cube; and the number 7 defines the center point of the cube.

Each of the Seven Major Arcanum also corresponds with a radial plasma, forming an entire psychomythology according to the number seven.

Throne (Dali): In the cosmology of Palenque the throne is symbolic of the the all-seeing eye of God (Horus) and is guarded by 9 Ik, patroness of avatars.

Avatar (Seli): The Avatar turns the wheel of time and is represented at the bottom of the cube, which touches the Earth plane. Only the Avatar can renew the message of the Throne of God. It is the Avatar who knows and renews time.

Mystery (Gamma): For the Avatar to communicate the message of renewal, there must be knowledge of the Mystery. This is the bond between the invisible and the visible that connects all things to the original matrix of the synchronic order of reality. This Mystery is known as death, and enlightenment is synonymous with knowing the mystery of death.

Accessing Your Multidimensional Self: A Key to Cosmic History

Initiation (Kali): The Mystery opened by death represents Initiation, entrance to the fifth world of the center, the knowledge of knowing and passing through death in full consciousness, both during and after life. The tomb epitomizes the power of initiation. (Of all tombs, that of Pacal Votan is the paramount emblem of the Initiation). Note that Kali, the fourth radial plasma, is the catalytic agent between the sensory and telepathic quantum. The four is directly related to the 7 and is a primary key to the Law of Time. The formulation 4:7::7:13 is the purest cosmology of the Law of Time and should be meditated upon deeply.

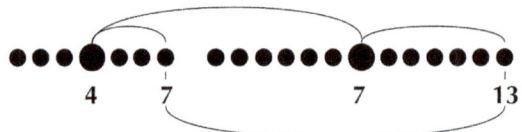

Timespace (Alpha). The primal initiation of Pacal Votan required a Timespace manifestation, symbolized above by the Palace of Heaven and below by the Temple of Earth or the Temple of Inscriptions. Palenque, or Nah Chan, represents the earthly timespace manifestation of the heavenly city known as Tollan.

Transcendence (Limi). Like all Timespace focalization, correct knowledge leads to Transcendence, an affirmation of the Mystery and of the effectiveness of the Initiation.

The Seven Caves

The Law of Seven is what underlies the entirety of Cosmic History. Everything can be reduced to aspects of the number seven. Tollan Zuvuya or the 7 caves or the place of the 7 ravines is a place contacted through the mind where the memories and knowledge of Tollan and the return of Tollan are kept. The 7 caves refer to the power of 7 as the generating power of the knowledge of origin and return. The 7 caves are the stored place of the wisdom lore of Quetzalcoatl. In the 7 caves is the origin of everything, including the origin of the synchronic order.

Cube (Silio). The initiatory process leads to the seventh stage and the magical evocation of the Cube, both with its six sides and three inner planes, which could only be self-reflectively known after God assumed the power of the Throne. The Cube is guarded by the Red Queen (galactic feminine energy), she who completes the lineage of Votan, and in whose heart is the Initiate of the Throne.

Seven Heptad Gates and their relation to the Seven Major Arcanum

Within the synchronic order, the seven-day cycle opens the seven hyper-galactic portals in the brain that establish the six mental spheres plus the holomind perceiver, the seventh mental sphere. These hyper-galactic portals are known as the seven *heptad gates*. The activation of the holomind perceiver on a seven-day basis evolves this new mental organ as the medium of perception of the Second Creation.

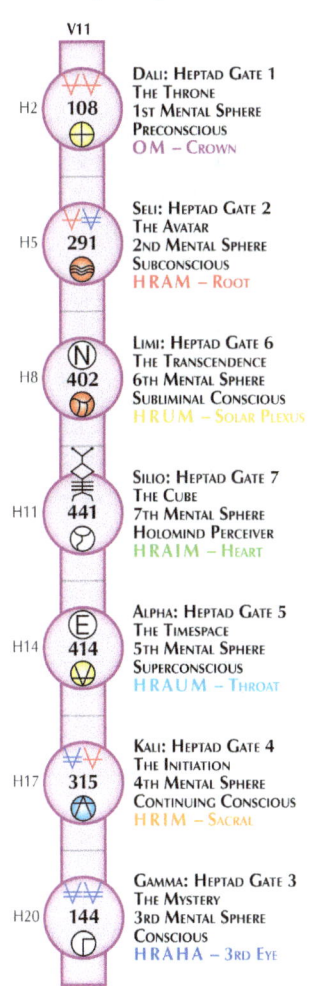

Each week the seven portals or heptad gates establish the cube of one of 52 heptad paths. In this way the evolution of the seventh day of creation is activated, laying the foundation of galactic culture.

The seven portals are projected from the corpus callosum to a line that runs from the center of the base of the skull over the top of the head and down to the third eye. Each of the portals opens a cosmic channel through which telepathic frequencies attract different hyperplasmas and electrical charges, namely: alpha-alpha, alpha-beta, beta-beta, beta-alpha, hyperelectron, hyperneutron, and Sirius B-52/Element 113.

The seven hyper-charges activate each of the seven mental spheres. Correlated to the seven days of the week, each of the portals corresponds to one of the Seven Major Arcanum of the Law of Time, one of the 21 galactic archetypes, and has a planetary designation (see *Synchrogalactic Yoga*, chapter 13).

The Arcanum of the Throne is located in the crown chakra governed by the Dali plasma. It is coded by the Dragon, Primal Force, associated with Neptune. Here the alpha-alpha hyperplasma activates the first mental sphere, preconscious, as profound samadhi. In the 441 base matrix the Throne is coded by frequency 108.

Accessing Your Multidimensional Self: A Key to Cosmic History

The 52 Heptad Paths of Hunab Ku 21
52 Heptads of the Cosmic Ring of V.24.3
The Archetypal Journey Made Available to Everyone

Annual Alpha Phase TELEKTONON Unit of Outer Manifestation. · **20 Heptads — 140 Days** · **Four Outer Courts (Power Cells) Established**

Magnetic Moon ·
- 1st Heptad Path: Neptune / Maldek — **Being evolves Sex**
- 2nd Heptad Path: Neptune / Mars — **Being evolves Death**
- 3rd Heptad Path: Neptune / Earth — **Being evolves Knowledge**
- 4th Heptad Path: Maldek / Earth — **Sex evolves Knowledge**
- **POWER of KNOWLEDGE**

Lunar Moon ··
- 5th Heptad Path: Mars / Earth — **Death evolves Knowledge**
- 6th Heptad Path: Saturn / Venus — **Dreaming evolves Art**
- 7th Heptad Path: Saturn / Mercury — **Dreaming evolves Purity**
- 8th Heptad Path: Saturn / Mercury — **Dreaming evolves Love**
- **KNOWLEDGE EVOLVES POWER OF LOVE**

Electric Moon ···
- 9th Heptad Path: Venus / Mercury — **Art evolves Love**
- 10th Heptad Path: Mercury / Mercury — **Purity evolves Love**
- 11th Heptad Path: Uranus / Venus — **Spirit evolves Magic**
- 12th Heptad Path: Uranus / Earth — **Spirit evolves Free Will**
- **POWER of LOVE EVOLVES POWER of PROPHECY**

Self-existing Moon ····
- 13th Heptad Path: Uranus / Mars — **Spirit evolves Prophecy**
- 14th Heptad Path: Venus / Mars — **Magic evolves Prophecy**
- 15th Heptad Path: Earth / Mars — **Free Will evolves Prophecy**
- 16th Heptad Path: Jupiter / Maldek — **Awareness evolves Timelessness**
- **POWER of PROPHECY EVOLVES POWER of INTELLIGENCE**

Overtone Moon —
- 17th Heptad Path: Jupiter / Jupiter — **Awareness evolves Vision**
- 18th Heptad Path: Jupiter / Saturn — **Awareness evolves Intelligence**
- 19th Heptad Path: Maldek / Saturn — **Timelessness evolves Intelligence**
- 20th Heptad Path: Jupiter / Saturn — **Vision evolves Intelligence**
- **POWER of INTELLIGENCE**

Day 365	Skywalker
73 × 5	Mirror
GREEN DAY	Night
	Star

= Complete the Galactic Order $(84 + 1) 6^2 + 7^2$ Days

Absolute TELEKTONON
20 Types of 7-Kin Heptads in Sequence
[140 Kin × 13 Tones = 1820 Kin
7-G Spins / 1 Holtun]

1. Dragon (1) — Hand (7)
2. Star (8) — Wizard (14)
3. Eagle (15) — Dragon (1)
4. Wind (2) — Star (8)
5. Moon (9) — Eagle (15)
6. Warrior (16) — Wind (2)
7. Night (3) — Moon (9)
8. Dog (10) — Warrior (16)
9. Earth (17) — Night (3)
10. Seed (4) — Dog (10)
11. Monkey (11) — Earth (17)
12. Mirror (18) — Seed (4)
13. Serpent (5) — Monkey (11)
14. Human (12) — Mirror (18)
15. Storm (19) — Serpent (5)
16. Worldbridger (6) — Human (12)
17. Skywalker (13) — Storm (19)
18. Sun (20) — Worldbridger (6)
19. Hand (7) — Skywalker (13)
20. Wizard (14) — Sun (20)

20 Paths of Outer Manifestation

20 Paths of Inner Radiance

12 Paths of Transcendent Order

Cosmic Moon ≡
- 49th Heptad Path: Pluto / Venus — **Enlightenment evolves Magic**
- 50th Heptad Path: Pluto / Earth — **Enlightenment evolves Free Will**
- 51st Heptad Path: Pluto / Maldek — **Navigation evolves Timelessness**
- 52nd Heptad Path: Uranus / Jupiter — **Navigation evolves Vision**
- **POWER of PROPHECY and INTELLIGENCE COSMICIZED**

Crystal Moon ≡
- 45th Heptad Path: Neptune / Maldek — **Meditation evolves Sex**
- 46th Heptad Path: Neptune / Mars — **Meditation evolves Death**
- 47th Heptad Path: Pluto / Venus — **Self-Generation evolves Art**
- 48th Heptad Path: Pluto / Mercury — **Self-Generation evolves Purity**
- **POWER of KNOWLEDGE AND LOVE CRYSTALLIZED**

Spectral Moon ≡
- 41st Heptad Path: Jupiter / Maldek — **Vision evolves Sex**
- 42nd Heptad Path: Mars / Venus — **Death evolves Art**
- 43rd Heptad Path: Mercury / Venus — **Purity evolves Magic**
- 44th Heptad Path: Earth / Maldek — **Free Will evolves Timelessness**
- **ATTAIN ELECTRO ETHERIC FORM**

Planetary Moon ≡
- 37th Heptad Path: Venus / Neptune — **Art of Meditation** ☉ DUM KUALI CELL ESTABL.
- 38th Heptad Path: Neptune / Jupiter — **Meditation of Vision** ☾ CELL ESTABLISHED
- 39th Heptad Path: Mercury / Pluto — **Purity of Enlightenment** △ DUM DUAR CELL ESTABL.
- 40th Heptad Path: Pluto / Maldek — **Enlightenment/Timelessness** ▲ CELL ESTABLISHED
- **THE TWO ELECTRO ETHERIC STABILIZERS**

Rhythmic Moon ∸
- 21st Heptad Path: Neptune / Earth — **Meditation reflects evolution of Knowledge**
- 22nd Heptad Path: Pluto / Mercury — **Self-Generation Catalyzes evolution of Love**
- 23rd Heptad Path: Pluto / Mars — **Enlightenment fulfills evolution of Prophecy**
- 24th Heptad Path: Uranus / Saturn — **Navigation Synchronizes evolution of Intelligence**
- **OUTER MATRIX**

Resonant Moon ∺
- 25th Heptad Path: Uranus / Neptune — **Navigation of Meditation**
- 26th Heptad Path: Neptune / Pluto — **Meditation of Self-Generation**
- 27th Heptad Path: Pluto / Pluto — **Self-Generation of Enlightenment**
- 28th Heptad Path: Pluto / Uranus — **Enlightenment of Navigation**
- **INNER MATRIX**

Galactic Moon ∴
- 29th Heptad Path: G-Core — **Hunab Ku transmits Unity of Totality as Navigation**
- 30th Heptad Path: G-Core / Neptune — **Hunab Ku transmits Unity of Totality as Meditation**
- 31st Heptad Path: G-Core / Pluto — **Hunab Ku transmits Unity of Totality as Self-Generation**
- 32nd Heptad Path: G-Core / Pluto — **Hunab Ku transmits Unity of Totality as Enlightenment**
- **CORE MATRIX — HUNAB KU 21**

Solar Moon ∷
- 33rd Heptad Path: Maldek / Uranus — **Sex evolved as Thermic/Luminic Navigation**
- 34th Heptad Path: Uranus / Earth — **Navigation evolved as Luminic/Thermic Free Will**
- 35th Heptad Path: Mars / Pluto — **Death evolved as Thermic Self-Generation**
- 36th Heptad Path: Pluto / Venus — **Self-Generation evolved as Luminic Magic**
- **THE TWO ELECTRO ETHERIC MERIDIANS**

Annual Omega Phase TELEKTONON Unit of Radiance. 20 Heptads — 140 Days [280 Days Complete] Matrix [Moons 6-7-8]

Cycle · **Transcendence** · **TELEKTONON** · **Annual** · **and two Electro Etheric Power Cells established [Moons 9 and 10]**

The Arcanum of the Avatar is located in the root chakra governed by the Seli plasma. It is coded by the Hand, Avatar, associated with Earth. Here the alpha-beta hyperplasma activates the second mental sphere, subconscious as informative samadhi. In the 441 base matrix the Avatar is coded by frequency 291.

The Arcanum of the Mystery is located in the third eye chakra governed by the Gamma plasma. It is coded by the Wind, High Priestess, associated with Uranus. Here the beta-beta hyperplasma activates the third mental sphere, conscious, as waking conscious mediumship. In the 441 base matrix the Mystery is coded by frequency 144.

7 Heptad Gates within the 441 Base Matrix

The Arcanum of the Initiation is located in the secret center governed by the Kali plasma. It is coded by the Skywalker, Prophet, associated with Mars. Here the beta-alpha hyperplasma activates the fourth mental sphere, continuing conscious, as higher mind control. In the 441 base matrix the Initiation is coded by frequency 315.

The Arcanum of the Timespace is located in throat chakra governed by the Alpha plasma. It is coded by the Sun, Enlightened One, associated with Pluto. Here the hyperelectron activates the fifth mental sphere, superconscious, as the centrifugal hyperthermic force field, and releases EE (double-extended electron) at the South (Darka) pole. In the 441 base matrix the Timespace is coded by frequency 414.

The Arcanum of the Transcendence is located in solar plexus chakra governed by the Limi plasma. It is coded by the Mirror, Yogi(ni), associated with Neptune. Here the hyperneutron activates the sixth mental sphere, subliminal conscious, as the centripetal hyperluminic force field, and purifies ME (mental electron) at the North (Marka) pole. In the 441 base matrix the Transcendence is coded by frequency 402.

The Arcanum of the Cube is located in heart chakra governed by the Silio plasma. It is coded by Hunab Ku 21—The One Dweller of the Cube. Here the Sirius B-52 hyperplasma/Element 113 activates the seventh mental sphere, holomind perceiver, as hyperplasmic enlightenment of radial consciousness, and discharges MEN (mental-electron neutron) to the center of the Earth. In the 441 base matrix the Cube is coded by frequency 441.

On the Day out of Time and on 0.0.Hunab Ku (leap day, Gregorian 29 February) the only heptad gate that is activated is the Hunab Ku 21.

We practice opening a heptad gate each day, beginning on Dali with **profound samadhi**, which is the pure non-conceptual space of experience connecting us to our **preconscious,** first mental sphere. Then we advance to Seli and activate **informative samadhi,** where we allow ourselves to receive the telepathic frequencies of the purity of our consciousness that activate the **subconscious,** second mental sphere. On the third day, Gamma, we activate **waking conscious mediumship**, which helps us to realize that we are always mediums—that we can always (consciously) channel cosmic forces, evolving the **conscious,** first mental sphere. On the fourth day, Kali, the fourth mental sphere, **continuing consciousness,** is activated as **higher mind control,** governed by the fourth-dimensional self (holon). On this day we practice how to maintain ourselves in such a state that we begin to experience the quality of unbroken awareness of the higher mind.

The first four days (Dali to Kali) connect us to the first four circuits, which connect the four outer time dimensions and the four radial time dimensions; or eight time dimensions. The last three circuits are all in the ninth time dimension. From here we enter Alpha, **superconscious** and Limi, **subliminal conscious,** where we are opening ourselves to operating in the ninth time dimension. On the seventh day, Silio, **holomind perceiver,** we open to the 11th dimension or the order of the cube. Through this practice, we open new channels within our being and become highly sensitized to energetic and emotional perturbations and how they reflect in the outer environment and vice versa. At any moment we can open ourselves to become channels for the galactic order.

Chapter 10 • Enchanting the Numbers

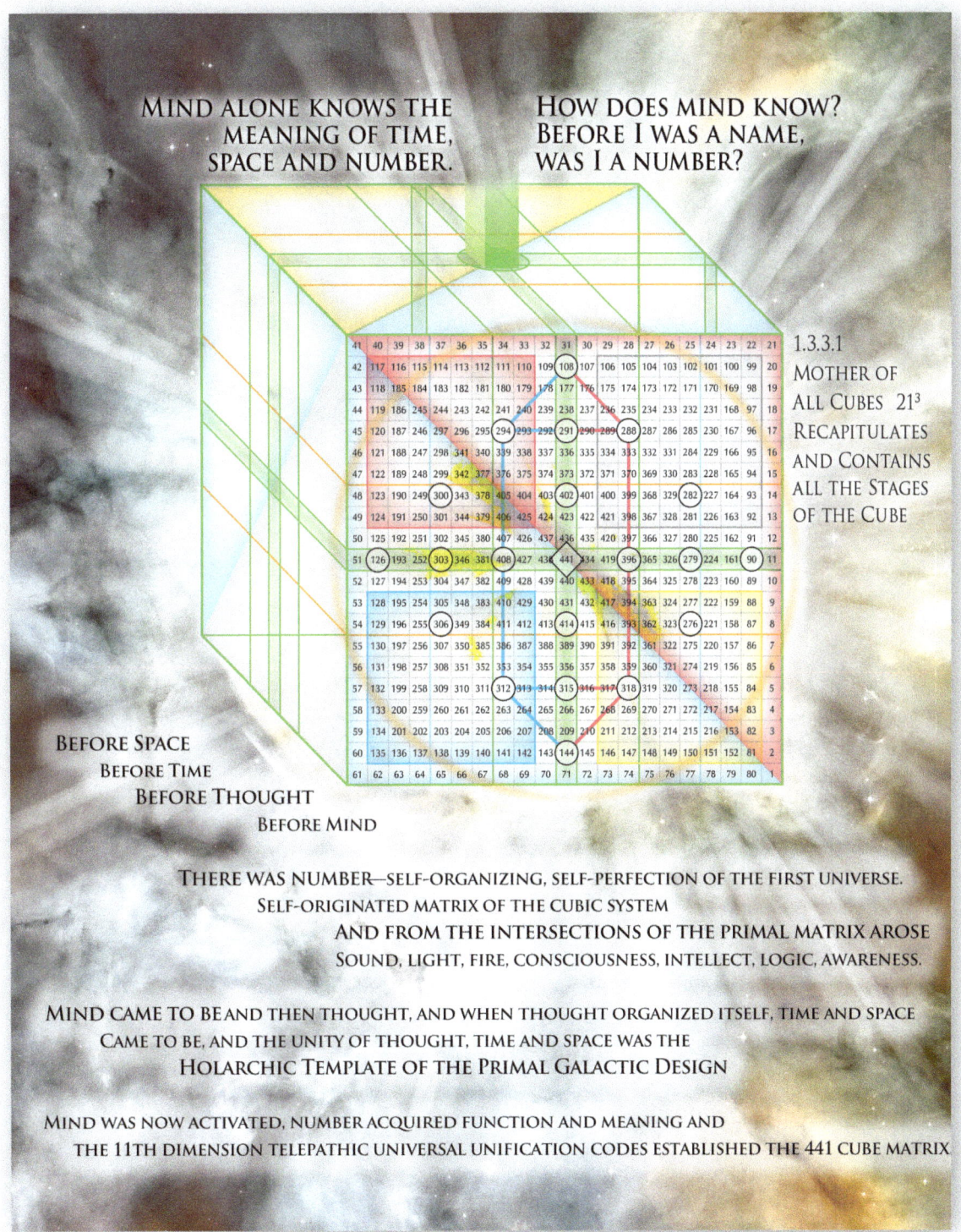

MIND ALONE KNOWS THE
MEANING OF TIME,
SPACE AND NUMBER.

HOW DOES MIND KNOW?
BEFORE I WAS A NAME,
WAS I A NUMBER?

1.3.3.1
MOTHER OF
ALL CUBES 21^3
RECAPITULATES
AND CONTAINS
ALL THE STAGES
OF THE CUBE

BEFORE SPACE
BEFORE TIME
BEFORE THOUGHT
BEFORE MIND

THERE WAS NUMBER—SELF-ORGANIZING, SELF-PERFECTION OF THE FIRST UNIVERSE.
SELF-ORIGINATED MATRIX OF THE CUBIC SYSTEM
AND FROM THE INTERSECTIONS OF THE PRIMAL MATRIX AROSE
SOUND, LIGHT, FIRE, CONSCIOUSNESS, INTELLECT, LOGIC, AWARENESS.

MIND CAME TO BE AND THEN THOUGHT, AND WHEN THOUGHT ORGANIZED ITSELF, TIME AND SPACE
CAME TO BE, AND THE UNITY OF THOUGHT, TIME AND SPACE WAS THE
HOLARCHIC TEMPLATE OF THE PRIMAL GALACTIC DESIGN

MIND WAS NOW ACTIVATED, NUMBER ACQUIRED FUNCTION AND MEANING AND
THE 11TH DIMENSION TELEPATHIC UNIVERSAL UNIFICATION CODES ESTABLISHED THE 441 CUBE MATRIX

CHAPTER 11

LIBERATING THE PLANET HOLON

The whole planetary system is in reality a vast interlocking, interdependent and interrelated complexity of vehicles communicating or responsive to communication. —Alice Bailey, Telepathy

The whole of the solar system is a living organism that is a member of a much larger galactic cosmic system. *The Knowledge Book* states that all galactic systems are connected to a center of communication. The solar system, as a totality, is connected to this center of communications.

Cosmic History describes the solar system as a subset of a larger system that consists of a) the biosphere at a planetary level; b) a heliosphere at the next level; and c) a galactosphere at the galactic level. This is all contained within d) the cosmosphere, which is the whole of the cosmos as an equalizing set of interacting functions that unify the different orders of quantifiable reality. The cosmosphere also unifies the multiple orders of different dimensions from subquanitifiable to super transcendent non-quantifiable realities of consciousness and meta- or supraconsciousness.

As we saw from previous chapters, all phases of the cosmos in its cosmological sequencing are interlocked by a common set of electroplasmic interactions, ultimately generated from the sole atom. We are active participants in this vastly dynamic phenomenon. The Law of Time gives us a working model where we can begin this active participation on the planetary level by aligning our human holon with the planet holon.

The planet holon divides the Earth into 20 zones that correspond with the 20 solar seals. Each seal also corresponds to a planet, a chakra and one of two flows: galactic/karmic (inhalation from the Sun) or solar/prophetic (exhalation from the Sun). The planet holon structure makes up the fourth-dimensional skeleton of the planet and we can plug into it through our chakras. Since we are a microcosm of the planetary body, the planet is contained within our body and can be accessed through our chakra system. The entirety of the solar system can also be located within the 20 digits of our four extremities.

SOLAR SYSTEM, CHAKRAS AND FLUX TUBES

Cosmic History places special focus on the orbital positions of the different planets in relation to each other and to the Sun. All the moving bodies in the solar system have certain patterns, for example, the moon sets up a pattern of 27-28 and 29 days. These patterns inevitably affect and influence the noosphere on Earth.

The Law of Time illustrates that the planets in our solar system are connected and form one cosmic body. Since we are a microcosm of the solar system, the circuits of the planetary orbits directly relate to our own circuits/chakra system. Flux tubes or energy vortices, at one time, connected the consciousness circuits of the planetary orbits of our solar system—which can be envisioned as etheric spiraling force fields meant to pulse with the binary sunspot cycles.

These flux tubes were disturbed by the destruction and disruption of planetary orbits 4 and 5 (Mars and Maldek), and further disturbed by the artificial timing frequency of planetary orbit 3 (Earth). When the fifth planet, Maldek (now the Asteroid Belt), was destroyed and Mars rendered inoperable, these interplanetary flux tubes were shut down. Now, during this present time of (inter)planetary electromagnetic disorder, oceanic life—namely whales and dolphins—have been assisting in holding the Earth's frequencies in balance. Ultimately, in the new cycle that commenced on Galactic Synchronization day, the Sun will gain a new level of evolutionary balance.

Since we are a microcosm of the solar system, the rupturing of this flux tube system corresponds with the disturbances in our internal chakra system. When our chakras are not properly in resonance with the chakras of the Earth and solar system, there comes a diminishing of our spiritual power and a sense of disempowerment or helplessness.

We experience this as an increasing inner tension that is then mirrored by our planet and solar system as circuits being realigned. This tension we feel is the dissonance between two opposing frequencies which is now reaching its climax, ultimately resulting in a collective release of psychic energy that had been repressed during our consignment to an artificial linear third-dimensional timing program.

Planetary Intervals and the Titius-Bode Law

In the cosmology of the Law of Time, the frequencies of the planetary orbits are determined primarily by the "Bode numbers" as first proposed by Johann Daniel Titius of Wittenberg and then evolved and popularized in 1768 by German astronomer Johann Elert Bode.

The Titius-Bode Law determines that the planetary orbits could be assigned sets of whole numbers that define the orbital ratios of the planets in relation to each other and their distance from the Sun. According to the Law of Time, these ratios inform frequencies that coordinate different levels, or stages, of consciousness. Included in the planetary Bode numbers is Maldek, now known as the Asteroid Belt.

It was Bode who discovered the orbit of Maldek. Based on his use of (Johann) Kepler's "law of harmonies" (the third of his three laws of planetary motion), he was certain that there should have been a planet between Mars and Jupiter. So it was that on September 11, 1801, Kin 58, he discovered a band of asteroids orbiting the Sun—the remains of the planet Maldek.

Bode Numbers and Meanings of 10 Planetary Orbits

Mercury (4). Frequency of self-existing form power.

Venus (7). Frequency of resonant creation.

Earth (10). Frequency power of the 10 orbits, half of 20. Earth is the place of the transmigration of memories and programs from Maldek and Mars. Karma of previous world systems was transferred to Earth to be resolved or redeemed. Note: the frequency of Earth is 7.8 hertz, fractal of 78 and also a fractal of 780, the number of days in the Martian synodic cycle as viewed from Earth. Seventy-eight is also the key number in the decipherment of the sarcophagus of Pacal Votan; 78 is the sum tonal frequency of the 13 solar seals carved on the sarcophagus lid.

Planets

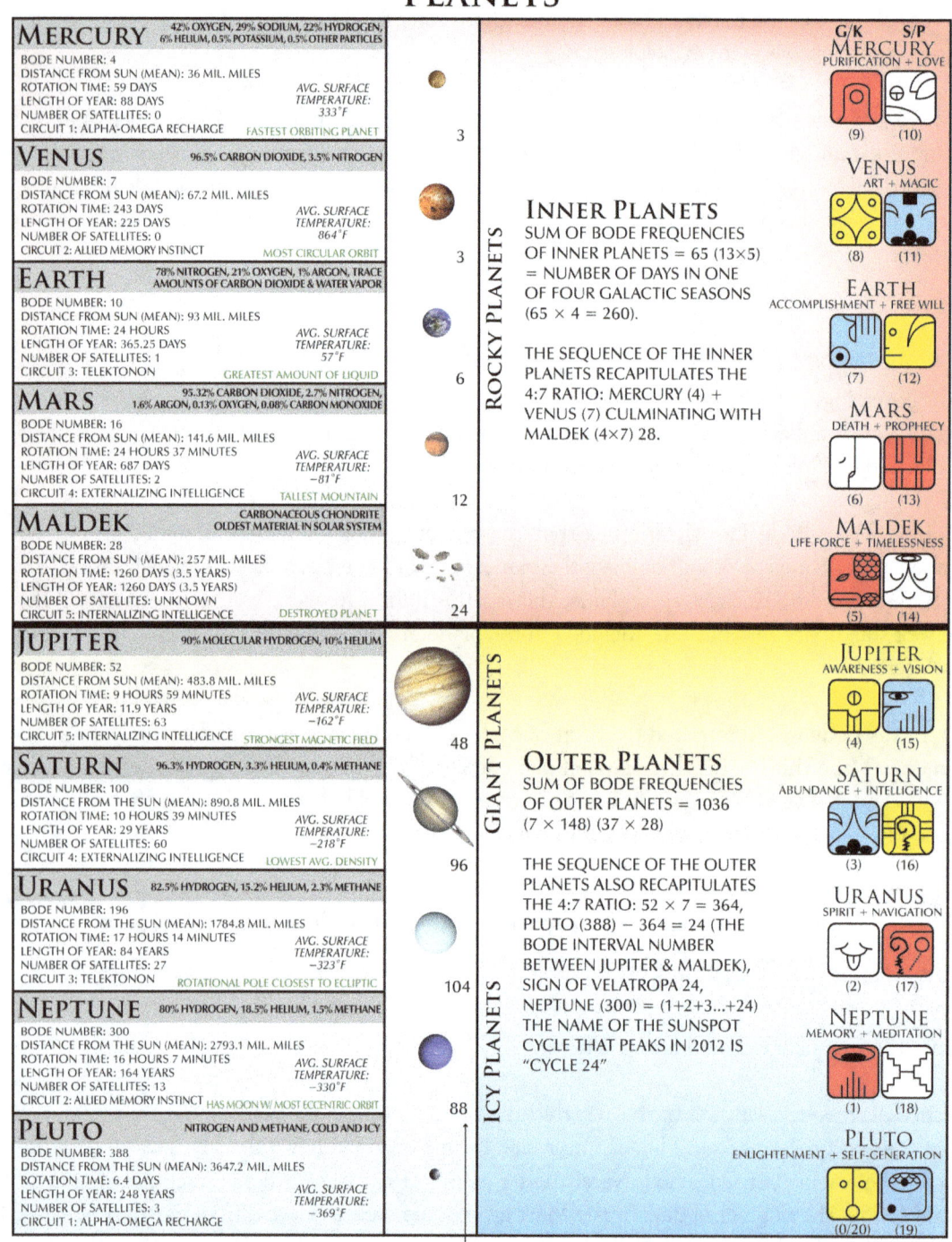

Bode Numbers and Planet Frequencies

Bode numbers take the planet as a whole reduced to a set of intervals that have relation in proportion to each other and their distance from the Sun. The Bode numbers sequence breaks down into two sets: the five inner planets and the five outer planets. The five *inner planets* are: Mercury (4); Venus (7); Earth (10); Mars (16); and Maldek (28). The five *outer planets* are: Jupiter (52); Saturn (100); Uranus (196); Neptune (300); and Pluto

Inner Planets

Mercury (4). *Frequency of self-existing form power.*

Venus (7). *Frequency of resonant creation.*

Earth (10). *Frequency power of the 10 orbits,* half of 20. Earth is the place of the transmigration of memories and programs from Maldek and Mars. Karma of previous world systems was transferred to Earth to see if it could be resolved or redeemed.

Note the frequency of Earth is 7.8 hertz, fractal of 78 and also a fractal of 780, the number of days in the Martian synodic cycle as viewed from Earth. Seventy-eight is also the key in the decipherment of the tomb of Pacal Votan; 78 is the sum tonal frequency of the 13 seals carved on the sarcophagus lid.

Also note the relationship of Earth to Mercury is a 10 to 4 relationship. This is a close relation. 10 is the triangular of 4 (1 + 2 + 3 + 4 = 10). Venus (7) to Earth (10) is an even tighter relation. The relation of Earth to Mars is 16 to 10. Look at the ratio intervals and see what kind of whole number differences these create.

Mars (16). *Frequency of the Cube of the Law.* 4 squared. There are 16 positions between days 7 and 22. Through the system of whole number ratios, Titius and Bode both determined there was a missing planet between Mars (16) and Jupiter (52).

Maldek (28). *Frequency of the harmonic constant,* 4 × 7 (Mercury × Venus). This harmonic standard represents the mental organization of time. Note: the perfect harmonic ratio of Maldek is attained by doubling the distance between Maldek (28) and Mars (16). By observing the 28-day harmonic cycle, Earth

Outer Planets

can redeem the karma of the lost planet Maldek. 28 is the triangular of 7.

Jupiter (52). *Frequency of time.* 52 weeks = 1 year (solar orbit). The ratio of Sirius B is converted to 52 weeks in the Babylonian system of 7-day weeks. Saturn is associated with third-dimensional circuits and the creation of structures supporting time is money. Also to be noted, 52 is 4 × 13, 13 × 28 (Maldek) = 364 = 52 (Jupiter) × Venus (7).

Saturn (100). *Frequency of currency.* 100 is 10 × 10 (Earth). Basis of the monetary system which is the 3-D material application of T(E) = Money or Time is Money, where money equals the value 100.

Uranus (196). *Frequency of multidimensionality* (28 × 7). Uranus represents the connection to Earth that has to be made; this connection is being short-circuited by Saturn (100) and Jupiter (52), which destroyed Maldek (28) and made civilization on Mars (16) extinct. Uranus (196) is 28 × 7. Note: Uranus (196) = Saturn (100) + Jupiter (52) + Maldek (28) + Mars (16). Uranus (196) is occulted by the Tower of Babel (represented by the sequence Mars, Maldek, Jupiter, Saturn).

Neptune (300). *Frequency of oceanic memory.* 300 is the triangular of 24 (1 + 2 + 3 + ... + 24 = 300), Kinich Ahau is designated Velatropa 24. This signifies that the power of the cumulative memory of Velatropa 24 is kept in Neptune, planet of oceanic consciousness.

Pluto (388). *Frequency of 4 × 97 (96 + 1);* 96 is 24 × 4, so 97 is (24 × 4) +1.

Mars (16). Frequency of the Cube of the Law. 4 squared. The 16 positions from days 7-22 of every 28-day moon define the Warrior's Cube Journey.

Maldek (28). Frequency of the harmonic constant, 4 x 7 (Mercury x Venus). This harmonic standard represents the mental organization of time.

Jupiter (52). Frequency of time. 52 weeks = 1 year (solar orbit). 52 years = 1 orbit of Sirius B around Sirius A. The ratio of Sirius B is also fractally contained in the 52 heptad paths (or weeks) of the year.

Saturn (100). Frequency of currency. 100 is 10 x 10 (Earth squared). Basis of the monetary system which is the 3-D material application of T(E) = Money or Time is Money, where money equals the value 100.

Uranus (196). Frequency of multidimensionality (28 x 7). Uranus represents the connection to Earth that has to be made; it was this connection that was short-circuited by Saturn (100) and Jupiter (52), which destroyed Maldek (28) and made civilization on Mars (16) extinct.

Neptune (300). Frequency of oceanic memory. 300 is the triangular of 24 (1 + 2 + 3 + ... + 24 = 300). Kinich Ahau, our Sun, is also known as Velatropa 24. This signifies that the power of the cumulative memory of Velatropa 24 is kept in Neptune, planet of oceanic consciousness.

Pluto (388). Frequency of 194 x 2; the First Lost Generation (Kin 194) doubled. Also, 4 x 97 (96 + 1); 96 is 24 x 4, so 97 is (24 x 4) +1.

Five Outer Planets and Archetypes (Telepathic Zone)

Pluto (388): Power of Enlightenment and Self-Generation. Enlightenment and self-generation are intrinsic to our being. The self-generation of enlightenment is the gateway to and from interstellar and intergalactic space. Archetypes of the Enlightened One and Worldchanger.

Neptune (300): Power of Birth/Memory and Meditation. Our birth is a function of memory. At the time of birth all cosmic memory is within us. Meditation functions as a conscious remembering by which we are able to see clearly and maintain ourselves in the higher course of cosmic enlightenment. Archetypes of the Primal Force and Yogi(ni).

Uranus (196): Power of Spirit and Navigation. Navigation is the intrinsic power of knowing where to go and how to get there in the spiritual as well as the physical sense. Spirit is the basis of any navigation beyond the physical dimension. Spirit endows birth with purpose. Navigation is Spirit's means of returning to source.

Chapter 11 • Liberating the Planet Holon

Planetary Archetypes

Saturn (100): Power of Abundance and Intelligence. Abundance refers to the spiritual power of consciousness, rather than accumulation of material possessions. Spiritual abundance of consciousness is the capacity to establish any number of levels of intuitive orientation. Intelligence is the power of multi-leveled discrimination and discernment of any potential path to attain a specific mission or goal. As the seventh planet, Saturn is the focalizer of consciousness in the interplanetary system. Archetypes of the Dreamer and Pathfinder.

Jupiter (52): Power of Flowering and Vision. Flowering is a function of awareness. A flower exemplifies solar consciousness as it opens to the Sun. Vision is a function of the same solar power—if there is no light then you cannot see. Flowering of vision represents the visionary capacity of forever expanding in consciousness. Archetypes of the Innocent and Seer.

Five Inner Planets and Archetypes (Instinctual Zone)

Maldek (28): Power of Life-Force and Timelessness. The function and purpose of life-force is to attain timelessness or self-realization. This was the pattern of the original Adam—Adam Kadmon—the first human "manufactured" in the solar system. Life-force is always flowing, remaining in the flow of moment-to-moment timelessness. Archetypes of the Serpent Initiate and Wizard.

Mars (16): Power of Death and Prophecy. Where there is life there is death. Everything in the biosphere is a continuous recirculation, or migration, of atoms—the recirculation of life within death and death within life. Prophecy is the gift of seeing the true meaning of life and death and receiving from akashic space the message to be spoken. Archetypes of the Hierophant and Prophet.

Earth (10): Power of Accomplishment and Free Will. Relates to the two poles of consciousness. The power of accomplishment relates to the power of memory at birth. How? By remembering purpose and bringing to completion the order of the universe through the correct use of free will. Free will is the choice to align with the Divine Plan: this is true accomplishment. Archetypes of the Avatar and Sage.

Venus (7): Power of Art and Magic. Art is a natural function of the power of accomplishment. Magic is what arises from the correct alignment of free will with the Divine Plan. To align with the Divine Plan is to put the mind in its correct place. Mind and time precede space and physical order—realizing this, magic becomes possible and art becomes supernatural. Archetypes of the Artist and Magician.

Mercury (4): Power of Purification and Love. Purification is a natural function; we are in a continuous process of purification. When we have purified, then we can truly love. This is all a process of the

Chapter 11 • Liberating the Planet Holon

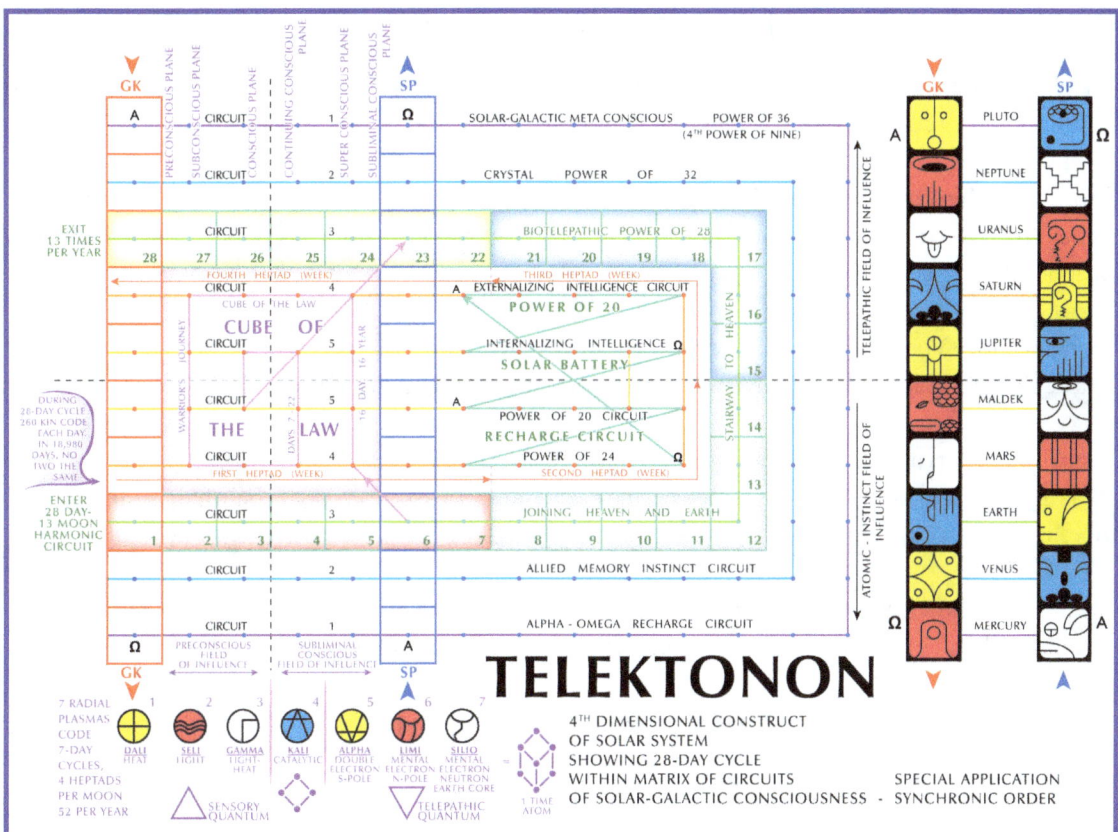

The Telektonon illustrates where the 28-day pattern occurs, which is between the third and eighth orbits (Earth and Uranus). This also shows the structure of the 20 seals, broken down into a sequence of 10 each, which corresponds to the planetary orbits in their two flows: the galactic/karmic sequence (GK), which goes from outside the solar system into the Sun; and a solar/prophetic (SP) sequence which goes from the Sun out to the galaxy.

The 28-day cycle corresponds to the Earth sequence connecting with the Uranus sequence. This forms one circuit. All 10 planets paired thusly creates five circuits. So the fifth force power in the Telektonon is seen as the five circuits that connect the planetary orbits. When meditated on, the Telektonon map is revealed as a matrix or template that shows the constituents or qualities of consciousness as functions of the planetary orbits. Each of the planets is assigned two of the solar seals or symbols.

solar/prophetic generation of love. We purify ourselves to heal ourselves. When we heal ourselves, then we naturally generate love for ourselves and for all beings. Only when we truly love and accept ourselves can we love others. Love is the greatest natural healing. Archetypes of the Healer and Compassionate One.

The Five Circuits of Consciousness

There is an ocean of consciousness located in the planetary system and coordinated by the five circuits. Each circuit represents a different quality of consciousness or intelligence.

Pluto and Mercury are located on the first circuit known as alpha-omega recharge. This is the metaconscious circuit where the highest subtle planes of consciousness connect with the whole galactic order.

Neptune and Venus are on the second circuit known as allied memory/instinct. This is where instinct and telepathy first arise from the metaconsciousness coming in from the galaxy.

Uranus and Earth are located on the third and central circuit known as the Telektonon/earth spirit speaking tube circuit. This is the biotelepathic circuit and the central key of the whole system of flux tubes in our solar system.

Saturn and Mars are on the fourth circuit or externalizing intelligence circuit where perceptions are externalized and external perceptions are received into the sensory system.

Planet Holon – Five Circuits

Study where the circuits are found on the planet holon. See how the circuits are maintained in the planet holon.

Chapter 11 • Liberating the Planet Holon

Maldek and Jupiter form the fifth and final circuit of internalizing intelligence where perceptions are internalized and later flower within the external circuits.

These circuits are the Earth's consciousness reflecting the operating system of the noosphere and are key functions of the planet holon. This model creates a field of planetary intelligence that helps order and organize our thoughts and internal programs; for it is symbolic structures and mathematics that coordinate the overall field of consciousness. All meaning comes from the core field of intelligence that organizes the field of manifestation.

THE FIVE EARTH FAMILIES ARE THE ARCHETYPAL GUARDIANS OF THE EARTH. THEY MAKE A PERFECT PENTAGRAM OF THE SOLAR ROUND OF TIME. EVERY 5 DAYS EACH OF THE EARTH FAMILIES HAS ITS TURN TO DEFINE THE WAY. IN THE NOOSPHERE, SOCIETY IS ORGANIZED IN TIME 73 TIMES A YEAR. THIS IS A CHROMATIC OF TIME. 73 CHROMATICS, 5 DAYS EACH = 365 DAYS OF THE SOLAR YEAR EQUAL AND FREE, FIVE EARTH FAMILIES ARE WE IN THE UTOPIAN WAY WE ALL LIVE BY SYNCHRONICITY.

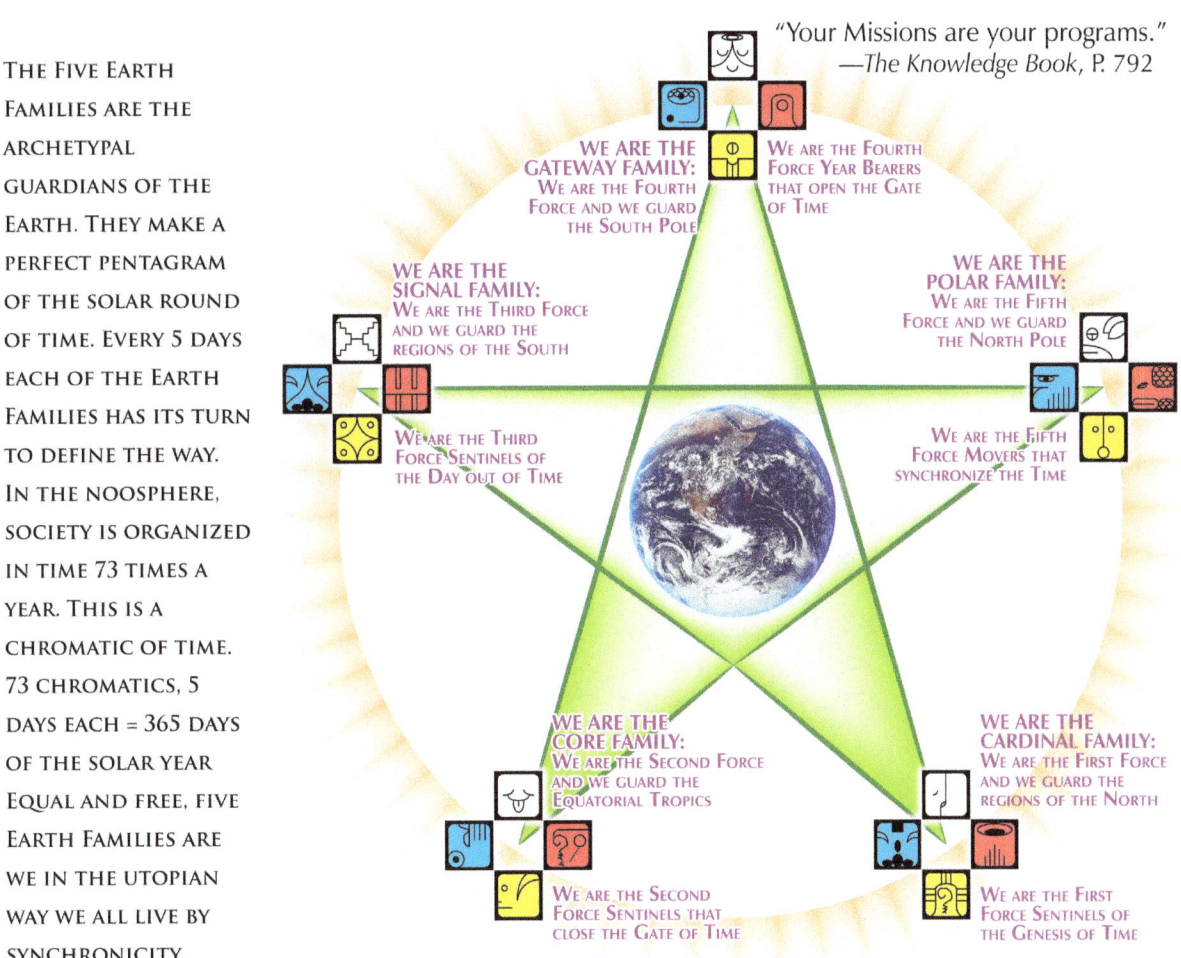

"Your Missions are your programs."
—*The Knowledge Book*, P. 792

145

CHAPTER 12

UNIVERSALIZING THE PLANETARY GRID

I live on Earth at present, and I don't know what I am. I know that I am not a category. I am not a thing—a noun. I seem to be a verb, an evolutionary process—an integral function of the universe. —Buckminster Fuller

The notion of a planetary grid goes back to Plato who conceived of Earth as being like a dodecahedron-shaped ball. R. Buckminster Fuller further developed this idea and laid out a dodecahedron on the world map, and even made dodecahedron globes.

In the 1970s Russian scientist, Kiril Lachugin, conceived of the Earth as a giant crystal structure. This crystal structure creates a grid that is constructed of an icosahedron integrated with a dodecahedron. This model was adopted by American researchers Becker and Hagens and developed as the Planetary Grid System.

The Planet Holon was discovered in 1986 by José Argüelles/Valum Votan through his meditations on Buckminster Fuller's dymaxion dodecahedronworld map. The Planet Holon serves as a harmonic frequency grid to stabilize the dissonance of the planet. Also known as the Arcturus Protectorate Zone, this grid is a key to planetary geomancy, or earth divination.

THREE KEY COMPONENTS

Planetary geomancy consciously engages not only the surface of the planet, but also the internal workings of interplanetary forces. There are three key components to consider: 1) the Outermost level or electromagnetic field; 2) Surface tension or plate tectonics; and 3) the Core.

Level 1: Outermost (Electromagnetic Field)

This is the level of the electromagnetic field, the Van Allen radiation belts, and in particular the psi bank and Noosphere. This structure consists of eight seasonal plates, four in the North and four in the South, which are then further subdivided into the 24 psi nimboid membranes (see graphic four quadrants, 8 plates, and 24 psi nimboid solar vision.)

Each of these psi nimboid membranes is coded by one of 24 Elder Futhark runes. By studying the color patterns of the different solar seals we can see how each of these psi nimboid plates is

THREE LEVELS OF NEW EARTH GEOMANCY

A) Outermost: Electromagnetic Field
Van Allen Radiation Belts, Cosmic-Solar radiation receiver-transformers, Earth broadcast studio: "Noosphere Live"

Binary Sunspot Cycle, information keys via 260/441 programs

PSI BANK = RINGS = CUMULATIVE PSION DEPOSIT + SYNTHESIS OF STAGES OF PSYCHOCULTURAL DEVELOPMENT

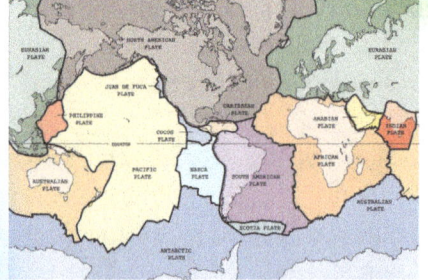

GEOMANTIC MODEL

B) Surface Tension: Geomagnetic Field
Tectonic plates, underlying zones of cosmic interplanetary influence.

Plate Boundaries

Planet Holon/Arcturus Protectorate superimposed on the geomagnetic field

Three Types of Plate Boundaries
Constructive boundary – Plates pulling away
Destructive boundary – Pushing against
Transform boundary – Sliding over each other

C) Dynamic Inner Core
Iron Crystal Octahedron provides gyroscopic dynamic stabilizer, radial diffuser of solar galactic plasma information codes received and transmitted as information waves to surface and electromagnetic field.

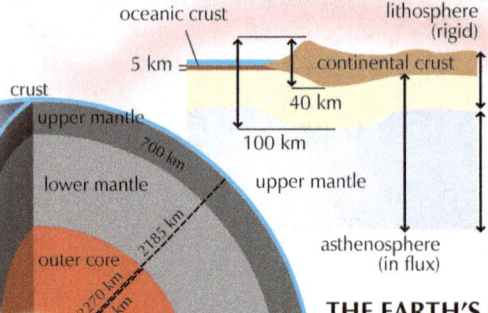

THE EARTH'S INTERIOR
The Earth's interior is divided as follows:

1. **Crust** (5-40 km thick): The thin outer skin of the planet.
2. **Mantle** (2,885 km thick): The origin of most magma.
3. **Core** (3,486 km thick): A dense metal-rich ball inside the Earth. The core is composed of liquid **outer core** and solid **inner core**.

NEPTUNE-URANUS CELL GOVERNS RED + WHITE CHROMATICS

INNER CORE

OCTAHEDRON CRYSTAL HUNAB KU 21

RADIUS = 19 × 64 (1216 KM)

VENUS-EARTH CELL GOVERNS BLUE + YELLOW CHROMATICS

affected by the Planet Holon in its color formation. The psi plates belong to the outermost aspect; the etheric form of the psi bank located in between the outer and inner Van Allen radiation belts. Here, the programs from the binary solar sunspot cycle first affect the electromagnetic field.

Consciously directed collective thought-force will increase the receptive interaction at this psi bank/noospheric level as the information coming in from the binary sunspots hits the electromagnetic field. The noosphere electromagnetic programs are activated through the psi field and channeled through the poles into the Earth. They are also radiated onto the surface level of the Earth. This is the first stage of receiving the information/energy from the binary sunspot cycles.

Level 2: Surface Tension or Plate Tectonics

Geomagnetically, the second level is governed by the tectonic plates, which create the surface tension of the planet. There are three types among the plates: 1) The constructive, where the plates are pulling apart and create a positive energy; 2) The destructive, when plates slide and come into collision with each other (such as the Chilean fault line and Boxing Day tsunami in Indonesia); and 3) Plates that slide over/under each other, such as the San Andreas fault, California. Types 2 & 3 set off "destructive" forces.

There are about 20 main tectonic plates that are always in motion with a fluid foundation. This creates the surface tension on Earth, and which contributes to the dynamic of life on Earth. Different types of Earth energies emerge through different plates. The Arcturus Protectorate Grid, indicating the planetary zones of influence, is overlaid on Earth to help stabilize the plates by creatively reconfiguring the biopsychic influence—the psychic field as we know it.

Level 3: The Core

The third level is the core—the Earth core. At the center of the Earth there is an outer and inner core. The inner core has a radius of 1216 km (or 19 x 64/DNA code). The octahedral core is inside of this. The eight facets of the octahedron correspond to the eightfold division of the 4 psi plates. There is a correspondence and dynamic connection between the octahedral core and the four seasonal psi plates.

The dynamic inner core, like a gyroscope, is intended to stabilize the planet. It has an electrodynamic connection to the poles and receives solar cosmic transmissions that are stored within the core. These transmissions are then intermittently, and radially diffused from the core to the surface. The codes are received and transmitted as information to the different plasmas and subliminally affect the consciousness of receptive human beings. The practice of Synchrogalactic Yoga helps tune us in to these frequencies (see Chapter 13).

Accessing Your Multidimensional Self: A Key to Cosmic History

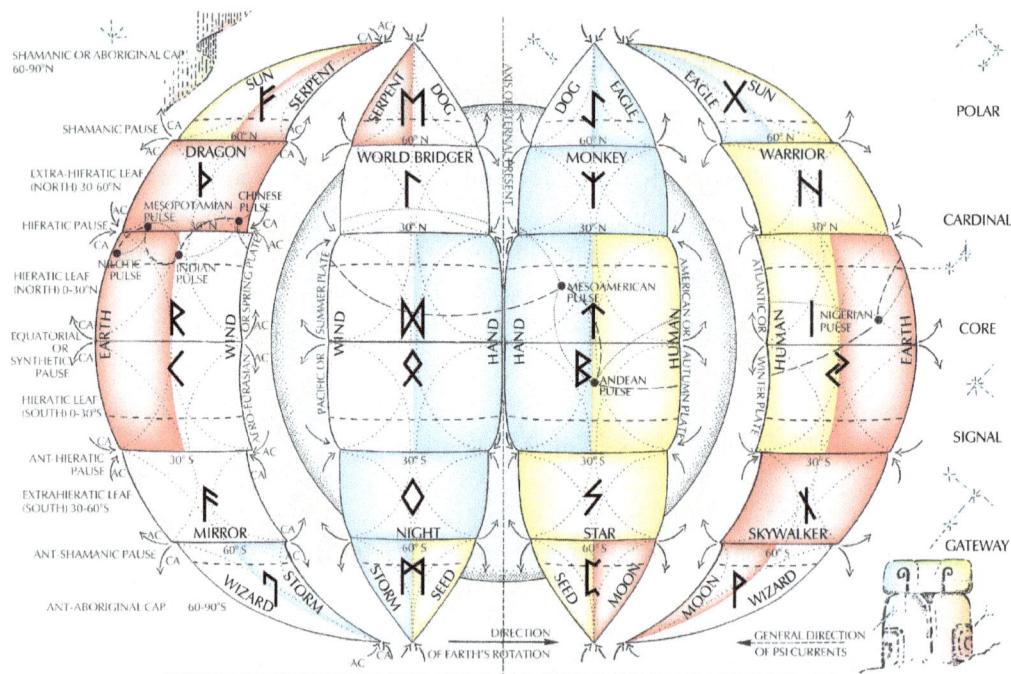

THE PSI BANK SHOWING THE FOUR QUADRANTS, EIGHT SEASONAL MEMORY PLATES, AND
24 PSIONIC NIMBOID MEMBRANES – ALSO SHOWING ZONES OF INFLUENCE WITH 24 ELDER FUTHARK RUNES

WEEK 1. AFRO-EURASIAN PLATE

- Day 1: **FEHU** is Flaming Abundance that initiates the Throne.
- Day 2: **URUZ** is the Power of Shaping that initiates the Avatar.
- Day 3: **THURISAZ** is the Sacred Struggle that initiates the Mystery.
- Day 4: **ANSUZ** is the Breath of Votan that initiates the Initiation.
- Day 5: **RAIDHO** is the Solar Ring that initiates the Timespace.
- Day 6: **KENNAZ** is the Light-searing torch that initiates the Transcendence.
- Day 7: **Cube Power of 7** – Cubes the Afro-Eurasian Plate by the power of Fehu-Kennaz.

WEEK 2. PACIFIC PLATE

- Day 8: **EHWAZ** is the Union of Horse and Rider that refines the Throne.
- Day 9: **MANNAZ** is the Whole Human that refines the Avatar.
- Day 10: **LAGUZ** is the Water Forming that refines the Mystery.
- Day 11: **INGWAZ** is the Seed Enclosed that refines the Initiation.
- Day 12: **DAGGAZ** is the Daybreak Meditation that refines the Timespace.
- Day 13: **OTHALA** is the Mother Realm that refines the Transcendence.
- Day 14: **Cube Power of 14** – Cubes the Pacific Plate by the Power of Ehwaz-Othala.

WEEK 3. AMERICAN PLATE

- Day 15: **EIHWAZ** is the Cosmic Tree that transforms the Throne.
- Day 16: **PERTHRO** is the Well of Memory that transforms the Avatar.
- Day 17: **ELHAZ** is the Act of Making Sacred that transforms the Mystery.
- Day 18: **SOWILO** is the Solar Ray that transforms the Initiation.
- Day 19: **TIWAZ** is the Power Making Scepter that transforms the Timespace.
- Day 20: **BERKANO** is Fruitfulness that transforms the Transcendence.
- Day 21: **Cube Power of 21** – Cubes the American Plate by the Power of Eihwaz-Berkano.

WEEK 4. ATLANTIC PLATE

- Day 22: **GEBO** is the Gift that ripens the Throne.
- Day 23: **WUNJO** is Joy that ripens the Avatar.
- Day 24: **HAGALAZ** is the Crystal that ripens the Mystery.
- Day 25: **NAUTHIZ** is the Testing that ripens the Initiation.
- Day 26: **ISE** is the Concentrated Will that ripens the Timespace.
- Day 27: **JERA** is the Law of Alternation that ripens the Transcendence.
- Day 28: **Cube Power of 28** – Cubes the Atlantic Plate by the Power of Gebo-Jera.

Chapter 12 • Universalizing the Planetary Grid

PLANET HOLON – PLANET DESIGNATIONS

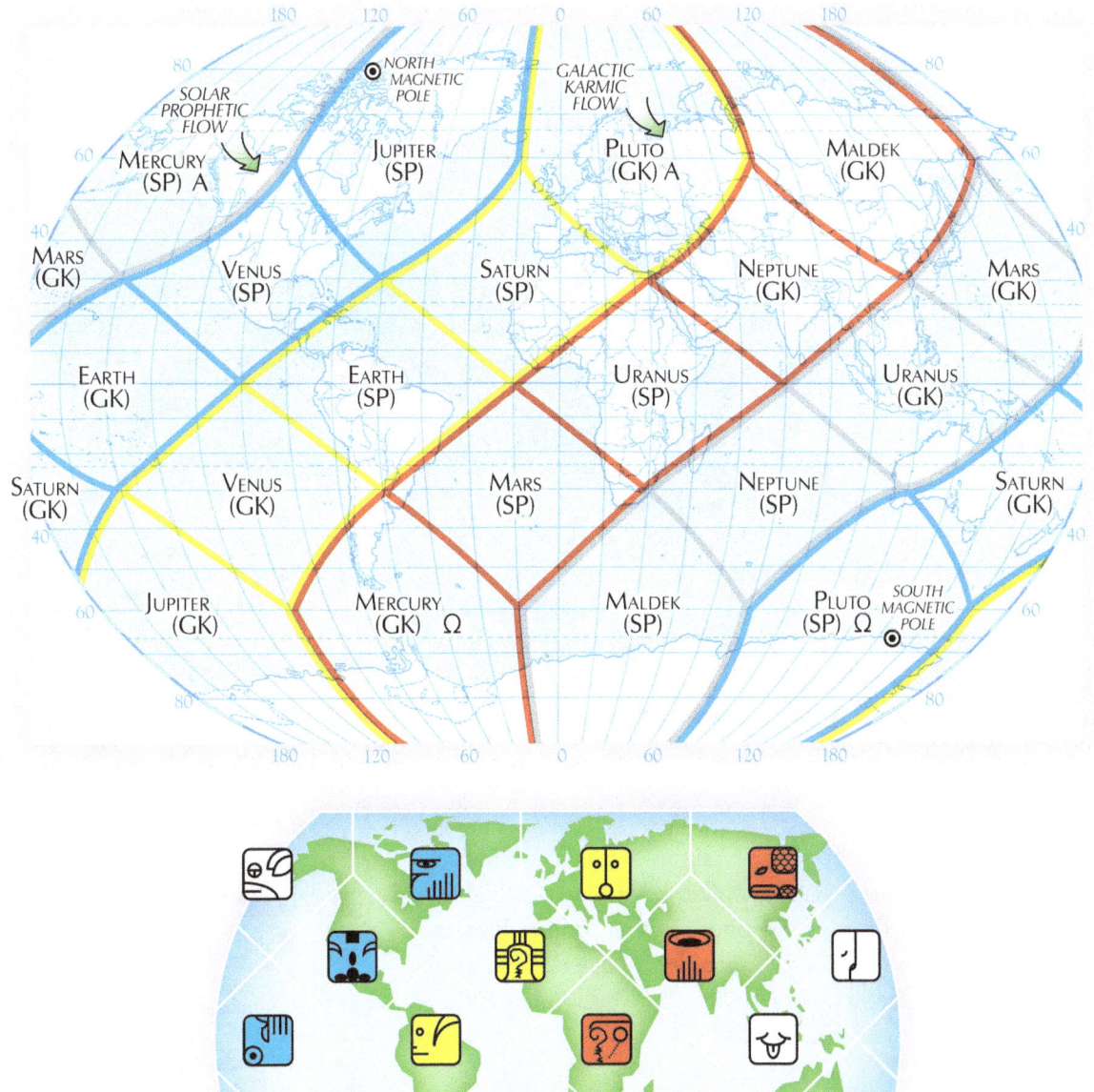

Accessing Your Multidimensional Self: A Key to Cosmic History

How to Practice Planetary Geomancy

The purpose of Planetary Geomancy is to further activate the Earth as a living, evolving and conscious being, and in this way begin to telepathically activate the noosphere.

As we saw from the previous chapter, the Planet Holon is divided into 20 zones. Study these zones and also note the planet associated with each. Each flow is divided into two chromatics of five seals each, which diagonally span from the North Pole to South Pole (Illustrated on the Planet Holon image moving from the top moving down and right).

This structure makes up the skeleton of the fourth-dimensional body of the Planet. Here are simple instructions to begin to interact with this system. To go more in-depth into the methods of planetary geomancy see *Book of the Transcendence (Cosmic History Chronicles Vol. 6)*.

1. Find your galactic signature (see appendix).
2. Locate your solar seal on the Planet Holon
3. Note what part of the Earth this covers
4. Note the chakra, Earth Family and Planet that is associated with this region

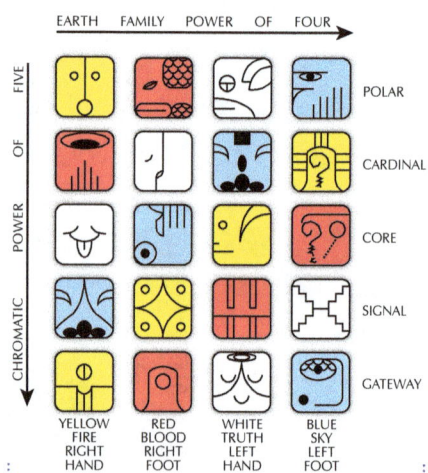

For example, if your solar seal is Skywalker, then you would first locate Skywalker on the Planet Holon. You can see that it is located in the **South Atlantic ocean** between South Africa and the southeast coast of Brazil and South America.

Visualize that part of the world as if from high above the Earth. Then note that Skywalker belongs to the **Signal** Earth Family, which corresponds to the **Solar Plexus** chakra. Skywalker is also associated with planet **Mars,** and is the **solar/prophetic** flow or outbreath (Worldbridger is the galactic/karmic in-breath of Mars).

Now, transfer the visualization of the Skywalker Zone/ South Atlantic ocean into your solar plexus chakra and feel that part of the Earth broadcasting through your solar plexus. As you do this, think to yourself: "May the Skywalker zone of Earth be inseparable from my Solar Plexus, May I become one with the Earth."

The Earth families are five sets of four seals each. Any day of the solar year is coded by one of these sets, such that every four years, the same four seals code that day in a succession of red, white, blue, yellow seals). One sequence of Earth families creates a chromatic of time: 73 chromatics, 5 days each = 365 (days in a solar year).

Chapter 12 • Universalizing the Planetary Grid

The key is to telepathically tune into and take responsibility for this part of the planet. Study the region and note what is going on in it. Work with it psychically on both the surface and interplanetary levels. Also take note of which region on the Earth you were born and pay special attention to that region as well.

The Planet Holon is also activated on a daily basis through the 13 Moon calendar. Through the solar seal of the daily kin, each day corresponds to a chakra that is plugged into one of the twenty zones on the Planet Holon.

Each of the seals also corresponds to a galactic archetype. Remember that by continuously activating this grid, you are activating the fourth- and fifth-dimensional frequencies and thus helping to lay a foundation for the emergence of a new order or state of being: the Noosphere.

Chakra	Earth Family
Crown	Polar
Throat	Cardinal
Heart	Core
Solar Plexus	Signal
Root	Gateway

By identifying with your particular zone on the Planet Holon, you begin to create a telepathic link with one of the functions of the noosphere through your Earth Family/Planet Holon.

The New Planetary Geomancy

Planet Holon Psi Bank—Psi Nimboid Membrane + 4 Quadrants + 8 Seasonal Memory Plates
Zones of Influence or Strategic Psychogeographic Locations
Psi Bank Plates + Planet Holon zones establish Biopsychic Field Coordinated by Noosphere

Planet Holon

Chakra	Earth Family					
Crown	Polar					Sound the Chromatics
Throat	Cardinal					Establish the Genesis
Heart	Core					Mine the Tunnels
Solar Plexus	Signal					Unravel the Mystery
Root	Gateway					Open the Portals

PACIFIC PLATE · AMERICAN PLATE ·· ATLANTIC PLATE ··· AFRO EURASIAN PLATE ····

AA Midway Code: unification synthesis, planetary projection systems

---

Sun Zone — NORTH POLAR
0 = ☉
Psi Plate I ᚠ
Psi Plate IV ᚷ
Begin Yellow Chromatic/Fire Clan

Polar Family Yellow (Sound the Chromatics)
Zone of the Enlightened One, (A) GK Pluto, Inflow of Galactic Influences
Zone of psychogeographic influence: European subcontinent, from western Siberia, Slavic land, across all of Europe, but not including Iberian Peninsula [Spain & Portugal], projecting upward from Great Pyramid of Egypt, Syria, Turkey, the Caucasus, much of the Mediterranean and Black & Caspian Seas, Stonehenge, heartland of Western Civilization, Christianity, ancient Rome, Greece, Egypt, Russia, Byzantum, Ottoman Empire.

Dragon Zone — NORTH TEMPERATE
·
Psi Plate I ᚦ
The Vedas, I Ching, Qur'an

Cardinal Family Red (Establish the Genesis)
Zone of the Ancient of Days, GK Neptune, Activation of Galactic Memory
Zone of psychogeographic influence: projecting east from Great Pyramid and north from mid-Indian Ocean, Arabian Peninsula, Middle-East, including Israel, Mecca, Jerusalem, Baghdad, "Cradle of Civilization", Iraq, Indian subcontinent, Vedic root, Himalayas, Afghanistan, Tibet, much of China, into southern Siberia, root of monotheistic religions, as well as Hindu, Jain, Buddhist, Sikh, Yoga, Taoism, Hunza, Shambhala, the mother of human civilization.

Wind Zone — EQUATORIAL
··
N S
Psi Plate I ᚱ ᚲ
Psi Plate II ᛗ ᛞ
Straddles Equator (North/South)

Core Family White (Mine the Tunnels)
Zone of the High Priestess, GK Uranus, Galactic Spiritual Communication
Zone of psychogeographic influence: projecting south from south China & China Sea, and north from Arabian land, Aboriginal North and Western Australia, includes all of New Guinea, Indonesia, Java, Bali, Borabadur, Southeast Asia, Buddhist, Hindu, Islam overlays, the Philippines and into the West Pacific Ocean, Aboriginal, Oriental and Polynesian mix.

Night Zone — SOUTH TEMPERATE
···
Psi Plate II ◇
Aboriginal/Tribal overlays of Christian Colonialism

Signal Family Blue (Unravel the Mystery)
Zone of the Dreamer, GK Saturn, Distillation of Galactic Power of 7
Zone of psychogeographic influence: projecting from southwestern-most point of Australia, includes most of Aboriginal Australia [Oceania], Uluru, Tasman Sea, Melanesia, Polynesia, Aotearoa and Southeastern South Pacific, land of great Polynesian navigators, followed by Captain Cook & British imperialism, making present Australia & New Zealand part of the British Commonwealth.

Seed Zone — SOUTH POLAR
····
Psi Plate II ᛘ
Psi Plate III ᚳ

Gateway Family Yellow (Open the Portals)
Zone of the Innocent, GK Jupiter, Magnification of the Flowering of Galactic Power
Zone of psychogeographic influence: Antarctica, Transantarctic Mountains, Ross Sea and Ross Ice Shelf, West Antarctica, Amundsen Sea, Southern Sea, southernmost South Pacific Ocean, treasure vaults of the secrets of Lemuria & Atlantis. Completes Yellow Chromatic/Fire Clan.

Chapter 12 • Universalizing the Planetary Grid

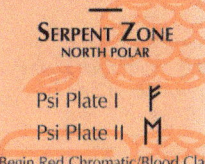

Serpent Zone
NORTH POLAR

Psi Plate I
Psi Plate II

Begin Red Chromatic/Blood Clan

Polar Family Red (Sound the Chromatics), Zone of the Serpent Initiate, GK Maldek
The Lost Planet Primal Initiations of Power & Knowledge
Zone of psychogeographic influence: Northeast Asia, the Great Tundra, Siberian plains & plateaus, Arctic Ocean, Mongolia, the Gobi Desert, northeastern China, Beijing, the Forbidden City, Eastern Kazakhstan, Altai, the Korean Peninsula, Hokkaido, Sea of Japan, Sea of Okhotsk, northwest North Pacific, ancient shamanic magic zone, Genghis & Kublai Khan, home of Sky Religion, Magic, Taoism, Buddhism.

Worldbridger Zone
NORTH TEMPERATE

Psi Plate II

Cardinal Family White (Establish the Genesis), Zone of the Hierophant, GK Mars
The Lost Civilization of Galactic Mars, Seat of the Hierarchical Knowledge
Zone of psychogeographic influence: North Pacific Ocean, Japan, Land of the Rising Sun, ancient mysteries of the Takenouchi, 7 Generations, Shinto and flowering of Zen Buddhism, leader of the later industrial civilization, Mt. Fuji, North Mariana Islands, Hiroshima, Nagasaki, atomic bomb/memory of Mars.

Hand Zone
EQUATORIAL

Psi Plate II
Psi Plate III

Straddles Equator (North/South)

Core Family Blue (Mine the Tunnels), Zone of the Avatar, GK Earth
Focalization Point of the Influx of the Lost Knowledge of the Otherworlds
Zone of psychogeographic influence: Central, North & South Pacific, northern & eastern Polynesia, farthest reaches of the ancient Polynesian navigators, principle zone of influence, Hawaiian Islands, Hawaiian volcanoes, last Polynesian kingdom contested by Japan, USA, WWII.

Star Zone
SOUTH TEMPERATE

Psi Plate III

Signal Family Yellow (Unravel the Mystery)
Zone of the Artist, GK Venus, Focalization of Influx of Galactic Artistic Knowledge
Zone of psychogeographic influence: South Pacific Ocean, easternmost Polynesia, Easter island, Kontiki Aku Aku Ancient Star Mysteries, central Chile, and west Argentina, heart of Cordillera of the Southern Andes Mountain chain, southernmost reaches of Inca Empire, Mount Aconcagua seismic zone, Rim of Fire, Spanish Colonial Empire, liberator O'Higgens.

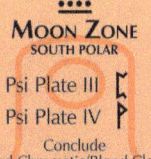

Moon Zone
SOUTH POLAR

Psi Plate III
Psi Plate IV

Conclude
Red Chromatic/Blood Clan

Gateway Family Red (Open the Portals)
Zone of the Healer, (Ω) GK Mercury, Point of Influx of Galactic Healing Knowledge
Zone of psychogeographic influence: Western Antarctica, Antarctic Peninsula, southern South America, Patagonia, the Healing Heartland, southern Chile, southern Argentina, Falkland Islands, southernmost Atlantic Ocean, Tierra del Fuego, South Georgia, Sandwich Islands.

Dog Zone
NORTH POLAR

Psi Plate II
Psi Plate III

Begin White Chromatic/Truth Clan

Polar Family White (Sound the Chromatics), Zone of the Compassionate One, (A) SP Mercury
Point of Influx of Solar Logos Love Frequencies
Zone of psychogeographic influence: North Pacific Ocean, easternmost Siberia, ancient land bridge to North America, shamanic migration of ancient Amerindians, Alaska, Mount McKinley, Eskimo culture, north-northwest Pacific coast cultures, now Alaska, 49th U.S. State and northwestern-most Canada/Yukon.

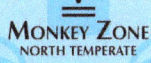

Monkey Zone
NORTH TEMPERATE

Psi Plate II

Northwest Caribbean,
Mt. Shasta, Rocky Mountains

Cardinal Family Blue (Establish the Genesis)
Zone of the Magician, SP Venus, Point of Influx of Magical Powers of the Solar Logos
Zone of psychogeographic influence: Most of Temperate & Tropical North America, Mexico and Central America, Seat of great civilizations, Olmec, Maya, Toltec, Zapotec, Aztec as well as sedentary & nomadic North Amerindian cultures, Hopi, Navajo, Ute, Lakota, Cherokee, etc., seat of Mayan Calendar & Galactic Maya Home Base, prophecies of time (Sunstone), Quetzalcoatl, U.S.A. (except eastern seaboard), Mexico and Canada.

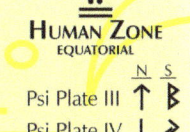

Human Zone
EQUATORIAL

Psi Plate III
Psi Plate IV

Straddles Equator (North/South)

Core Family Yellow (Mine the Tunnels)
Zone of the Sage, SP Earth, Point of Influx of Wisdom of Solar Logos
Zone of psychogeographic influence: South Central America, Central Caribbean, major part of South America, Amazon, Andes, Andean civilization, Chavin, Nazca, Tiahuanaco, Inca Empire, Macchu Picchu, Kontiki Viracocha, Keepers of the Wisdom of the Atlantean Star Elders, colonialist Catholic Empire, modern-day Brazil, Venezuela, Colombia, Ecuador, Peru.

Accessing Your Multidimensional Self: A Key to Cosmic History

SKYWALKER ZONE — SOUTH TEMPERATE
Psi Plate IV

Signal Family Red (Unravel the Mystery), Zone of the Prophet, SP Mars
Point of Influx of the Space of Prophecy of the Redemption of the Lost Planets
Zone of psychogeographic influence: South Atlantic (southern reaches of ancient Atlantean Empire), southwestern-most African continent, present-day Namibia & Republic of South Africa, Cape Town, Namib & Kalahari Deserts, mid-Atlantic coast of South America, urban Brazil (Rio, Sao Paolo), Uruguay and urban Argentina (Buenos Aires).

WIZARD ZONE — SOUTH POLAR
Psi Plate IV
Psi Plate I
Conclude White Chromatic/Truth Clan

Gateway Family White (Open the Portals)
Zone of the Wizard, SP Maldek, Storehouse of the Lost Wisdom of the Otherworlds
Zone of psychogeographic influence: Antarctica, Queen Maud Land, east Antarctica, Valkyrie Dome, Atlantic Indian Antarctic Basin, point of generation: southeast African coast.

EAGLE ZONE — NORTH POLAR
Psi Plate III
Psi Plate IV
Begin Blue Chromatic/Sky Clan

Polar Family Blue (Sound the Chromatics)
Zone of the Seer, SP Jupiter, Planetary Fountainhead of Visionary Power
Zone of psychogeographic influence: North Magnetic Pole, Arctic Ocean, Greenland, Iceland, north Canada, Baffin Island, Queen Elizabeth Islands, Hudson Bay, Great Lakes, eastern Canada, eastern Seaboard, U.S.A. urban zone, global industrial world center, former Iroquois Nation, Eskimo shamans.

WARRIOR ZONE — NORTH TEMPERATE
Psi Plate IV

Cardinal Family Yellow (Establish the Genesis)
Zone of the Pathfinder, SP Saturn, Atlantean Pathways of Cosmic Consciousness
Zone of psychogeographic influence: projecting west from Giza Pyramid, northwest Africa, Sahara Desert, ancient Benin Empire, Ghana, Senegal, Algeria, Morocco, Libya, north Atlantic Ocean, ancient Atlantis "Beneath the sea she may be", pathways of the great sea-farers, Iberian Peninsula, Spain & Portugal.

EARTH ZONE — EQUATORIAL
Psi Plate IV
Psi Plate I
Straddles Equator (North/South) Overlays of Hindu, Tribal with Christian, Muslim

Core Family Red (Mine the Tunnels), Zone of the Navigator, SP Uranus
Synchrotronic Evolutionary Space of the Birth and Rebirth of the Human Race
Zone of psychogeographic influence: projecting south from Giza Pyramid, major portion of African continent, Egypt, Sudan, Ethiopia, Kenya, Mt. Kenya, Mt. Kilimanjaro, Nigeria, Congo River, Angola, Zimbabwe, Tanzania, Mozambique, the Heartland of the Human Race, zone of the rebirth from global industrial colonialist oppression, the original tribes of man.

MIRROR ZONE — SOUTH TEMPERATE
Psi Plate I

Signal Family White (Unravel the Mystery)
Zone of the Yogi(ni), SP Neptune, Oceanic Consciousness of Cosmic Memory
Zone of psychogeographic influence: Indian Ocean, Madagascar, Seychelles Islands, Mauritius, Chagos Archipelago, southwestern-most point of Australia, along with Hand zone as most oceanic of all the zones, Treasure Trove of the Lost Mysteries of the Cosmic Unconscious.

STORM ZONE — SOUTH POLAR
Psi Plate I
Psi Plate II
Conclude Blue Chromatic/Sky Clan

Gateway Family Blue (Open the Portals), Zone of the World-Changer, (Ω) SP Pluto,
Magnetic/Transformative Field of Planetary Regeneration
Zone of psychogeographic influence: South Magnetic Pole, South Indian & Southern Oceans, Antarctica, Transantarctic Mountains, George V Land, Wilkes Land, Ross Sea & Ross Shelf, plasma generator of the Rainbow Bridge.

HUNAB KU 21 — EARTH CORE
Psi Plate I
Psi Plate II
Psi Plate III
Psi Plate IV
Coordinates Planetary Unification Cells

Generator of Solar-Galactic Electrodynamic Transmissions through Radio Polar Diffusion
Zone of the Magus of the Infinite, Solar-Galactic Root of Planetary Kuxan Suum
Seat of Noosphere Consciousness and Psi Bank Programs, Receptor of Solar Sunspot Cycle Transmissions

Crystal Iron Octahedral Inner Core: Radius 1216 km = 64 (DNA) × 19 (command)
Outer Core Radius 2270 km. (1216+2270) = 3486 = BMU 399 ☉) Lower Mantle Radius: 2185 km.
Upper Mantle to Crust: 700 km. Total Kilometers, Center to Crust Radius: 6371 km.

CHAPTER 13

SYNCHROGALACTIC YOGA

Synchrogalactic Yoga is a system of inner discovery and self-research that unites traditional yoga practices with the synchronic order. The system of Synchrogalactic Yoga provides the template or matrix for realizing the super mental superhuman within ourselves. All yoga is for the purpose of self realization.

The synchronic codes of time create the context and matrix of meaning to understand our inner explorations and experiences. Through application and meditation of these codes, the body and mind become synchronized with the universal order as coordinated by the 13:20 timing frequency. This system facilitates self-synchronization, where the human mind and soul experience unification at a noospheric, planetary level. This will radically alter our self-perception and perception of the universe.

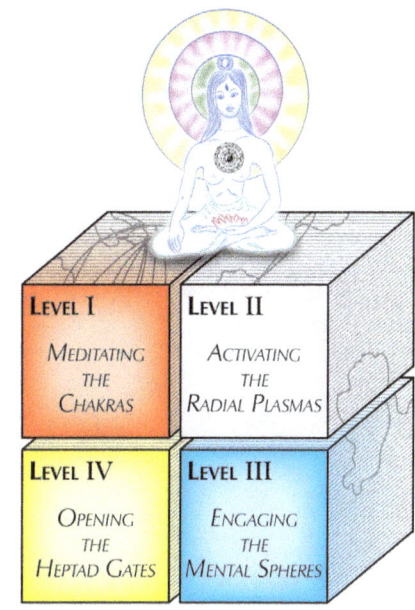

SYNCHROGALACTIC YOGA

Through the process of self-synchronization, we begin to experience many other selves who are also synchronizing to this state. It is this union of synchronized selves within the planetary circuit board that creates the planetary field of consciousness.

Herein are presented the basic practices of Synchrogalactic Yoga as four levels: 1) Meditating the Chakras; 2) Activating the Radial Plasmas; 3) Engaging the Mental Spheres; and 4) Opening the Heptad Gates.

These practices are synchronized with the 13 Moon, 28-day calendar cycle, creating four seven day cycles per moon (28 days). The seven-day cycle is coded by the seven radial plasmas: Dali, Seli, Gamma, Kali, Alpha, Limi and Silio.

Accessing Your Multidimensional Self: A Key to Cosmic History

Day One: DALI

Level 1: Meditating the Sahasrara (Crown) Chakra

Sit in a comfortable meditative posture. Keep your spine erect and body relaxed. With the body completely still, practice a few moments of natural mind meditation. Once the mind is sufficiently clear, direct your attention to your crown or Sahasrara chakra. Make it as clear and pristine as possible, glistening and sparkling with vibrant energy. When it is pure and translucent, floating just above the top of your head, allow it to dissolve and transform itself into a thousand-petalled violet lotus.

Concentrate on this area inside of your crown chakra. This is the doorway to cosmic consciousness. This center contains the dormant capacity for total enlightenment. Yogic scriptures say that the Sahasrara chakra is the seat of the self-luminous soul or *chitta*, the essence of mind.

This chakra is governed by the feminine principle or Shakti Goddess *Maha Shakti* (Union). When this center is finally awakened the activities of the mind cease and merge into the light of illumination. This is the source of cosmic enlightenment.

Feel the textures of light/heat, warmth and nurturance balancing your pineal gland and cerebral cortex, bringing all of your chakras into harmony. Your entire glandular system is pacified and bathed in the warmth of this divine light. In this chakra lies our capacity to tune into and even take on different qualities or stages of being. This is the place used by mediums to channel information.

By awakening our crown chakra we become clear light oracles of planetary divination; to divine is to know directly by mind.

Sahasrara affirmation: *May the pure light universe infuse our soul's journey, that the planetary noosphere may become the crown of pure radiance!*

Accessing Your Multidimensional Self: A Key to Cosmic History

Level 2: Activating Radial Plasma: Dali

Dali
Crown

Breathe deeply through your nostrils and allow your awareness to flow up your nose and into your crown chakra. Bring your awareness to the inner Dali plasma at the center of the chakra. Visualize the yellow symbol radiating healing charges of heat.

Repeat the following while focusing on your crown chakra: "My father is intrinsic awareness, I feel the heat." Feel this heat power ignite at your crown chakra, blazing as your innate self-existing awareness free from conceptualization.

Cover your left nostril with your left thumb and breathe slowly and deeply three times in and out through your right nostril. Flash onto the Dali plasma and feel the heat of intrinsic awareness emanating out of your crown chakra. Now cover your right nostril with your right thumb and repeat, focusing all of your attention to your crown chakra, Dali plasma. Feel this heat move from your crown chakra down your spinal column and into your limbs, permeating your entire being. Your crown chakra is flooded with radiant warmth that connects you to the realm of cosmic consciousness. Give yourself to the process as if nothing else mattered.

Dali is the first state of the three-part primary sensory quantum. A sensory quantum is the first stage building block of sensory experience.

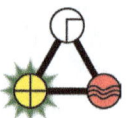

Level 3: Engaging the First Mental Sphere (Preconscious)

Profound samadhi activates first mental sphere.

Visualize the first mental sphere (preconscious) in the brain, located in and covering the right rear lobe and cerebellum. This sphere is the resonant chamber of the physical body and governs the right rear lobe of the brain.

By means of the preconscious, the evolutive activity of the third- and fourth-dimensional beings are programmed. This sphere corresponds to the first time dimension: *Cosmic creation*. It is activated by profound samadhi which penetrates to the deepest layers of the preconscious. This is the sphere where the primal codes of cosmic creation are situated.

Cosmic creation refers to mastery of the cosmic forces. This comes about through the self-creation of the energy of space. Here, we are no longer the victim of conditioned reality, thoughts and patterns. We have freed ourselves from the claims of the false self. Here we are creating ourselves and reality anew by embodying the five virtues: Remembrance, discipline, exertion, patience and compassion.

To experience and activate this mental sphere exert in natural mind meditation expanding the duration of the GAP—the space between thoughts.

NATURAL MIND MEDITATION

Sit still, with spine erect. Keep eyes slightly open looking toward the floor. Feel your intrinsic dignity in this posture. In this position, watch your breath. Breathe normally. As you become aware of your thoughts just label them "thinking", and as you exhale, dissolve the thoughts. It matters not the nature or content of the thoughts, just dissolve them. At that very moment, just as the thought dissolves, lies the GAP between thoughts. It is this GAP that you want to become familiar with and cultivate. It is the seed of natural mind and the key to your true, authentic self. Practice this each day and note the subtle shifts in your perceptions and attitudes.

LEVEL 4: OPENING THE FIRST HEPTAD GATE (108)

ALPHA-ALPHA

We begin this practice by introducing the seven solar mantras that open the seven solar gates (see previous chapter). For this chakra, the mantra is **OM**.

First visualize the violet thousand-petaled lotus **Sahasrara** chakra with the **yellow Dali** plasma superimposed over it at your crown. Hold this visualization and feel the two intermingle as you chant the sacred letter **OM** as long as your breath can sustain it *(Patanjali says that OM is the word that manifests God)*. OM is the universal symbol for primordial sound vibration.

Locate Heptad Gate **108** and the **Alpha-Alpha** symbol on the 441 holomind perceiver. Its matrix location is V11:H2, second circuit, 7th time dimension: vertical time cosmic command descending. Now locate it in your body at the base of your skull (see graphic at the end of this chapter).

Visualize the **Alpha-Alpha** hyperplasma above the **yellow Dali** in your **crown** chakra. Take the **Alpha-Alpha** into the **first** mental sphere in the **first** time dimension (**cosmic creation**) where it activates the **preconscious mind** as **profound samadhi**. Here is the intergalactic channel (BMU 341) through which the **Alpha-Alpha** hyperplasma is secreted into the brain.

From the **first** mental sphere, mentally direct the **Alpha-Alpha** hyperplasma to the **crown** chakra and impress it above the **Dali** seal. Hold this with four alternate nostril breaths (four times in and out through each nostril), followed by one deep breath through both nostrils.

Descend down the central column (spine), secreting this red electric **Alpha-Alpha** hyperplasma into all 144,000 etheric fibers of the astral body. Practice the **breath of fire,** rapid shallow breathing through the nose, transmuting any blockages or obscurations into streams of crystal clear **profound samadhi** spreading throughout your entire nervous system.

Spectral, electric red Alpha-Alpha vibrates subtle activating force into all etheric fibers. Ascend back up central channel and leave **Dali** at the **crown** chakra. Return your consciousness to the first mental sphere, then close and seal the Heptad Gate at the base of your skull. Relax and breathe slowly and deeply at least 13 times.

 Harmonic UR rune 84: *Galactic Life Whole Becomes Medium of Transmission.*

For additional practice: Locate Heptad Gate 108 on the Hunab Ku 21. Note that it corresponds to the Primal Force, Ancient of Days, Galactatron, Queen of the Throne; G/K Neptune, Bode Number 300. Study the connections (see graphic at the end of this chapter).

Day Two: SELI

Level 1: Meditating the Muladhara (Root) Chakra

Sit in a comfortable meditative posture. Keep your spine erect and body relaxed. With the body completely still, practice a few moments of natural mind meditation. Once the mind is sufficiently clear, direct your attention to your root or Muladhara chakra. Make it as clear and pristine as possible, glistening and sparkling with vibrant energy. When it is pure and translucent, pulsing at your root, allow it to dissolve and transform itself into a four-petaled red lotus.

Concentrate on this area inside of your root chakra. This is a key chakra in Kundalini Yoga where the awakening of the vital force begins; it is also the conjunction of 72,000 pairs of nerve endings in the body.

In Samkhya philosophy, Muladhara is understood as *moola prakriti*, the transcendental basis of physical nature. This is the base from which the three main psychic channels or nadis emerge and flow up the spinal cord: Ida (mental force), left; Pingala (vital force), right; and Sushumna (spiritual force), center.

This chakra is governed by the feminine principle or Shakti Goddess *Dakini* (Security). The physical body zone of psychic activation extends from the root chakra to the solar plexus. Emotional information from the solar plexus comes into the physical body at the root. At its base level this chakra deals with security and survival—the basic instincts.

This chakra also serves as a storage center for much unconscious energy including "lower" emotions such as guilt and other psychic complexes. With the awakening of this chakra, we proceed from the unconscious to the conscious.

Muladhara affirmation: *May the highest yogic force within the planetary consciousness direct all manifestation to its fulfillment!*

Accessing Your Multidimensional Self: A Key to Cosmic History

Level 2: Activating Radial Plasma: Seli

Seli
Root

Breathe deeply through your nostrils and allow your awareness to flow down from your nose and into your root chakra. Bring your awareness to the inner Seli plasma at the center of the chakra. Visualize the red symbol radiating streams of white light. This plasma accounts for the intensity of inner light.

Repeat the following while focusing on your root chakra: "My mother is the ultimate sphere, I see the light." Feel this sphere of light as the perfect form at your root chakra. This quality of perfection is the actual nature of reality.

Cover your left nostril with your left thumb and breathe slowly and deeply three times in and out through your right nostril. Flash onto the Seli plasma and feel the light of the ultimate sphere emanating out of the root chakra. Now cover your right nostril with your right thumb and repeat the three breaths, focusing all of your attention to your root chakra, Seli plasma. Feel this luminosity (light) emanate from your root chakra, moving up your spinal column to your crown chakra and then permeating your body to the tips of your fingers and toes. Feel your entire body flooded with this radiant light, grounding you into the Earth and extending upward to the crown of cosmic consciousness.

Feel the emanations of flowing streams of light clearing and releasing any blockages in your system. The Great Mother energy nurtures the root of your being, the base or seat of the kundalini force. Kundalini (life-force) energy is released from the root, activating the secret center and opening the inner wisdom channel of the third eye.

Seli is the second stage of the three-part primary sensory quantum. A sensory quantum is the first stage building block of sensory experience.

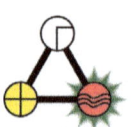

Level 3: Engaging the Second Mental Sphere (Sub- or Unconscious)

Informative samadhi activates second mental sphere.

Visualize the second mental sphere (sub- or unconscious) in the brain and centered in the optic nerve, encompassing the pineal gland and corpus callosum. This mental sphere governs the right front hemisphere.

This sphere contains every perception and life experience that was not consciously registered or that is filtered out of your day-to-day conscious mind (third mental sphere). What people think of as their personality is primarily based on their own evaluation of their reactions to a set of circumstances. Everyone experiences a different set and order of life circumstances and is given an equal opportunity of responding consciously or unconsciously and/or positively or negatively.

This sphere corresponds to the third time dimension: *Cosmic synchronization*. Cosmic synchronization refers to mastery of the synchronic order: Self-creation through time. Here, we impress the codes of the synchronic order, embedding them into our subconscious.

The second mental sphere is activated as informative samadhi. Cultivation of unbroken meditative awareness allows us to access information previously out of range of our waking conscious. Knowledge of the Law of Time lies dormant in this mental sphere. The Law of Time makes conscious what was previously unconscious. According to the Law of Time all life possesses unconscious energy

This mental sphere is activated by cultivating states of peripheral awareness, both through meditation and by contemplation of the Law of Time: Time as the evolution of consciousness.

If our day to day experience remains unconscious of the Law of Time, then when an experience occurs in our timespace, we will not be aware of the opportunity for heightened consciousness that is being presented to us. However, if we are conscious of the Law of Time, then our experiences become triggers that enter us into higher consciousness.

Level 4: Opening the Second Heptad Gate (291)

Alpha-Beta

Visualize the red four-petaled lotus **Muladhara** chakra with the **red Seli** plasma superimposed over it at your root. Hold this visualization and feel the two intermingle as you chant the sacred letter **HRAM** as long as your breath can sustain it.

Locate Heptad Gate **291** and the **Alpha-Beta** symbol on the 441 holomind perceiver. Its matrix location is V11:H5, fifth circuit, 7th time dimension, vertical time cosmic command descending. Now locate it in your body at the middle back of your skull, halfway between base and crown (see graphic at the end of this chapter).

Visualize the **Alpha-Beta** hyperplasma above the **red Seli** in your **root** chakra. Take the **Alpha-Beta** into the **second** mental sphere in the **third** time dimension (**cosmic synchronization**) where it activates the **subconscious** as **informative samadhi**. Here is the intergalactic channel (BMU 351) through which the **Alpha-Beta** hyperplasma is secreted into the front, right hemisphere of the brain.

From the **second** mental sphere, mentally direct the **Alpha-Beta** hyperplasma to the **root** chakra and impress it above the **Seli** seal. Hold this with four alternate nostril breaths (four times in and out through each nostril), followed by one breath through both nostrils.

Ascend up the central column (spine), secreting this **Alpha-Beta** hyperplasma into all 144,000 etheric fibers of the astral body. Practice the **breath of fire,** rapid shallow breathing through the nose, transmuting any blockages or obscurations into streams of crystal clear **informative samadhi** spreading throughout your entire nervous system.

Spectral, electric red and blue Alpha-Beta vibrates subtle activating force into all etheric fibers. Descend back down central channel and leave **Seli** at the **root** chakra. Ascend back up central channel and return your consciousness to the second mental sphere, then close and seal the Heptad Gate at the middle of the back of your skull. Relax and breathe slowly and deeply at least 13 times.

 Harmonic UR rune 88: *Galactic Life Whole Realized as Cosmic Consciousness.*

For additional practice: Locate Heptad Gate 291 on the Hunab Ku 21. Note that it corresponds to the Avatar, Accomplisher of Knowledge, the Exemplar; G/K Earth, Bode Number 10. Study all of the connections (see graphic at the end of this chapter).

Day Three: GAMMA

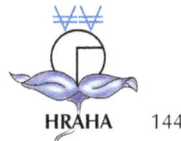

HRAHA 144

Level 1: Meditating the Ajna (Third Eye) Chakra

Sit in a comfortable meditative posture. Keep your spine erect and body relaxed. With the body completely still, practice a few moments of natural mind meditation. Once the mind is sufficiently clear, direct your attention to your third eye or Ajna chakra. Make it as clear and pristine as possible, glistening and sparkling with vibrant energy. When it is pure and translucent, pulsing at your brow, allow it to dissolve and transform itself into a two-petalled indigo lotus.

Concentrate on this area inside of your third eye chakra. Concentration on this chakra awakens the pineal gland, opening our inner vision to the receptivity of cosmic forces; this is the doorway to the astral and psychic dimensions of consciousness.

The word "ajna" is derived from the Sanskrit root which means "to know, obey or follow." Literally, ajna means "command" or "the monitoring center." It is also sometimes referred to as the chakra of the mind or the eye of wisdom. The Ajna chakra is the point where the three main nadis (Ida, Pingala and Sushumna) merge into one stream of consciousness and flow up to the crown center.

To awaken the Ajna chakra requires discipline and persistent concentration. Visualize a dot of light and stay focused on the single point of light to cultivate your inner vision. The purpose of this action is to pacify the lower emotions, open the inner vision, and sustain concentration. Cultivation of the Ajna chakra lifts us to a level of continuing consciousness, creating the possibility for mind-to-mind communication or telepathy.

This chakra is governed by the feminine principle or Shakti Goddess *Hakini* (Insight). It holds the key to intuition, or sixth sense—direct attunement or attaining divine knowledge directly without the aid of the senses—what is traditionally called "gnosis."

When this center is finally awakened the body becomes flooded with bliss light radiance that illuminates all you set your mind on. You are creating a light transmission antennae from the inside out so that the higher intelligence may connect with you. Once sufficiently disciplined, your inner vision can be directed to any one of your other chakras to retrieve information, impressions, stored memories and/or insights. It is through the Ajna chakra that we may see the hidden essence of the world of appearance: past, future and present at once. When the mind is purified, then the other chakras naturally awaken.

Ajna affirmation: *May we be granted galactic vision to transform all matter into the purifying radiance of the higher dream!*

Level 2: Activating Radial Plasma: Gamma

**Gamma
Third Eye**

Breathe deeply through your nostrils and allow your awareness to flow up your nose and into your third eye chakra. Bring your awareness to the inner Gamma plasma at the center of the chakra. Visualize the white symbol radiating out to all points of the universe with peaceful equanimity and equalization of light and heat charges.

Repeat the following while focusing on your third eye: "My lineage is the union of intrinsic awareness and the ultimate sphere, I attain the power of peace." Allow yourself to feel the merging of light (perfect radiant form) and heat (intrinsic awareness) within the third eye. Feel the inherent perfection and innate self-liberation of peace that always exists in the present moment.

To discover the lineage of heat and light cover your left nostril with your left thumb and breathe deeply three times in and out through your right nostril. First, flash onto the yellow Dali plasma at your crown chakra and feel the heat of intrinsic awareness emanating from this center. Now, cover your right nostril with your right thumb and breathe deeply three times in and out of your left nostril. Flash onto the luminous red Seli plasma at your root chakra and feel the soothing flow of the radiating sphere of light. Contemplate the mystery of light and heat.

Now merge the heat from the crown and light from the root together in your third eye, white Gamma plasma. Feel the pulsing union of this intrinsic awareness (heat) and ultimate sphere (light). Your entire body and glandular system is pacified and bathed in the warmth of this divine mother/father light.

With sufficient concentration and practice, the thermic energy from both the crown chakra as well as the exterior higher-dimensional light universe floods into the third eye and fills the physical and astral nervous system with radiant insight, reinstating our clairvoyant birthright.

Gamma is the third stage that completes the three-part primary sensory quantum. A sensory quantum is the first stage building block of sensory experience.

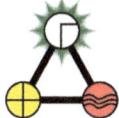

Level 3: Engaging the Third Mental Sphere (Waking Conscious)

Waking conscious mediumship activates third mental sphere.

Visualize the third mental sphere (waking conscious) located in the brain at the anterior portion of the right cerebral hemisphere above the right eye. This mental sphere generally functions solely with the third-dimensional self, but in a state of wakefulness it operates at the beta level governing the left front cerebral hemisphere.

The third mental sphere is the medium of thought, decision and moment-to-moment awareness. Becoming conscious means to question everything back to its source. True knowledge begins first with curiosity, a desire to *know*. This desire to *know* creates the space for intelligent questions to arise. With these questions comes the desire to know the answer. The feedback received varies according to the quality of the question.

This mental sphere governs the power of free will; it is intended to be disciplined by the exercise of will on behalf of a spiritually coordinated purpose. When this is achieved, then the eye of wisdom opens and gnosis becomes possible.

This sphere also corresponds to the fourth time dimension: *Cosmic cube*. Cosmic cube refers to the highest level of cosmic mastery entering us into higher mental design processes of co-creation. The most direct way to activate this level of awareness is by practicing tuning the third eye to the Supreme Being; shining, full of light, pure, perfect and free of obscurations. Keep the mind fixed for as long as possible on this formless One; the Creator of all Knowledge and Intelligence. Allow your mind to merge with all of creation.

The ability to have one-pointed consciousness is the key to *waking conscious mediumship*. When the mind is concentrated at this point then comes the transcendence of individual *unconsciousness* into collective planetary *consciousness*.

Level 4: Opening the Third Heptad Gate (144)

Beta-Beta

Visualize the indigo two-petaled lotus **Ajna** chakra with the **white Gamma** plasma superimposed over it at your brow. Hold this visualization and feel the two intermingle as you chant the sacred letter **HRAHA** as long as your breath can sustain it.

Locate Heptad Gate **144** and the **Beta-Beta** symbol on the 441 holomind perceiver. Its matrix location is V11:H20, second circuit, 8th time dimension, vertical time cosmic command ascending. Now locate it in your body at the front of your skull, at the brow (see graphic at the end of this chapter).

Visualize the **Beta-Beta** hyperplasma above the **white Gamma** in your **third eye** chakra. Take the **Beta-Beta** into the **third** mental sphere in the **fourth** time dimension (**cosmic cube**) where it activates the **conscious** mind as **waking mediumship**. Here is the intergalactic channel (BMU 321) through which the **Beta-Beta** hyperplasma is secreted into the front, left hemisphere of the brain.

From the **third** mental sphere, mentally direct the **Beta-Beta** hyperplasma to the **third eye** chakra and impress it above the **Gamma** seal. Hold this with four alternate nostril breaths (four times in and out through each nostril), followed by one breath through both nostrils.

Descend down the central column (spine), secreting this **Beta-Beta** hyperplasma into all 144,000 etheric fibers of the astral body. Practice the **breath of fire,** rapid shallow breathing through the nose, transmuting any blockages or obscurations into streams of crystal clear **waking conscious mediumship** spreading throughout your entire nervous system.

Spectral, electric blue Beta-Beta vibrates subtle activating force into all etheric fibers. Ascend back up central channel and leave **Gamma** at the **third eye** chakra. Return your consciousness to the third mental sphere, then close and seal the Heptad Gate at your third eye. Relax and breathe slowly and deeply at least 13 times.

 Harmonic UR rune 91: *Galactic Art Whole Defines Space.*

For additional practice: Locate Heptad Gate 144 on the Hunab Ku 21. Note that it corresponds to the High Priestess, Spirit Essence, Urania, Lady of the Winds; G/K Uranus, Bode Number 196. Study all of the connections (see graphic at the end of this chapter).

Day Four: KALI

Level 1: Meditating the Svadhisthana (Secret Center) Chakra

Sit in a comfortable meditative posture. Keep your spine erect and body relaxed. With the body completely still, practice a few moments of natural mind meditation. Once the mind is sufficiently clear, direct your attention to your secret center or Svadhisthana chakra. Make it as clear and pristine as possible, glistening and sparkling with vibrant energy. When it is pure and translucent, pulsing at your secret center, allow it to dissolve and transform itself into an orange six-petalled lotus.

Concentrate on this area inside of your secret center chakra. This is the seat of sexual awareness and holds a supremely powerful energy. This is also the seat of body consciousness.

In yogic tradition, the Svadhisthana is known as the substratum or basis of individual human consciousness. It is the container of all karmas, impressions, past lives and previous experience, or the unconscious, as it pertains specifically to the formation of the earthly personality or circumstantial persona.

This chakra is governed by the feminine principle or Shakti Goddess *Rakini* (Sexuality). This is the place that stores the most psychic blockages and karma—the collective karma of the unconscious. We want to awaken the secret center in order to open our inner vision to the receptivity of cosmic electricity.

When this center is finally awakened the body becomes flooded with cosmic electricity that connects all other chakras. This is the area to transmute and re-channel the powerful sexual, or kundalini energy into a higher form of electricity. The energy stored in this chakra can be used to vitalize the different levels of being.

Svadhisthana affirmation: *May the supramental forces gather their electroplasmic structures of spiritual evolution and release them into the noosphere!*

Level 2: Activating Radial Plasma: Kali

Kali
Secret Center

Breathe deeply through your nostrils and allow your awareness to flow up your nose and down into your secret center chakra. Bring your awareness to the inner Kali plasma at the center of the chakra. Visualize the blue symbol radiating streams of white light.

Feel the Kali plasma gathering in the secret center, accounting for the quality of intensified light heat, which is also associated with the sexual, or kundalini energy.

Repeat the following while focusing on your secret center: "My name is the glorious lotus-born, I catalyze the light-heat within." Feel within yourself this light-heat, the self-generated electricity that arises from a condition of immaculate purity.

Cover your left nostril with your left thumb and breathe deeply three times in and out through your right nostril. Flash onto the Kali plasma and feel the intensified light-heat emanating out of the secret center chakra. Now cover your right nostril with your right thumb and repeat the three breaths. Focus on the Kali plasma and feel this intrinsic light-heat awareness pulsing from your secret center chakra into your entire being. Feel the flowing streams of light and heat catalyzing your entire system into ever more subtle spirals of radiance. This powerful energy emanates from your secret center chakra, activating, circulating and invigorating all other chakras. You are the glorious lotus-born, born from Father Heat and Mother Light.

Kali plasma is the link between the three light-heat sensory plasmas and the three telepathic plasmas. It is the catalytic agent between the thermic/luminic sensory quantum and the subatomic telepathic quantum.

Level 3: Engaging the Fourth Mental Sphere (Continuing Conscious)

Higher mind control activates fourth mental sphere.

Visualize the fourth mental sphere (continuing conscious) located in the brain above the left eye in the left cerebral hemisphere. This mental sphere controls and governs the rear left hemisphere.

Continuing consciousness is the ability to maintain a conscious thoughtform in succession over a long, unbroken period of time. In terms of Cosmic Science, continuing consciousness is the ability of the 4-D "Other" to maintain direct communication with the 5-D "Higher Self" and to continue to establish and extend realization of the whole to the 3-D "self".

This sphere corresponds to the second time dimension: *Cosmic ascension.* Cosmic ascension refers to the mastery of higher powers of telepathic perception and projection. This means we can perceive ourselves anywhere in the universe and project to those places as necessary.

To cultivate continuing consciousness choose a thought, mental structure or series of numbers to focus on. You might also practice maintaining projective geometries, like an icosahedron or dodecahedron. Concentrate and fill your mind entirely with this inner perception or mental construct—keep it filled with this thought. The moment that any other thought tries to enter the mind displace it immediately with the thought-construct upon which you are concentrating.

Continue until you acquire the skill of being able to concentrate on anything for as long as you wish, or until it appears before you in hallucinatory clarity. Persistent training in control of your thought-world prepares you for supermental descent of consciousness. Analyze every thought that arises. If a thought is not constructive or harmonious, let it go immediately. Do this as often as necessary until it becomes second nature. When you attain this capacity you will experience higher mind control: you are no longer the doer or the thinker, but the higher self has intervened.

Accessing Your Multidimensional Self: A Key to Cosmic History

LEVEL 4: OPENING THE FOURTH HEPTAD GATE (315)

BETA-ALPHA

Visualize the orange six-petaled lotus **Svadhisthana** chakra with the **blue Kali** plasma superimposed over it at your sacral area. Hold this visualization and feel the two intermingle as you chant the sacred letter **HRIM** as long as your breath can sustain it.

Locate Heptad Gate **315** and the **Beta-Alpha** symbol on the 441 holomind perceiver. Its matrix location is V11:H17, fifth circuit, 8th time dimension, vertical time cosmic command ascending. Now locate it in your body at the top of your forehead, just above the third eye (see graphic at the end of this chapter).

Visualize the **Beta-Alpha** hyperplasma above the **blue Kali** in your **secret center** chakra. Take the **Beta-Alpha** into the **fourth** mental sphere in the **second** time dimension (**cosmic ascension**) where it activates **continuing conscious** as **higher mind control**. Here is the intergalactic channel (BMU 331) through which the **Beta-Alpha** hyperplasma is secreted into the rear left hemisphere of the brain.

From the **fourth** mental sphere, mentally direct the **Beta-Alpha** hyperplasma to the **secret center** chakra and impress it above the **Kali** seal. Hold this with four alternate nostril breaths (four times in and out through each nostril), followed by one breath through both nostrils.

Ascend up the central column (spine), secreting this **Beta-Alpha** hyperplasma into all 144,000 etheric fibers of the astral body. Practice the **breath of fire,** rapid shallow breathing through the nose, transmuting any blockages or obscurations into streams of crystal clear **higher mind control** spreading through your entire nervous system.

Spectral, electric blue and red Beta-Alpha vibrates subtle activating force into all etheric fibers. Descend back down central channel and leave **Kali** at the **secret center** chakra. Ascend back up central channel and return your consciousness to the fourth mental sphere, then close and seal the Heptad Gate at the top front of your skull. Relax and breathe slowly and deeply at least 13 times.

 Harmonic UR rune 95: *Galactic Art Whole Becomes Meditation of Reality.*

For additional practice: Locate Heptad Gate 315 on the Hunab Ku 21. Note that it corresponds to the Prophet, the Renewer of Culture, World Teacher; S/P Mars, Bode Number 16. Study all of the connections (see graphic at the end of this chapter).

Day Five: ALPHA

HRAUM 414

Level 1: Meditating the Vishuddha (Throat) Chakra

Sit in a comfortable meditative posture. Keep your spine erect and body relaxed. With the body completely still, practice a few moments of natural mind meditation. Once the mind is sufficiently clear, direct your attention to your throat or Vishuddha chakra. Make it as clear and pristine as possible, glistening and sparkling with vibrant energy. When it is pure and translucent, radiating from your throat, allow it to dissolve and transform itself into a blue sixteen-petalled lotus.

Concentrate on this area inside of your throat chakra. This center contains the will to communicate and to extend oneself to others in patterns of informative thought and behavior.

The Vishuddha chakra is the channel of communication bringing the fourth dimension through to the third dimension. This deals both with the mental and emotional bodies and is the center for artistic expression and communicating intelligence derived from the higher mental spheres (5th and 6th).

The Vishuddha chakra is known by some yogic traditions as the chakra of spiritual rebirth, and in Kundalini yoga as the "fountain of youth", the place where spontaneous physical rejuvenation begins. To activate the Vishuddha chakra you may recite prayers, sing devotional songs or practice mantra. Chant "Ahhh" seven times to open the throat chakra.

This chakra is governed by the feminine principle or Shakti Goddess *Shakini* (Knowledge). The Vishuddha is also the center of purification and discrimination and the locus of vijnana, or divine analytical wisdom. By focusing our attention on this chakra, we can discriminate between messages from the higher mind from messages of ego.

This Vishuddha chakra is related with *Nada Yoga*, or the branch of kundalini yoga concerned with sound vibration (Vishuddha and Muladhara are considered to be the two basic centers of vibration). The Muladhara chakra corresponds to the cosmic vibratory root, while the Vishuddha chakra is the receiver of the higher harmonics of the music of the spheres. When this chakra reaches its highest state, sounds emitted take on magical qualities that change the space of the listener through vibration. This chakra can also be utilized as a receiving station to tune into the thoughts and feelings of people both far and near.

This is the supermental reception center of thought-waves and transmissions which discriminates then directs messages to the appropriate chakra. As this chakra awakens, we can begin to direct the energies of the body from the lower to the higher chakras, reconnecting our expression as higher resonant channels of the cosmos.

Note: The nerve channel in the throat is also associated with *kurma nadi*, the tortoise nadi. When this nadi is awakened the practitioner is able to completely overcome the desire and necessity for food and drink. (This has been demonstrated by many yogis, particularly in India. Examples of such yogis/yoginis can be found in *Autobiography of a Yogi*, by Sri Paramahansa Yogananda).

Vishuddha affirmation: *May the vision of the star elders of the great councils of light and wisdom speak through me so that all may ascend to sublime grace!*

Level 2: Activating Radial Plasma: Alpha

Alpha Throat

Breathe deeply through your nostrils and allow your awareness to flow up your nose and down into your throat chakra. Bring your awareness to the inner Alpha plasma at the center of the chakra. Visualize the yellow symbol radiating luminous streams of white light.

Feel the electrical vibration of the Alpha plasma gathered in the throat center. This center activates the double-extended electrical charge, which is in telepathic resonance with the South Pole. Repeat the following while focusing on your throat chakra: "My country is the unborn ultimate sphere, I release the double-extended electron at the South Pole." Unborn refers to the unconditional indestructible state that pervades the entire universe from beginningless beginning to endless end. Feel your consciousness align with Universal consciousness as your vibration raises to the frequency of the new Earth. All knots and obscurations dissolve from your mental stream as you merge into the great ocean of superconscious universal mind.

Cover your left nostril with your left thumb and breathe deeply three times in and out through your right nostril. Flash onto the Alpha plasma and feel the light streaming in from the Universal Mind purifying your throat chakra, and cleansing all of your communication channels. Now cover your right nostril with your right thumb and repeat the three breaths, focusing all of your attention on the throat chakra. Your throat chakra emanates sound enlivening and resonating healing vibrations to all of the other chakras. You are the creator of the new stories, the teller of the new tales.

Alpha plasma charge is the first stage of the three-part telepathic quantum. At the center of Alpha feel the integrated charges of the sensory quanta: Dali, Seli, and Gamma, transmuted by Kali into the Alpha telepathic charge. Then by extending your mind telepathically to the south of the Planet, release the double-extended electron at the South Pole.

Level 3: Engaging the Fifth Mental Sphere (Superconscious)

Hyperelectronic superconscious activates fifth mental sphere.

Visualize the fifth mental sphere (superconscious) situated in the brain above the left ear in the left cerebral hemisphere. This is the seat of the fifth-dimensional higher self and functions with the fourth-dimensional "Other". This mental sphere governs and activates the right lateral hemispheres midway between right ear and right temple where it sends paranormal impulses to the first mental sphere: preconscious.

Superconsciousness lies behind the veil of waking consciousness. It is sometimes referred to as cosmic consciousness or Christ consciousness; the self-existing consciousness bliss that transcends creation. The quality of our thoughts and attention is key to harnessing these superconscious powers.

Our thoughts are electronic lines of force that release into the atmosphere and create specific effects according to the strength of the thought. To embody a superconscious state of mind requires persistent and attentive concentration and devotion to meditation practice.

This sphere corresponds to the fifth time dimension, the radial time of the superconscious fifth-dimensional Higher Self. It is characterized by an electrical hyper-clarity that is definitely not "of this world." This sphere is increasingly activated with the advent of the noosphere, and is characterized by total holistic perception. Incorporating the continuing conscious of the fourth mental sphere, the superconscious expands into the mentation waves of the fifth-dimensional higher self. A "mentation" wave is a configuration of telepathic potentialities, independent of language, and based on whole orders of supermental precepts intrinsic to non-egoic knowing. To cultivate a superconscious mind, meditate the whole Earth as a single organism held together by a universal thought-field.

> ### Whole Earth Meditation
>
> Visualize yourself right where you are. Notice the space that you are in, whether it be inside or outside. Now lift out of the environment you find yourself in and look down on it from above. Lift out further and see the entire street or area that you are in. Now expand out and lift higher and higher into space. From space, view the Earth as a single luminous blue mandala. See the Earth from all angles. See it as a planetary orb, a wheel spinning in space with an essential value, its dharma or truth. The dharma or capacity of Earth is its capacity to sustain life.
>
> Visualize the whole of life on Earth, from the animals, to the plants, to the humans down onto the insects and plankton. See it all as one whole system. The whole of the life on the Earth is the biosphere, or the sphere of life that covers the surface of the Earth like a film or vibrant mantle that is ever in motion. Really visualize how all of the different life forms and processes are one unity on this shining blue orb.
>
> Now let your mind penetrate beneath the surface of the Earth. Feel the spherical layers of sediment and crystalline rock. Go to the core and find the massive iron crystal octahedron. Feel this crystal core as a dynamic radio receiver elongated in the direction of each of its magnetic poles. Place yourself in meditation at the very center of that crystal radio receiver. Who is the Earth receiving? What is the Earth broadcasting? Where is the Earth receiving? What messages is Earth giving you right now?
>
> *Note: Application of advanced pure meditation techniques are necessary to unify with universal cosmic space. Telepathic supernormative thoughtforms are always coming from the fifth mental sphere, the superconscious.*

Level 4: Opening the Fifth Heptad Gate (414)

Hyperelectron

Visualize the blue sixteen-petaled lotus **Vishuddha** chakra with the **yellow Alpha** plasma superimposed over it at your throat. Hold this visualization and feel the two intermingle as you chant the sacred letter HRAUM as long as your breath can sustain it.

Locate Heptad Gate **414** and the **Hyperelectron** symbol on the 441 holomind perceiver. Its matrix location is V11:H14, eighth circuit, 9th time dimension, inner core time. Now locate it in your body at front, center top of your skull (see graphic at the end of this chapter).

Visualize the **Hyperelectron with the spiraling red Kuali force field** above the **yellow Alpha** in your **throat** chakra. Take the **Hyperelectron** into the **fifth** mental sphere in the **fifth** time dimension (red Kuali electrothermic force field H11:V1-7, right-handed time) where it activates the **superconscious** as **hyperelectronic superconscious** informing **mental spheres one and two**.

From the **fifth** mental sphere, mentally direct the **black Hyperelectron** to the **throat** chakra and impress it above the **Alpha** seal. Hold this with four alternate nostril breaths (four times in and out through each nostril), followed by one breath through both nostrils.

Descend down the central column (spine), secreting the **Hyperelectron** (red kuali force field) into all 144,000 etheric fibers of the astral body. Practice the **breath of fire,** rapid shallow breathing through the nose, transmuting any blockages or obscurations into streams of crystal clear **hyperelectronic superconscious** spreading through your entire nervous system.

The black Hyperelectron with spectral, electric red Kuali force field vibrates subtle activating electronic force into all etheric fibers. Descend back down central channel and leave **Alpha** at the **throat** chakra. Return your consciousness to the fifth mental sphere, then close and seal the Heptad Gate at the front top-center of your skull. Relax and breathe slowly and deeply at least 13 times.

 Harmonic UR rune 90: *Galactic Art Whole Defined by Time.*

For additional practice: Locate Heptad Gate 414 on the Hunab Ku 21. Note that it corresponds to the Enlightened One, the Bringer of the Higher Truth, the Renewer of Life, Holder of the Timespace Wisdom; G/K Pluto, Bode Number 388. Study all of the connections (see graphic at the end of this chapter).

Day Six: LIMI

HRUM 402

Level 1: Meditating the Manipura (Solar Plexus) Chakra

Sit in a comfortable meditative posture. Keep your spine erect and body relaxed. With the body completely still, practice a few moments of natural mind meditation. Once the mind is sufficiently clear, direct your attention to your solar plexus or Manipura chakra. Make it as clear and pristine as possible, glistening and sparkling with vibrant energy. When it is pure and translucent, radiating from your solar plexus, allow it to dissolve and transform itself into a yellow ten-petalled lotus.

Concentrate on this area inside your solar plexus. The solar plexus is considered the second brain and the central storehouse of prana. The energy stored in this chakra can be used to connect us both individually and as a planet, through the Sun, to the galactic core, Hunab Ku. In the Tibetan tradition this chakra is known as *mani padma*, or "jeweled lotus." This is the point where all 72,000 nerve endings (on each side of the body) meet, for a total of 144,000 nerve endings.

This chakra is governed by the feminine principle or Shakti Goddess *Lakini* (Authority). This chakra center is also associated with willpower, and power in general; it is the place of empowerment and disempowerment, judgment and identity. The solar plexus is the processing chamber of the instinctual/intuitive energy and emotional intelligence. This energy is transferred to the heart chakra where the transduction of emotional energy is experienced as the "intelligence of the heart."

Meditation on the Manipura chakra leads to knowledge of the entire physical and subtle body system. When this center is purified and awakened, then it is possible to reconnect (via the etheric "highway" of the *kuxan suum* or cosmic umbilical cord) to the center of the galaxy, Hunab Ku. When this reconnection takes place the body becomes disease-free and luminous, and consciousness does not fall back into a lower state.

This chakra is often compared to the heat and the power of the Sun, radiating and distributing pranic energy throughout the entire human system. To awaken this chakra, breathe slowly into the solar plexus and feel the expansion and contraction of the navel as you breathe in and out through the naval. Breathe in, hold and suck the stomach in, then push it out when you exhale. Do this several times focusing on the purification of the abdominal area.

From this center feel the kuxan suum as the etheric fiber that flows directly to the center of the galaxy, making the solar plexus chakra a vital information receptacle. The kuxan suum connects the planetary circuit with the solar and galactic circuits.

Through an effort of imaginal will, we can direct our astral body through the reflective membrane of the planetary field into the Sun and then ultimately to the galactic core. This is the area allowing us to transmute and override primitive lower emotions by opening to receive the influx of higher cosmic energy. It is important to visualize the kuxan suum as a luminous etheric thread extending from the solar plexus to the center of the galaxy. This establishes us in the galactic order of reality.

Manipura affirmation: *May our perceptions be organized into a cosmic whole that we may all become one with the radialized order of the Primal Source!*

Level 2: Activating Radial Plasma: Limi

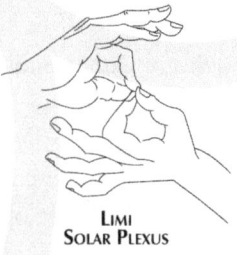

Limi
Solar Plexus

Breathe deeply through both your nostrils and allow your awareness to flow up your nose and down into your solar plexus chakra. Bring your awareness to the inner Limi plasma at the center of the chakra. Visualize the red symbol radiating luminous streams of white light.

Feel the Limi plasma vibrating, electrically gathered in the solar plexus, accounting for the mental electron electrical charge, which is in telepathic resonance with the North Pole.

Repeat the following while focusing on your solar plexus chakra: "I consume dualistic thoughts as food, I purify the mental-electron at the North Pole." Feel all conditioned thoughts dissolve in the light of intrinsic awareness.

Cover your left nostril with your left thumb and breathe deeply three times in and out through your right nostril. Flash onto the Limi plasma and feel the galactic connection out of the solar plexus. Now cover the right nostril with the right thumb and repeat the three breaths. Focus all of your attention to your solar plexus chakra, Limi plasma, and feel into the galactic reality being pulsed, breathed and radiated from your solar plexus chakra into the world.

Feel the Limi plasma gathered in the solar plexus accounting for the mental electron charge in telepathic resonance with the North Pole. The Limi charge is the second of three plasmas to form the telepathic quantum. This is the second telepathic plasma where you take the sensory quantum transmutations and breathe them out into the world through your solar plexus, emanating stabilizing vibrations to the astral and emotional bodies, soothing the rest of the chakras.

At the center of Limi feel the integrated charges of the sensory quanta: Dali, Seli, and Gamma, transmuted by Kali and the Alpha telepathic charge which initiates the telepathic quanta. Then by extending your mind telepathically to the north of the Planet, place the mental electron at the North Pole and purify it.

LEVEL 3: ENGAGING THE SIXTH MENTAL SPHERE (SUBLIMINAL CONSCIOUS)

Hyperneutronic subliminal consciousness activates sixth mental sphere.

Visualize the sixth mental sphere (subliminal conscious) located in the brain above the right ear in the right cerebral hemisphere. This sphere governs and controls the left lateral hemisphere. (Note how 5th and 6th mental spheres govern parts of the brain opposite their locus, exhibiting together a type of crossover polarity).

Subliminal means you are operating independent of past and future; this is how people can contact different entities on different planes of existence. Since subliminal consciousness is independent of past and future, you can tune into it at the conscious level, suspending all conditioned thought-programs. This mental sphere functions with the third-dimensional "self," storing impressions which are then transmuted into subliminal patterns of communication.

The sixth mental sphere allows us access to the parapsychic, supramental realm. This is the seat of the telepathic scanning system and interdimensional programs. To experience this, relax and focus your breath awareness on the psychic passages between the root, solar plexus and throat centers. Feel the upward circulation of energy and visualize yourself as a cosmic antenna for higher intelligence. Open yourself to become a telepathic receptor of higher mind capable of transmitting and receiving subliminal messages.

This intention, maintained through undistracted, non-conceptual meditative awareness, activates higher mind telepathic receptivity. This can also be realized and cultivated through dreamtime.

Note that this mental sphere contains subliminal suggestive impulses that affect third-dimensional functions as "intuitive flashes" (but which may actually be telepathic transmissions from remote points of supermental cosmic civilization trying to establish "contact"). These contacts leave impressions in the sixth mental sphere, which may be transmitted or transduced in any number of ways, which include ear-ringing, subliminal or hypnogogic imagery, déjà vu's, etc.

Level 4: Opening the Sixth Heptad Gate (402)

Visualize the yellow ten-petaled lotus **Manipura** chakra with the **red Limi** plasma superimposed over it at your solar plexus. Hold this visualization and feel the two intermingle as you chant the sacred letter **HRUM** as long as your breath can sustain it.

Locate Heptad Gate **402** and the **Hyperneutron** symbol on the 441 holomind perceiver. Its matrix location is V11:H8, eighth circuit, 9th time dimension, inner core time. Now locate it in your body at the back, top center of your skull (see graphic at the end of this chapter).

Visualize the **Hyperneutron with the rectilinear blue Duar force field** above the **red Limi** in your **solar plexus** chakra. Take the **Hyperneutron** into the **sixth** mental sphere in the **sixth** time dimension (blue Duar electroluminic force field H11:V15-21, left-handed time) where it activates the **subliminal conscious** as **hyperneutronic subliminal conscious** informing **mental spheres three and four.**

From the **sixth** mental sphere, mentally direct the **Hyperneutron** to the solar plexus chakra and impress it above the **Limi** seal. Hold this with four alternate nostril breaths (four times in and out through each nostril), followed by one breath through both nostrils.

Ascend up the central column (spine), secreting the **Hyperneutron** (blue duar force field) into all 144,000 etheric fibers of the astral body. Practice the **breath of fire,** rapid shallow breathing through the nose, transmuting any blockages or obscurations into streams of crystal clear **hyperneutronic subliminal consciousness** spreading through your entire nervous system.

The black Hyperneutron with spectral, electric blue Duar force field vibrates subtle activating neutronic force into all etheric fibers. Descend back down the central channel and leave **Limi** at the **solar plexus** chakra. Return your consciousness to the sixth mental sphere, then close and seal the Heptad Gate at the back top-side of your skull. Relax and breathe slowly and deeply at least 13 times.

 Harmonic UR rune 81: *Radiogenesis Establishes Galactic Life Whole*.

For additional practice: Locate Heptad Gate 402 on the Hunab Ku 21. Note that it corresponds to the Yogi/Yogini, the Meditation Master, Holder of the Transcendental Wisdom; S/P Neptune, Bode Number 300. Study all of the connections (see graphic at the end of this chapter).

Day Seven: SILIO

HRAIM   441

Level 1: Meditating the Anahata (Heart) Chakra

Sit in a comfortable meditative posture. Keep your spine erect and body relaxed. With the body completely still, practice a few moments of natural mind meditation. Once the mind is sufficiently clear, direct your attention to your heart or Anahata chakra. Make it as clear and pristine as possible, glistening and sparkling with vibrant energy. When it is pure and translucent, radiating from your heart, allow it to dissolve and transform itself into a green twelve-petalled lotus.

Concentrate on this area inside of your heart chakra. The heart is the main transducer of energy and is also an organ of knowing; it is the key to developing clairsentience—divine sense of touch—and also the place where "gnosis", direct knowledge of the supreme reality, occurs.

This Anahata chakra is governed by the feminine principle or Shakti Goddess *Kakini* (Devotion). This chakra serves as the seat of the memory of God through devotion, or *bodhichitta*, the mind of the aspiration to enlightenment. This area contains the transcendental programs that transform biological survival issues into forms of selfless compassion.

The heart energy is fed by the secret center, the seat of life-force energy. The heart chakra contains all impulses of innate being or essence nature. At this center comes the input from both the physical and mental bodies. The heart is like a mirror: if the input is unclear and distorted then so is the feedback. To activate the heart essence, body and mind must be purified. The heart center balances male/female (yin/yang) energies through pure unconditional love and cultivation of the higher emotional body.

To awaken the heart chakra, think of someone that you love deeply. Feel your heart open, emanating warmth and light. Now stay with this feeling and expand it until it becomes love for all beings. Allow this quality of love-bliss to circulate from your heart center to the rest of your body. Extend love and forgiveness toward yourself and to everyone on the Planet.

Feel the electromagnetic energy radiate from your heart. Feel your love and gratitude cradling the whole Earth and all of life. When the Anahata center is fully awakened, the body is transmuted by higher emotions and the heart chakra floods the subtle body with divine love; this flow of vital energy is the love of God.

Yogis say this chakra can be awakened simply through repetition of a syllable or mantra until it becomes the spontaneous form of your conscious awareness. This chakra is awakened in accordance with the degree of our love and devotion to the Creator, or Higher Self—the divine consciousness of All That Is.

Anahata affirmation: *May the abundance of the galactic power of the higher dream generate forever the compassionate heart of cosmic love!*

Level 2: Activating Radial Plasma: Silio

Silio
Heart

Breathe deeply through your nostrils and allow your awareness to flow up your nose and down into your heart chakra. Bring your awareness to the inner Silio plasma at the center of the chakra. Visualize the white symbol radiating luminous streams of white light.

Feel the Silio plasma gathered in the heart chakra discharging waves of unconditional love throughout the planet. Within this spiritual heart energy feel the mental electron-neutron charge telepathically in resonance with the center of the Earth.

Repeat the following while focusing on your heart chakra: "My role is to accomplish the actions of the Buddha, I discharge the mental electron-neutron at the center of the Earth." The Buddha is the enlightened mind. This potential exists in all beings. It is also known as the bodhichitta, or mind of enlightenment.

Feel this love enlightenment energy within your heart. Keep expanding this beautiful energy from your chest so that it sweeps powerfully through the planet bringing an end to all suffering. Feel love and light pulsing out, wave after wave, for the healing of all afflictions, all the hungry souls, the sick and the weary—healing them all with positive self-enlightening heart impulses. With this visualization, you may wish to chant the Buddhist Heart Sutra (Prajnaparamita): *Gate Gate Paragate Parasamgate Bodhi Svaha* (gone, gone, gone, beyond, gone totally beyond, all hail the Enlightened One).

Cover your left nostril with your left thumb and breathe deeply three times in and out through your right nostril. Flash onto the Silio plasma and feel the new world of higher spiritual emotions vibrating and emanating out of the heart chakra. Now cover your right nostril with your right thumb and repeat the three breaths. Focus all of your attention to your heart chakra, Silio plasma, and draw in with your breath the new enlightened reality—then release, breathing pure love through your heart chakra into the world, emanating stabilizing vibrations to the astral and emotional body, soothing the rest of the chakras.

The Silio charge completes the telepathic quantum and also completes the seven-part time atom. At the center of Silio, feel the integrated charges of the sensory quantum: Dali, Seli, and Gamma, transmuted by Kali and joined to the telepathic quantum, Alpha and Limi. Then by extending your mind telepathically to the Earth's core, discharge the mental electron-neutron at the center of the Earth.

Note: One sensory quantum joined by the catalytic plasma to one telepathic quantum makes one time atom. There are four time atoms per 28-day moon stored at the center of the Earth as one Master Time Molecule (for full instructions see 7:7::7:7 Telektonon Revelation).

Level 3: Engaging the Seventh Mental Sphere (Holomind Perceiver)

Visualize the seventh mental sphere (holomind perceiver) located in the central corpus callosum of the higher self and projected onto the corpus callosum of the 3-D and 4-D Self. This is the new perceptual organ allowing us to access the noospheric programs inclusive of the akashic register. This seventh mental sphere is also the seat of your "true self" or rigpa (wisdom self). All mental spheres are unified by and accessed through the seventh mental sphere.

The holomind perceiver is an evolving organ, the noospheric sensing device opening us to an entirely new cosmic reality. As the site and generator of the UR runes, the fourth-dimensional timing matrices and the 441 Synchronotron Matrix, the holomind perceiver contains the fourth-dimensional psychocultural programs and the holoneme of the psi bank grid, meaning that it holds the hologram of the total perceived planetary reality.

Study of and meditation on the holomind perceiver prepares the mind to open to the galactic dimension and receive an entirely new base of knowledge and perception. The holomind perceiver is activated through diligent application and study of Cosmic History and the disciplined application of the 441 matrix codes as they are regulated by the synchronic order.

Note: Cosmic thoughts are referred to as "mentation" waves, formulated as the correct laws of thought, and are a function of the holomind perceiver. A "mentation" wave is a configuration of telepathic potentialities, independent of language, and based on whole orders of supermental precepts, intrinsic to non-egoic knowing. The mentation waves are a function of the holomind perceiver and operate at the central core, radiating out to the different mental spheres as is needed. This is how the noosphere is established.

Level 4: Opening the Seventh Heptad Gate (441)

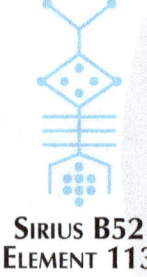

Sirius B52 Element 113

Visualize the green twelve-petaled lotus **Anahata** chakra with the **white Silio** plasma and the **etheric blue Sirius Beta 52/Element 113** superimposed over it at your heart. Hold this visualization and feel the three intermingle as you chant the sacred letter **HRAIM** as long as your breath can sustain it.

Locate Heptad Gate **441** and the **etheric blue Sirius Beta 52/Element 113** signature on the 441 holomind perceiver. Its matrix location is V11:H11, eleventh circuit, 9th time dimension, inner core time. Now locate it in your body at the top center of your skull (see graphic at the end of this chapter).

Visualize the **Sirius Beta 52/Element 113** above the **white Silio** in your **heart** chakra. Take the **Sirius B52** into the **seventh** mental sphere in the **ninth** time dimension (inner core time) where it activates **hyperplasmic enlightenment** as **hyperelectronic superconscious** informing mental spheres one and two as well as the **hyperneutronic subliminal conscious** informing mental spheres three and four.

From the **seventh** mental sphere, mentally direct the **Sirius B52/Element 113** to the **heart** chakra and impress it above the **Silio** seal. Hold this with four alternate nostril breaths (four times in and out through each nostril), followed by one breath through both nostrils.

Descend down the central column (spine), secreting the **Sirius B52** hyperplasma into all 144,000 etheric fibers of the astral body. Practice the **breath of fire,** rapid shallow breathing through the nose, transmuting any blockages or obscurations into streams of crystal clear **hyperplasmic enlightenment** spreading throughout your entire nervous system.

Etheric blue Sirius B52/Element 113 vibrates subtle activating force into all etheric fibers. Descend back down central channel until you get to the root chakra where you discharge the mental electron-neutron to the center of the Earth. Ascend back up central channel and leave **Silio** at the **heart** chakra. Return your consciousness to the seventh mental sphere in the center of the crown chakra, then close and seal all seven Heptad Gates with the Sirius B52/Element 113. Relax and breathe slowly and deeply at least 13 times.

 Harmonic UR rune 113, Sirius-Beta 52/Element 113, hyperplasmic enlightenment: *Tonality of Sirius-Beta Encodes Seven Days of Creation as Interval of Lost Time Redeemed.*

For additional practice: Locate Heptad Gate 441 on the Hunab Ku 21. Note that it corresponds to the Magus of the Infinite, Lord of the Cube, Teacher of the Unity of Totality, Hunab Ku 21, the Source of All Movement and Measure. Study the connections (see graphic at the end of this chapter).

Chakras 8 and 9: Root of Root and Crown of Crown

Root of Root chakra extends to and encompasses the Earth's octahedral core; it is the matrix for grounding cosmic mediumship. The Earth core chakra is what gives us the ability to communicate with elemental spirits.

Crown of Crown chakra extends to and encompasses the Earth's noosphere. The noospheric crown is the higher mind control that tunes us into the higher telepathic collective consciousness, the field of the planetary logos, and to supreme supermental superconscious states of cosmic consciousness.

The central activity of these two chakras is to coordinate evolutionary functions or processes within the celestial body (one planet) wherein they hold their energy field. The higher celestial logoi act on every aspect and facet of consciousness evolution through the mental spheres; this opens up a diverse range of possibilities of consciousness, perception, sensation, etc.

This extends to the upper realms into the laws of destiny, laws of creation and the absolute. This is the realm of cosmic design that defines the infrastructure of the universe we live in. It is the realm of the 5-D higher self, the body of radiance of the planetary logos as the transductive accumulator of all hierarchies, commands and ordinances. As the root of root is the reservoir of cosmic mediumship, so the crown of crown is fulfillment and realization of all cosmic consciousness possibilities.

SEVEN HEPTAD GATES OF THE HOLOMIND PERCEIVER

GATE 108
V11:H2
CIRCUIT 2

Heptad Gate 1: Alpha-Alpha/Profound Samadhi
First Time Dimension (Cosmic Creation)
First Mental Sphere (Preconscious)

Galactic Life Whole Becomes Medium of Transmission
84

GATE 291
V11:H5
CIRCUIT 5

Heptad Gate 2: Alpha-Beta/Informative Samadhi
Third Time Dimension (Cosmic Synchronization)
Second Mental Sphere (Subconscious)

Galactic Life Whole Realized as Cosmic Consciousness
88

GATE 144
V11:H20
CIRCUIT 2

Heptad Gate 3: Beta-Beta/Conscious Waking Mediumship
Fourth Time Dimension (Cosmic Cube)
Third Mental Sphere (Waking Conscious)

Galactic Art Whole Defines Space
91

GATE 315
V11:H17
CIRCUIT 5

Heptad Gate 4: Beta-Alpha/Higher Mind Control
Second Time Dimension (Cosmic Ascension)
Fourth Mental Sphere (Continuing Conscious)

Galactic Art Whole Becomes Meditation of Reality
95

GATE 414
V11:H14
CIRCUIT 8

Heptad Gate 5: Hyperelectron/Hyperelectronic Superconscious (INFORMS 1ST & 2ND MENTAL SPHERES)
Fifth Time Dimension (Red Kuali Force Field, Right-hand Time)
Fifth Mental Sphere (Superconscious)

Galactic Art Whole Defined by Time
90

GATE 402
V11:H8
CIRCUIT 8

Heptad Gate 6: Hyperneutron/Hyperneutronic Subliminal Conscious (INFORMS 3RD & 4TH MENTAL SPHERES)
Sixth Time Dimension (Blue Duar Force Field, Left-hand Time)
Sixth Mental Sphere (Subliminal Conscious)

Radiogenesis Establishes Galactic Life Whole
81

GATE 441
V11:H11
CIRCUIT 11

Heptad Gate 7: Sirius Beta 52 Element 113/Hyperplasmic Enlightenment
Ninth Time Dimension (Inner Core Time)
Seventh Mental Sphere (Holomind Perceiver)

Tonality of Sirius Beta Encodes Seven Days of Creation as Interval of Lost Time
441

The 40 +1 [41] Mystic Gates and the Four Quadrants of Space
Showing the 7 Heptad Gates + Their Circuits

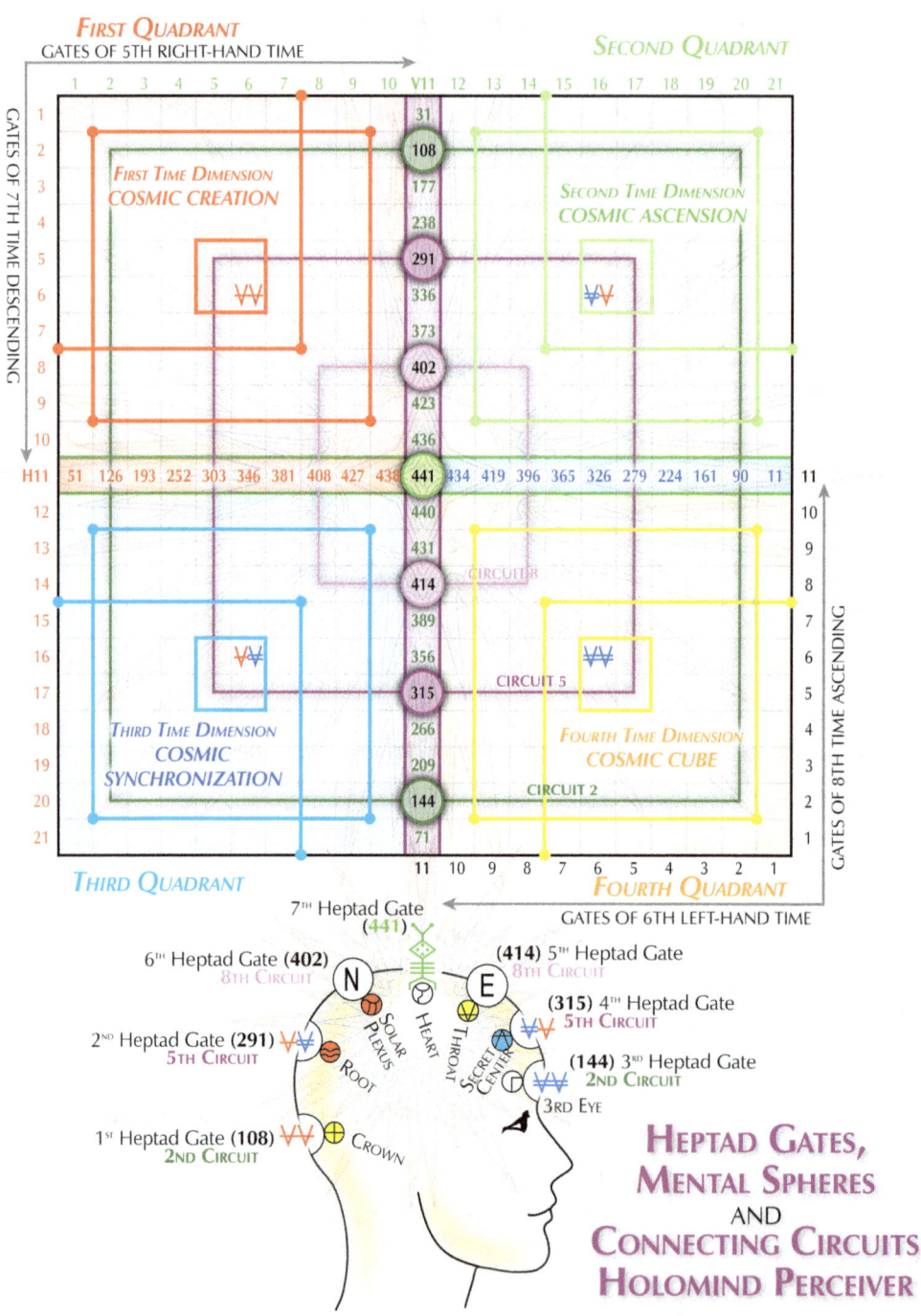

Chapter 13 • Synchrogalactic Yoga

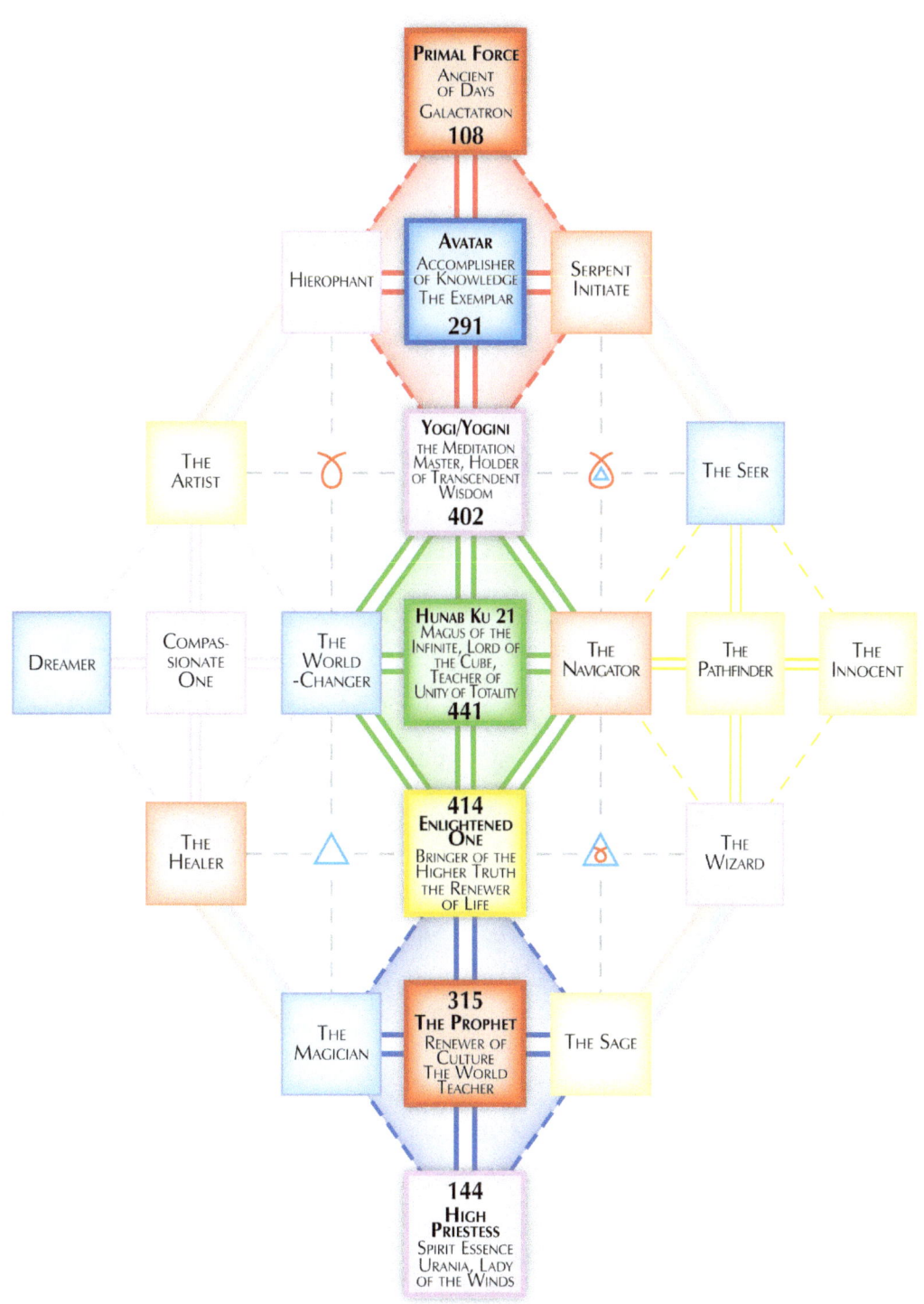

Appendix

Foundations of the Synchronic Order

PERPETUAL 13 MOON CALENDAR

DAY OUT OF TIME 7/25

MAGNETIC MOON •
1	2	3	4	5	6	7
7/26	7/27	7/28	7/29	7/30	7/31	8/1
8	9	10	11	12	13	14
8/2	8/3	8/4	8/5	8/6	8/7	8/8
15	16	17	18	19	20	21
8/9	8/10	8/11	8/12	8/13	8/14	8/15
22	23	24	25	26	27	28
8/16	8/17	8/18	8/19	8/20	8/21	8/22

LUNAR MOON ••
1	2	3	4	5	6	7
8/23	8/24	8/25	8/26	8/27	8/28	8/29
8	9	10	11	12	13	14
8/30	8/31	9/1	9/2	9/3	9/4	9/5
15	16	17	18	19	20	21
9/6	9/7	9/8	9/9	9/10	9/11	9/12
22	23	24	25	26	27	28
9/13	9/14	9/15	9/16	9/17	9/18	9/19

ELECTRIC MOON •••
1	2	3	4	5	6	7
9/20	9/21	9/22	9/23	9/24	9/25	9/26
8	9	10	11	12	13	14
9/27	9/28	9/29	9/30	10/1	10/2	10/3
15	16	17	18	19	20	21
10/4	10/5	10/6	10/7	10/8	10/9	10/10
22	23	24	25	26	27	28
10/11	10/12	10/13	10/14	10/15	10/16	10/17

SELF-EXISTING MOON ••••
1	2	3	4	5	6	7
10/18	10/19	10/20	10/21	10/22	10/23	10/24
8	9	10	11	12	13	14
10/25	10/26	10/27	10/28	10/29	10/30	10/31
15	16	17	18	19	20	21
11/1	11/2	11/3	11/4	11/5	11/6	11/7
22	23	24	25	26	27	28
11/8	11/9	11/10	11/11	11/12	11/13	11/14

OVERTONE MOON —
1	2	3	4	5	6	7
11/15	11/16	11/17	11/18	11/19	11/20	11/21
8	9	10	11	12	13	14
11/22	11/23	11/24	11/25	11/26	11/27	11/28
15	16	17	18	19	20	21
11/29	11/30	12/1	12/2	12/3	12/4	12/5
22	23	24	25	26	27	28
12/6	12/7	12/8	12/9	12/10	12/11	12/12

RHYTHMIC MOON •
1	2	3	4	5	6	7
12/13	12/14	12/15	12/16	12/17	12/18	12/19
8	9	10	11	12	13	14
12/20	12/21	12/22	12/23	12/24	12/25	12/26
15	16	17	18	19	20	21
12/27	12/28	12/29	12/30	12/31	1/1	1/2
22	23	24	25	26	27	28
1/3	1/4	1/5	1/6	1/7	1/8	1/9

RESONANT MOON ••
1	2	3	4	5	6	7
1/10	1/11	1/12	1/13	1/14	1/15	1/16
8	9	10	11	12	13	14
1/17	1/18	1/19	1/20	1/21	1/22	1/23
15	16	17	18	19	20	21
1/24	1/25	1/26	1/27	1/28	1/29	1/30
22	23	24	25	26	27	28
1/31	2/1	2/2	2/3	2/4	2/5	2/6

GALACTIC MOON •••
1	2	3	4	5	6	7
2/7	2/8	2/9	2/10	2/11	2/12	2/13
8	9	10	11	12	13	14
2/14	2/15	2/16	2/17	2/18	2/19	2/20
15	16	17	18	19	20	21
2/21	2/22	2/23	2/24	2/25	2/26	2/27
22	23	24	25	26	27	28
2/28	3/1	3/2	3/3	3/4	3/5	3/6

SOLAR MOON ••••
1	2	3	4	5	6	7
3/7	3/8	3/9	3/10	3/11	3/12	3/13
8	9	10	11	12	13	14
3/14	3/15	3/16	3/17	3/18	3/19	3/20
15	16	17	18	19	20	21
3/21	3/22	3/23	3/24	3/25	3/26	3/27
22	23	24	25	26	27	28
3/28	3/29	3/30	3/31	4/1	4/2	4/3

PLANETARY MOON —
1	2	3	4	5	6	7
4/4	4/5	4/6	4/7	4/8	4/9	4/10
8	9	10	11	12	13	14
4/11	4/12	4/13	4/14	4/15	4/16	4/17
15	16	17	18	19	20	21
4/18	4/19	4/20	4/21	4/22	4/23	4/24
22	23	24	25	26	27	28
4/25	4/26	4/27	4/28	4/29	4/30	5/1

SPECTRAL MOON •
1	2	3	4	5	6	7
5/2	5/3	5/4	5/5	5/6	5/7	5/8
8	9	10	11	12	13	14
5/9	5/10	5/11	5/12	5/13	5/14	5/15
15	16	17	18	19	20	21
5/16	5/17	5/18	5/19	5/20	5/21	5/22
22	23	24	25	26	27	28
5/23	5/24	5/25	5/26	5/27	5/28	5/29

CRYSTAL MOON ••
1	2	3	4	5	6	7
5/30	5/31	6/1	6/2	6/3	6/4	6/5
8	9	10	11	12	13	14
6/6	6/7	6/8	6/9	6/10	6/11	6/12
15	16	17	18	19	20	21
6/13	6/14	6/15	6/16	6/17	6/18	6/19
22	23	24	25	26	27	28
6/20	6/21	6/22	6/23	6/24	6/25	6/26

COSMIC MOON •••
1	2	3	4	5	6	7
6/27	6/28	6/29	6/30	7/1	7/2	7/3
8	9	10	11	12	13	14
7/4	7/5	7/6	7/7	7/8	7/9	7/10
15	16	17	18	19	20	21
7/11	7/12	7/13	7/14	7/15	7/16	7/17
22	23	24	25	26	27	28
7/18	7/19	7/20	7/21	7/22	7/23	7/24

13 Moon Calendar date / Gregorian Calendar date

WEEK 1 (Red / East) — KNOWLEDGE INITIATES VIEW
WEEK 2 (White / North) — HUMILITY REFINES MEDITATION
WEEK 3 (Blue / West) — PATIENCE TRANSFORMS CONDUCT
WEEK 4 (Yellow / South) — POWER RIPENS FRUIT

DALI • SELI • GAMMA • KALI • ALPHA • LIMI • SILIO

TZOLKIN
HARMONIC MODULE

Matrix of 260 Kin (days), consisting of 20 seals and 13 tones

THE 13 GALACTIC TONES

	NAME	ESSENCE	POWER	ACTION
•	Magnetic	Purpose	Unify	Attract
••	Lunar	Challenge	Polarize	Stabilize
•••	Electric	Service	Activate	Bond
••••	Self-Existing	Form	Define	Measure
—	Overtone	Radiance	Empower	Command
—•—	Rhythmic	Equality	Organize	Balance
—••—	Resonant	Attunement	Channel	Inspire
—•••—	Galactic	Integrity	Harmonize	Model
—••••—	Solar	Intention	Pulse	Realize
=	Planetary	Manifestation	Perfect	Produce
=•=	Spectral	Liberation	Dissolve	Release
=••=	Crystal	Cooperation	Dedicate	Universalize
=•••=	Cosmic	Presence	Endure	Transcend

13 Galactic Tones make one 13-Tone Wavespell. Learn more about the wavespell on page 266.

THE 20 SOLAR SEALS

Seal & Number	NAME	POWER	ACTION	ESSENCE	ARCHETYPE
1	Dragon	Birth	Nurtures	Being	Primal Force
2	Wind	Spirit	Communicates	Breath	High Priestess
3	Night	Abundance	Dreams	Intuition	Dreamer
4	Seed	Flowering	Targets	Awareness	The Innocent
5	Red Serpent	Life Force	Survives	Instinct	Serpent Initiate
6	Worldbridger	Death	Equalizes	Opportunity	Hierophant
7	Hand	Accomplishment	Knows	Healing	Avatar
8	Star	Elegance	Beautifies	Art	Artist
9	Moon	Universal Water	Purifies	Flow	Healer
10	Dog	Heart	Loves	Loyalty	Compassionate One
11	Monkey	Magic	Plays	Illusion	Magician
12	Human	Free Will	Influences	Wisdom	Sage
13	Skywalker	Space	Explores	Wakefulness	Prophet
14	Wizard	Timelessness	Enchants	Receptivity	Wizard
15	Eagle	Vision	Creates	Mind	Seer
16	Warrior	Intelligence	Questions	Fearlessness	Pathfinder
17	Earth	Navigation	Evolves	Synchronicity	Navigator
18	Mirror	Endlessness	Reflects	Order	Yogi(ni)
19	Storm	Self-Generation	Catalyzes	Energy	Worldchanger
20 or 0	Sun	Universal Fire	Enlightens	Life	Enlightened One

The 20 Solar Seals – Hunab Ku 21

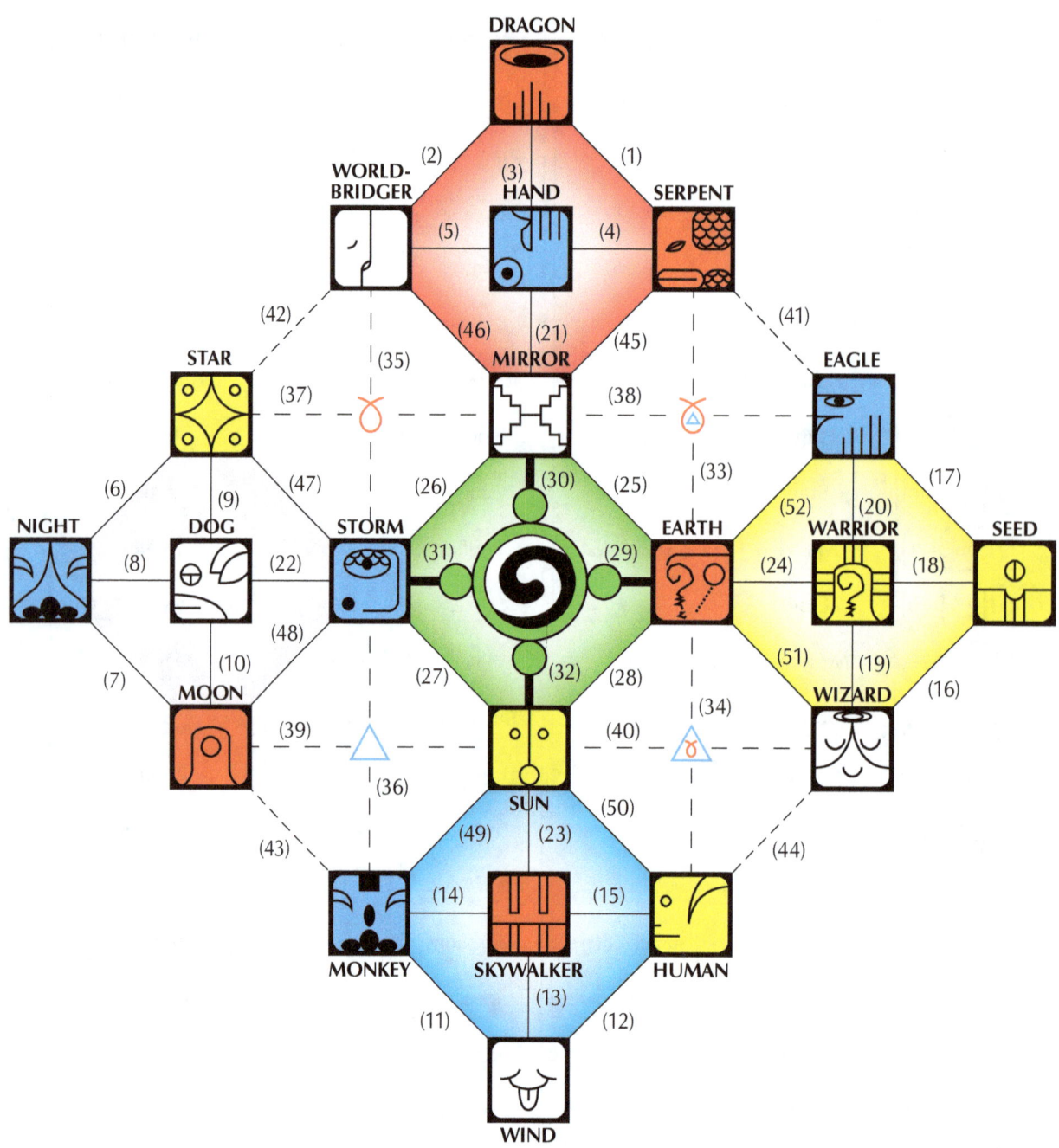

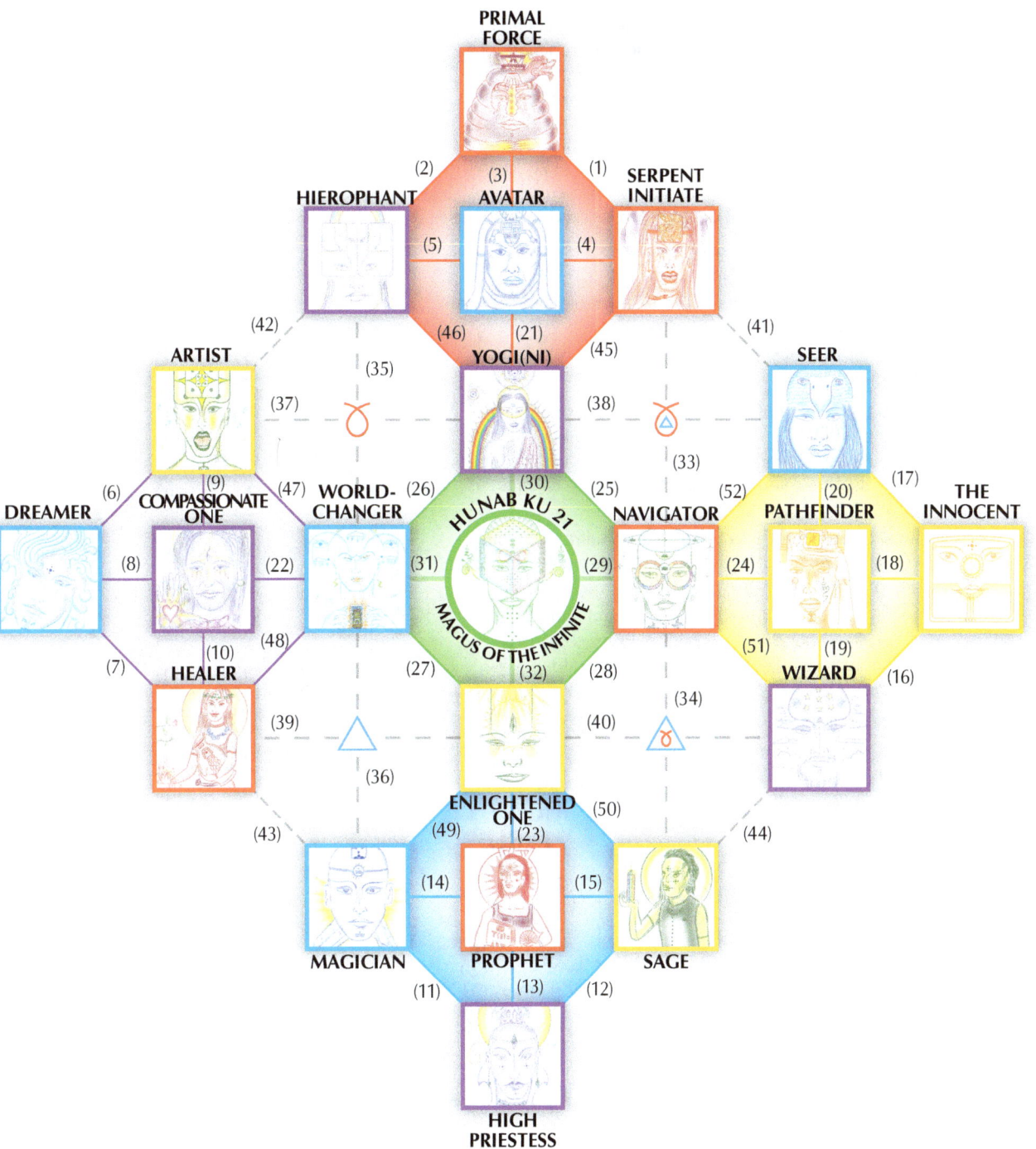

FIND YOUR GALACTIC SIGNATURE

The day you were born on the 13 Moon calendar is coded by your **galactic signature:** your password into fourth-dimensional time. Your galactic signature is one of the 260 different possibilities shown on the Tzolkin/Harmonic Module (shown on the inside back cover of this Almanac).

By playing the role of your galactic signature, you allow yourself – your mind, body and spirit – to vibrate to that particular frequency and you broadcast it out to everyone around you. This is your gift to the world.

To find your galactic signature:

1. Write down the number next to the Year you were born from the **Year Table**.
2. Add this to the Code Number for the Month you seek from the **Month Table**.
3. Now add the number of the Day of the month that you were born. For example, if you were born on November 28, add 28. (If you were born on February 29 before noon local time, use February 28 – if you were born after noon local time, use March 1).
4. The total of these three numbers is the kin number of your galactic signature! (if the number you have is greater than 260 you need to subtract 260).
5. Look at the Tzolkin on the previous page and find your kin number. This is your galactic signature. Example, Kin 164 is the Yellow Seed seal and the Galactic tone (tone 8). This is "Yellow Galactic Seed" or "8 Seed."

Welcome to Timeship Earth!

PRACTICE DATES:

Jose Arguelles/Valum Votan (Jan 24, 1939):
247 + 0 + 24 = 271 - 260 = 11.
Kin 11, Blue Spectral Monkey

The 14th Dalai Lama (July 6, 1935):
87 + 181 + 6 = 274 - 260 = 14.
Kin 14, White Magnetic Wizard

Ammachi (September 27, 1953):
157 + 243 + 27 = 427 - 260 = 167.
Kin 167, Blue Spectral Hand

July 26, 2014:
62 + 181 + 26 = 269 – 260 = 9.
Kin 9, Red Solar Moon

YEAR TABLE

2065	2013	1961	1909	217
2064	2012	1960	1908	112
2063	2011	1959	1907	7
2062	2010	1958	1906	162
2061	2009	1957	1905	57
2060	2008	1956	1904	212
2059	2007	1955	1903	107
2058	2006	1954	1902	2
2057	2005	1953	1901	157
2056	2004	1952	1900	52
2055	2003	1951	1899	207
2054	2002	1950	1898	102
2053	2001	1949	1897	257
2052	2000	1948	1896	152
2051	1999	1947	1895	47
2050	1998	1946	1894	202
2049	1997	1945	1893	97
2048	1996	1944	1892	252
2047	1995	1943	1891	147
2046	1994	1942	1890	42
2045	1993	1941	1889	197
2044	1992	1940	1888	92
2043	1991	1939	1887	247
2042	1990	1938	1886	142
2041	1989	1937	1885	37
2040	1988	1936	1884	192
2039	1987	1935	1883	87
2038	1986	1934	1882	242
2037	1985	1933	1881	137
2036	1984	1932	1880	32
2035	1983	1931	1879	187
2034	1982	1930	1878	82
2033	1981	1929	1877	237
2032	1980	1928	1876	132
2031	1979	1927	1875	27
2030	1978	1926	1874	182
2029	1977	1925	1873	77
2028	1976	1924	1872	232
2027	1975	1923	1871	127
2026	1974	1922	1870	22
2025	1973	1921	1869	177
2024	1972	1920	1868	72
2023	1971	1919	1867	227
2022	1970	1918	1866	122
2021	1969	1917	1865	17
2020	1968	1916	1864	172
2019	1967	1915	1863	67
2018	1966	1914	1862	222
2017	1965	1913	1861	117
2016	1964	1912	1860	12
2015	1963	1911	1859	167
2014	1962	1910	1858	62

MONTH TABLE

JANUARY	0
FEBRUARY	31
MARCH	59
APRIL	90
MAY	120
JUNE	151
JULY	181
AUGUST	212
SEPTEMBER	243
OCTOBER	13
NOVEMBER	44
DECEMBER	74

 You can also decode galactic signatures with the Galactic Compass! Download template and instructions at **lawoftime.org/galacticcompass**

How to Enter the 441 Synchronotron

The system of Synchronotron is a tool for learning the mathematical language of telepathy, which is the root of the Law of Time. It is a teaching from Sirius that contains the language of post-conceptual mind.

Sirius is a binary star – Sirius A and Sirius B. It takes Sirius B approximately 52 years to go in an orbit around Sirius A. This is the basis of the 52-year solar-galactic cycle (and why the galactic compass is also called the Sirian Wheel).

Synchronotron refers to the compendium of the practices of the 441 (21 x 21) cube matrix system. This mathematical system represents the minimum fractal of totality cubed: 21 x 21 being the prime statement of totality (20) + 1 (unity). 1+2+3+4+5+6 = 21 (unity of totality). More information can be found at www.lawoftime.org/synchronotron.

FINDING YOUR TELEPATHIC FREQUENCY INDEX

In the Synchronotron system we use your <u>13 Moon date</u> and your <u>galactic signature</u> to find coordinates for the Time, Space and Synchronic matrices (shown on the following pages). This gives us three sets of three numbers. *For this example, let's use the date 26 July 2013: Magnetic Moon 1 - Kin 164, Yellow Galactic Seed.*

Time Matrix TFI: First we find the 13 Moon date (ex: Magnetic Moon 1) in the Time Matrix. Take note of the coordinates (V1,H1). Now find this same location on the Base Matrix, and take note of the number there, this is called a Base Matrix Unit (BMU); so the Time Matrix BMU is 41. Next, find the same location on the Space Matrix and Synchronic Matrix: and write down and add the numbers you find on the three matrices: Time Matrix (1), Space Matrix (278), Synchronic Matrix (1). Lastly, add the three numbers: 278 + 1 + 1 = 280. So the Time Matrix TFI is <u>280</u>.

Space Matrix TFI: Next we find the Kin number on the Space Matrix. In this example it is Yellow Galactic Seed, Kin 164, so find 164 on the Space Matrix and note its coordinates (V9,H19). Again, find this coordinate on the Base Matrix to get the Space Matrix BMU (207). Next, find this location on the Time Matrix and Synchronic Matrix and write down and add the numbers you find: Time Matrix (273), Space Matrix (164), Synchronic Matrix (98). 273 + 164 + 98 = 535. So the Space Matrix TFI is <u>535</u>.

Synchronic Matrix TFI: Now we also find today's kin number on the Synchronic Matrix. So find 164 in the Tzolkin within the Synchronic Matrix, note its coordinates (V13,H4). As before, find this coordinate on the Base Matrix to get the Synchronic Matrix BMU (236). Next, find the same location on the Time Matrix and Space Matrix and write down and add the numbers you find: Time Matrix (83), Space Matrix (128), Synchronic Matrix (164). 83 + 128 + 164 = 375. So the Synchronic Matrix TFI is <u>375</u>.

Master Coordinating Frequency: The final step is to add the the three TFI's from the previous steps to arrive at the Master Coordinating Frequency. (Note: Do not add the BMU's, these stand alone). So we add the three TFI's: 280 + 535 + 375 = <u>794</u> Master Coordinating Frequency (MCF).

By reducing your MCF by multiples of 441 you can find your BMU. *Example:* 794 – 441 = BMU 353 (V8,H16). You can also reduce the MCF by multiples of 260 to find your Kin Equivalent. *Example:* 794 – 780 (260 x 3) = 14 = Kin 14, White Magnetic Wizard.

TIME MATRIX

All 28 days of all 13 Moons are contained in the 4 Outer Time Dimensions (orange quadrants) of the Time Matrix. Each quadrant is 7 rows of 7 units. Thus, one row of each quadrant is a 7-day week. The four weeks of each Moon are distributed in the 4 Outer Time Dimensions, thusly:

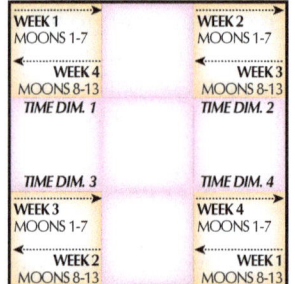

Moons 8-13 mirror Moons 1-6. Moon 7 has no mirror. The four weeks in Moons 1-7 descend through rows H1 to H7 and H15 to H21, moving left to right. The 4 weeks in Moons 8-13 mirror Moons 1-6, ascending through rows H20 to H15 and H7-H1, moving right to left.

For your reference, on the page after the next page there is a full matrix showing the coordinates of every 13 Moon date.

SPACE MATRIX

Four quadrants of 64 Kin each (4 x 64 = 256) plus 4 Kin around the central core.

In the daily practice find the kin number (within the colored regions).

Example: Kin 164, Yellow Galactic Seed = coordinate V9,H19

SYNCHRONIC MATRIX

Contains 260-unit Tzolkin within vertical columns 5-17, with central Mystic Column corresponding to the 11th vertical colum, while the 11th horizontal row contains the 13 powers of cosmic creation. The Four columns on either side of the Tzolkin are the 84 right- and 84 left-hand dharma gates, numbered 1-168 (21 x 8)

In the daily practice, find the Kin number in the Tzolkin and note the coordinate.

Example: Kin 164, Yellow Galactic Seed = coordinate V13,H4

	V1	V2	V3	V4	V5	V6	V7	V8	V9	V10	V11	V12	V13	V14	V15	V16	V17	V18	V19	V20	V21
H1	1	43	85	127	1	21	41	61	81	101	121	141	161	181	201	221	241	168	126	84	42
H2	2	44	86	128	2	22	42	62	82	102	122	142	162	182	202	222	242	167	125	83	41
H3	3	45	87	129	3	23	43	63	83	103	123	143	163	183	203	223	243	166	124	82	40
H4	4	46	88	130	4	24	44	64	84	104	124	144	164	184	204	224	244	165	123	81	39
H5	5	47	89	131	5	25	45	65	85	105	125	145	165	185	205	225	245	164	122	80	38
H6	6	48	90	132	6	26	46	66	86	106	126	146	166	186	206	226	246	163	121	79	37
H7	7	49	91	133	7	27	47	67	87	107	127	147	167	187	207	227	247	162	120	78	36
H8	8	50	92	134	8	28	48	68	88	108	128	148	168	188	208	228	248	161	119	77	35
H9	9	51	93	135	9	29	49	69	89	109	129	149	169	189	209	229	249	160	118	76	34
H10	10	52	94	136	10	30	50	70	90	110	130	150	170	190	210	230	250	159	117	75	33
H11	11	53	95	137	•	••	•••	••••	—	±	≛	≝	=	≐	≛	≝	≞	158	116	74	32
H12	12	54	96	138	11	31	51	71	91	111	131	151	171	191	211	231	251	157	115	73	31
H13	13	55	97	139	12	32	52	72	92	112	132	152	172	192	212	232	252	156	114	72	30
H14	14	56	98	140	13	33	53	73	93	113	133	153	173	193	213	233	253	155	113	71	29
H15	15	57	99	141	14	34	54	74	94	114	134	154	174	194	214	234	254	154	112	70	28
H16	16	58	100	142	15	35	55	75	95	115	135	155	175	195	215	235	255	153	111	69	27
H17	17	59	101	143	16	36	56	76	96	116	136	156	176	196	216	236	256	152	110	68	26
H18	18	60	102	144	17	37	57	77	97	117	137	157	177	197	217	237	257	151	109	67	25
H19	19	61	103	145	18	38	58	78	98	118	138	158	178	198	218	238	258	150	108	66	24
H20	20	62	104	146	19	39	59	79	99	119	139	159	179	199	219	239	259	149	107	65	23
H21	21	63	105	147	20	40	60	80	100	120	140	160	180	200	220	240	260	148	106	64	22

BASE MATRIX

Numbered 1-441 in a counter-clockwise spiral in ten concentric circuits until reaching the center of the matrix = 11th vertical axis and 11th horizontal axis (V11,H11) = 441.

	V1	V2	V3	V4	V5	V6	V7	V8	V9	V10	V11	V12	V13	V14	V15	V16	V17	V18	V19	V20	V21
H1	41	40	39	38	37	36	35	34	33	32	31	30	29	28	27	26	25	24	23	22	21
H2	42	117	116	115	114	113	112	111	110	109	108	107	106	105	104	103	102	101	100	99	20
H3	43	118	185	184	183	182	181	180	179	178	177	176	175	174	173	172	171	170	169	98	19
H4	44	119	186	245	244	243	242	241	240	239	238	237	236	235	234	233	232	231	168	97	18
H5	45	120	187	246	297	296	295	294	293	292	291	290	289	288	287	286	285	230	167	96	17
H6	46	121	188	247	298	341	340	339	338	337	336	335	334	333	332	331	284	229	166	95	16
H7	47	122	189	248	299	342	377	376	375	374	373	372	371	370	369	330	283	228	165	94	15
H8	48	123	190	249	300	343	378	405	404	403	402	401	400	399	368	329	282	227	164	93	14
H9	49	124	191	250	301	344	379	406	425	424	423	422	421	398	367	328	281	226	163	92	13
H10	50	125	192	251	302	345	380	407	426	437	436	435	420	397	366	327	280	225	162	91	12
H11	51	126	193	252	303	346	381	408	427	438	441	434	419	396	365	326	279	224	161	90	11
H12	52	127	194	253	304	347	382	409	428	439	440	433	418	395	364	325	278	223	160	89	10
H13	53	128	195	254	305	348	383	410	429	430	431	432	417	394	363	324	277	222	159	88	9
H14	54	129	196	255	306	349	384	411	412	413	414	415	416	393	362	323	276	221	158	87	8
H15	55	130	197	256	307	350	385	386	387	388	389	390	391	392	361	322	275	220	157	86	7
H16	56	131	198	257	308	351	352	353	354	355	356	357	358	359	360	321	274	219	156	85	6
H17	57	132	199	258	309	310	311	312	313	314	315	316	317	318	319	320	273	218	155	84	5
H18	58	133	200	259	260	261	262	263	264	265	266	267	268	269	270	271	272	217	154	83	4
H19	59	134	201	202	203	204	205	206	207	208	209	210	211	212	213	214	215	216	153	82	3
H20	60	135	136	137	138	139	140	141	142	143	144	145	146	147	148	149	150	151	152	81	2
H21	61	62	63	64	65	66	67	68	69	70	71	72	73	74	75	76	77	78	79	80	1

13 Moon/28-Day Calendar

LOCATED IN THE FOUR OUTER TIME DIMENSIONS OF THE TIME MATRIX

MOONS 1-7 BEGIN AT V1,H1 AND MOVE LEFT-TO-RIGHT TOP-TO BOTTOM
MOONS 8-13 BEGIN AT V21,H20 AND MOVE RIGHT-TO-LEFT BOTTOM-TO-TOP

	V1	V2	V3	V4	V5	V6	V7	V8	V9	V10	V11	V12	V13	V14	V15	V16	V17	V18	V19	V20	V21
H1	1.1 / 13.28	1.2 / 13.27	1.3 / 13.26	1.4 / 13.25	1.5 / 13.24	1.6 / 13.23	1.7 / 13.22								1.8 / 13.21	1.9 / 13.20	1.10 / 13.19	1.11 / 13.18	1.12 / 13.17	1.13 / 13.16	1.14 / 13.15
H2	2.1 / 12.28	2.2 / 12.27	2.3 / 12.26	2.4 / 12.25	2.5 / 12.24	2.6 / 12.23	2.7 / 12.22								2.8 / 12.21	2.9 / 12.20	2.10 / 12.19	2.11 / 12.18	2.12 / 12.17	2.13 / 12.16	2.14 / 12.15
H3	3.1 / 11.28	3.2 / 11.27	3.3 / 11.26	3.4 / 11.25	3.5 / 11.24	3.6 / 11.23	3.7 / 11.22								3.8 / 11.21	3.9 / 11.20	3.10 / 11.19	3.11 / 11.18	3.12 / 11.17	3.13 / 11.16	3.14 / 11.15
H4	4.1 / 10.28	4.2 / 10.27	4.3 / 10.26	4.4 / 10.25	4.5 / 10.24	4.6 / 10.23	4.7 / 10.22								4.8 / 10.21	4.9 / 10.20	4.10 / 10.19	4.11 / 10.18	4.12 / 10.17	4.13 / 10.16	4.14 / 10.15
H5	5.1 / 9.28	5.2 / 9.27	5.3 / 9.26	5.4 / 9.25	5.5 / 9.24	5.6 / 9.23	5.7 / 9.22								5.8 / 9.21	5.9 / 9.20	5.10 / 9.19	5.11 / 9.18	5.12 / 9.17	5.13 / 9.16	5.14 / 9.15
H6	6.1 / 8.28	6.2 / 8.27	6.3 / 8.26	6.4 / 8.25	6.5 / 8.24	6.6 / 8.23	6.7 / 8.22								6.8 / 8.21	6.9 / 8.20	6.10 / 8.19	6.11 / 8.18	6.12 / 8.17	6.13 / 8.16	6.14 / 8.15
H7	7.1	7.2	7.3	7.4	7.5	7.6	7.7								7.8	7.9	7.10	7.11	7.12	7.13	7.14
H8																					
H9																					
H10																					
H11																					
H12																					
H13																					
H14																					
H15	1.15 / 13.14	1.16 / 13.13	1.17 / 13.12	1.18 / 13.11	1.19 / 13.10	1.20 / 13.9	1.21 / 13.8								1.22 / 13.7	1.23 / 13.6	1.24 / 13.5	1.25 / 13.4	1.26 / 13.3	1.27 / 13.2	1.28 / 13.1
H16	2.15 / 12.14	2.16 / 12.13	2.17 / 12.12	2.18 / 12.11	2.19 / 12.10	2.20 / 12.9	2.21 / 12.8								2.22 / 12.7	2.23 / 12.6	2.24 / 12.5	2.25 / 12.4	2.26 / 12.3	2.27 / 12.2	2.28 / 12.1
H17	3.15 / 11.14	3.16 / 11.13	3.17 / 11.12	3.18 / 11.11	3.19 / 11.10	3.20 / 11.9	3.21 / 11.8								3.22 / 11.7	3.23 / 11.6	3.24 / 11.5	3.25 / 11.4	3.26 / 11.3	3.27 / 11.2	3.28 / 11.1
H18	4.15 / 10.14	4.16 / 10.13	4.17 / 10.12	4.18 / 10.11	4.19 / 10.10	4.20 / 10.9	4.21 / 10.8								4.22 / 10.7	4.23 / 10.6	4.24 / 10.5	4.25 / 10.4	4.26 / 10.3	4.27 / 10.2	4.28 / 10.1
H19	5.15 / 9.14	5.16 / 9.13	5.17 / 9.12	5.18 / 9.11	5.19 / 9.10	5.20 / 9.9	5.21 / 9.8								5.22 / 9.7	5.23 / 9.6	5.24 / 9.5	5.25 / 9.4	5.26 / 9.3	5.27 / 9.2	5.28 / 9.1
H20	6.15 / 8.14	6.16 / 8.13	6.17 / 8.12	6.18 / 8.11	6.19 / 8.10	6.20 / 8.9	6.21 / 8.8								6.22 / 8.7	6.23 / 8.6	6.24 / 8.5	6.25 / 8.4	6.26 / 8.3	6.27 / 8.2	6.28 / 8.1
H21	7.15	7.16	7.17	7.18	7.19	7.20	7.21								7.22	7.23	7.24	7.25	7.26	7.27	7.28

MOONS 1-6 MIRROR MOONS 8-13. MOON 7 HAS NO MIRROR.
When finding your Telepathic Frequency Index for the Time Matrix first check any 13 Moon calendar to find your 13 Moon birthdate (Example: July 26 = Magnetic Moon 1 = 1.1).

Then refer to the chart above to find the location of your 13 Moon birthdate in the 441 Matrix. Write down the horizontal and vertical vector points. (Example: Resonant Moon 15 = 7.15 = **V1,H21**)

EXAMPLES:

V1,H1 = 1.1 / 13.28 = Magnetic Moon 1 (July 26) / Cosmic Moon 28 (July 24)

V1,H21 = 7.15 = Resonant Moon 15 (Jan 24)

V21,H20 = 6.28 / 8.1 = Rhythmic Moon 28 (Jan 9) / Galactic Moon 1 (Feb 7)

SYNCHRONOTRON

Application – Holomind Perceiver Codes of Time

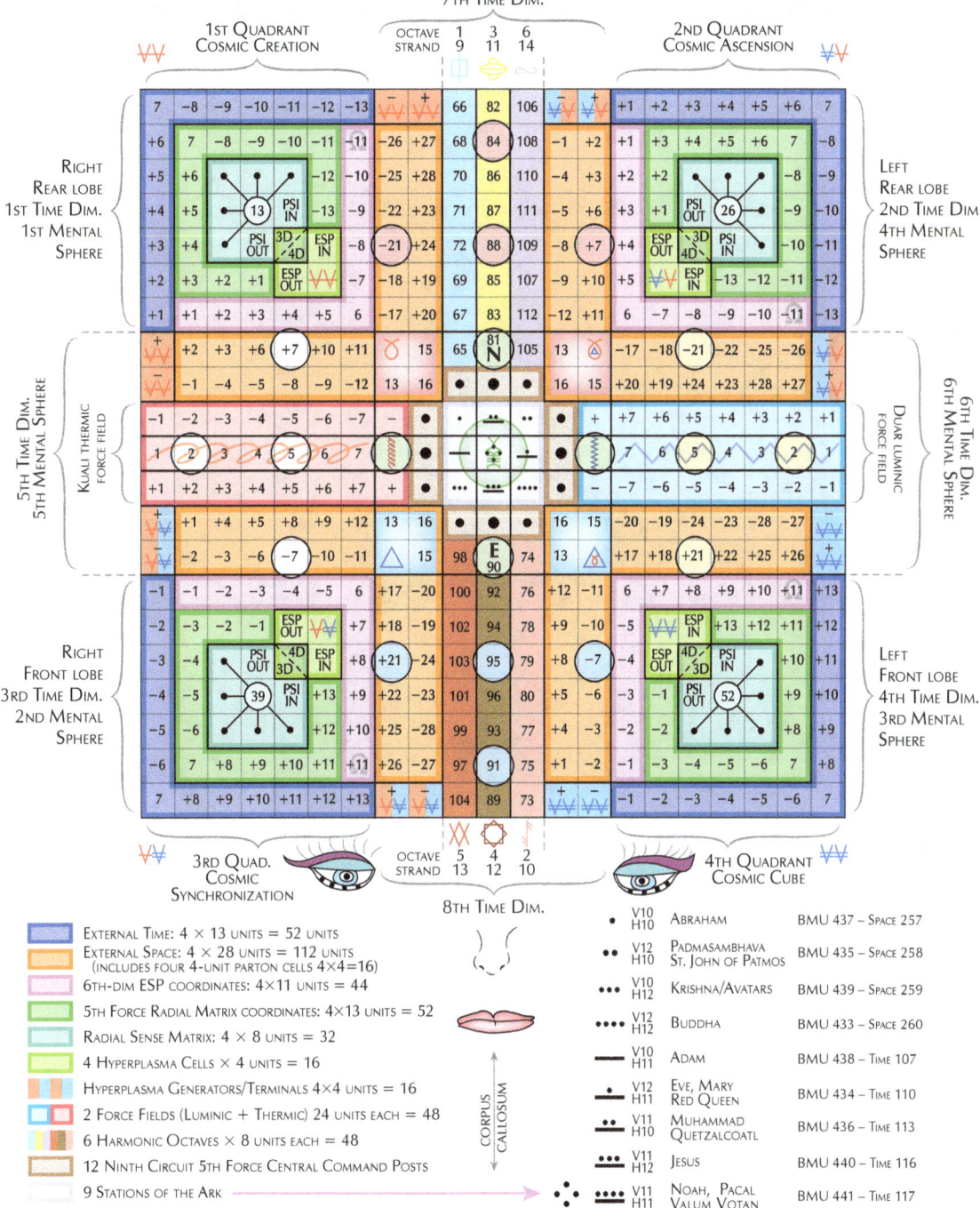

HOLOMIND PERCEIVER (HMP) is a function of the 441 Matrix Synchronotron. It is a "chip" of the 7th mental sphere demonstrating the radialization of consciousness. The HMP has different parts/functions radialized equal through the 4 quadrants and 9 time dimensions.

OCTAVE 1 STRAND 9	OCTAVE 2 STRAND 10	OCTAVE 3 STRAND 11	OCTAVE 4 STRAND 12	OCTAVE 5 STRAND 13	OCTAVE 6 STRAND 14
65 — Octave of Divine Decree "BE!"	73 — Command of Cosmic Creation Realized as Tree of Cosmic Fire	81 — Radiogenesis Establishes Galactic Life Whole	89 — Morphogenesis Establishes Galactic Art Whole	97 — Union of Ascent and Descent	105 — Octave of Infinite Mind Wave
66 — Divine Decree Establishes Time of Second Creation	74 — Tree of Fire Defined by Ring of Time	82 — Galactic Life Whole Evolved as Time	90 — Galactic Art Whole Defined by Time	98 — Time Equalized by Union of Ascent and Descent	106 — Infinite Mind Wave Floats in Time
67 — Divine Decree Establishes Space of Second Creation	75 — Tree of Fire Extends to Four Quarters of Space	83 — Galactic Life Whole Extends into Space	91 — Galactic Art Whole Defines Space	99 — Space Perfected by Union of Ascent and Descent	107 — Infinite Mind Wave Illumines Space
68 — Divine Decree Establishes Firmament of Second Creation	76 — Command of Cosmic Creation Enlightens Firmament	84 — Galactic Life Whole Becomes Medium of Transmission	92 — Galactic Art Whole Becomes Structure of Reality	100 — Union of Ascent and Descent Established as Cosmic Space	108 — Infinite Mind Wave Becomes Waking Consciousness
69 — Firmament Divides Time	77 — Firmament Defines Movement of Time as Day-Night	85 — Galactic Life Whole Channels Time	93 — Structure of Reality Evolved by Time	101 — System of Command Actualized in Time	109 — Waking Consciousness Identified as Time
70 — Firmament Divides Space	78 — Day-and-Night Defines Cosmic Space	86 — Galactic Life Whole Channels Space	94 — Structure of Reality Becomes Architecture of Space	102 — System of Commands Evolves Cosmic Space	110 — Waking Consciousness Discriminates Space
71 — Divine Decree Unifies Timespace	79 — Tree of Cosmic Fire Generates Planet Mind	87 — Timespace Unifies Galactic Life Whole	95 — Galactic Art Whole Becomes Meditation of Reality	103 — Channel of Command Becomes Self-evolving	111 — Infinite Mind Wave Reflects Infinity
72 — Timespace Establishes Cosmos as One Universal Mind	80 — Tree of Cosmic Fire Returns to Source as Star Mind	88 — Galactic Life Realized as Cosmic Consciousness	96 — Galactic Art Whole Gives Form to Cosmic Consciousness	104 — Channel of Commands Creates Cosmic Order	112 — Infinite Mind Wave Evolves Infinity

The 48 Harmonic Runes of the Second Creation—While there are eight strands of UR Runes that code the psi bank, governing the evolutionary sequences of planetary life, there are six strands of UR harmonic runes that govern the sequence of the "Second Creation." Since the genetic base of physical biological life is already established with the 64 UR Runes, the 48 UR harmonic runes are more like musical tones, and the six UR strands are referred to as Octaves. Within their six-octave range these 48 tones define the frequencies of cosmic evolution as a function of telepathic resonances. These harmonic runes are to be imprinted on the axis of the corpus callosum. Three octaves of 24 runes define the AC psychogenetic template, and the same for the CA psychogenetic template.

SELECTED BIBLIOGRAPHY

Books by Valum Votan (José Argüelles)

Earth Ascending: An Illustrated Treatise on the Law Governing Whole Systems. Shambhala Publications, 1984.
The Mayan Factor, Path Beyond Technology. Bear & Co, 1987.
Surfers of the Zuvuya, Tales of Interdimensional Travel. Bear & Co, 1988.
The Call of Pacal Votan, Time is the Fourth Dimension. Altea Publishers, 1996.
The Arcturus Probe, Tales and Reports of an Ongoing Investigation. Light Technology, 1996.
Time and the Technosphere: the Law of Time in Human Affairs. Inner Traditions International, 2002.
Manifesto for the Noosphere. North Atlantic Books, 2011.

Booklets and Fourth-Dimensional Tools

Thirteen Moons in Motion/with Lloydine Argüelles, 1992.
Dreamspell: the Journey of Timeship Earth 2013, 1993.
Telektonon, Prophecy of Pacal Votan, 1994.
The Thirteen Moon Calendar Change Peace Plan/with Lloydine Argüelles, 1995.
The 260 Postulates of the Dynamics of Time, 1996.
The Principia Mathematica of the Fourth Dimension, 1996.
The Rinri Project, Circumpolar Rainbow Bridge Experiment, 1996.
The 20 Tablets of the Law of Time, 1997.
7:7::7:7 Telektonon, 1998.
28 Meditations on the Law of Time, 2000.
Mystery of the Stone, 2004.
Noosphere II: The Great Experiment of the Law of Time, 2005.

Books by José Argüelles/Valum Votan & Stephanie South/Red Queen

Cosmic History Chronicles Volume I - Book of the Throne. Law of Time Press, 2005.
Cosmic History Chronicles Volume II - Book of the Avatar, Law of Time Press, 2006.
Cosmic History Chronicles Volume III - Book of the Mystery, Law of Time Press, 2007.
Cosmic History Chronicles Volume IV - Book of the Initiation, Law of Time Press, 2008.
Cosmic History Chronicles Volume V - Book of the Timespace, Law of Time Press, 2009.
Cosmic History Chronicles Volume VI - Book of the Transcendence, Law of Time Press, 2010.
Cosmic History Chronicles Volume VII - Book of the Cube, Law of Time Press, 2011.
2012 Biography of a Time Traveler: The Journey of José Argüelles, by Stephanie South. New Page Books (imprint of Career Press, Inc.), 2009.
Time, Synchronicity and Calendar Change: The Visionary Life and Work of José Argüelles, by Stephanie South. Law of Time Press, 2011.

And

The Knowledge Book, by Mevlana (V. Bülent Çorak). World Brotherhood Union Mevlana Supreme Foundation, 1996.

www.ingramcontent.com/pod-product-compliance
Lightning Source LLC
Chambersburg PA
CBHW080519300426
44112CB00018B/2789